Lecture Notes in Computer Science 2067

Edited by G. Goos, J. Hartmanis, and J. van Leeuwen

T0254134

Springer
Berlin
Heidelberg
New York
Barcelona
Hong Kong
London
Milan
Paris
Tokyo

Franck Cassez   Claude Jard
Brigitte Rozoy   Mark Dermot Ryan (Eds.)

Modeling and Verification of Parallel Processes

4th Summer School, MOVEP 2000
Nantes, France, June 19-23, 2000
Revised Tutorial Lectures

Springer

Series Editors

Gerhard Goos, Karlsruhe University, Germany
Juris Hartmanis, Cornell University, NY, USA
Jan van Leeuwen, Utrecht University, The Netherlands

Volume Editors

Franck Cassez
CNRS, IRCCyN
1 rue de la Noe, 44321 Nantes Cedex 3, France
E-mail: Franck.Cassez@irccyn.ec-nantes.fr

Claude Jard
CNRS, IRISA
Campus de Beaulieu, 35042 Rennes, France
E-mail: Claude.Jard@irisa.fr

Brigitte Rozoy
Université de Paris XI, Laboratoire de Recherche en Informatique
Bâtiment 490, 91405 Orsay Cedex, France
E-mail: rozoy@lri.fr

Mark Dermot Ryan
University of Birmingham, School of Computer Science
Edgbaston, Birmingham B15 2TT, UK
E-mail: m.d.ryan@cs.bham.ac.uk

Cataloging-in-Publication Data applied for

Die Deutsche Bibliothek - CIP-Einheitsaufnahme

Modeling and verification of parallel processes : 4th summer school /
MOVEP 2000, Nantes, France, June 19 - 23, 2000. Franck Cassez ... (ed.).
Berlin ; Heidelberg ; New York ; Barcelona ; Hong Kong ; London ; Milan ;
Paris ; Tokyo : Springer, 2001
    (Lecture notes in computer science ; Vol. 2067)
    ISBN 3-540-42787-2

CR Subject Classification (1998): D.2.4, F.3.1, F.4.1

ISSN 0302-9743
ISBN 3-540-42787-2 Springer-Verlag Berlin Heidelberg New York

Springer-Verlag Berlin Heidelberg New York
a member of BertelsmannSpringer Science+Business Media GmbH

http://www.springer.de

© Springer-Verlag Berlin Heidelberg 2001
Printed in Germany

Typesetting: Camera-ready by author, data conversion by PTP-Berlin, Stefan Sossna
Printed on acid-free paper   SPIN: 10781713   06/3142   5 4 3 2 1 0

Foreword

MOVEP 2000 was the fourth summer school in the series of MOVEP summer schools (MOdeling and VErification of Parallel processes), and was organized jointly by IRCCyN, IRISA, LRI (France), and the University of Birmingham (UK). It was held in Nantes, France on 19–23 June 2000 and continued the success of the first three MOVEP summer schools held in 1994, 1996, and 1998. MOVEP was originally a French-speaking school and was initiated by A. Arnold (LaBRI, Bordeaux), J. Beauquier (LRI, Orsay), and O. Roux (IRCCyN, Nantes) in 1994. MOVEP adopted English as its working language in 2000.

MOVEP is a school devoted to the wide area of modeling and verifying software or hardware systems. The goal of MOVEP is to gather students, academic researchers, and industrial researchers interested in the development of safety critical systems and to provide a forum for discussion among people from computer science and automatic control. More than 100 people from Europe, North America, North Africa, and India attended MOVEP 2000.

This volume contains tutorials and annotated bibliographies covering the main subjects adressed at MOVEP 2000. It gives a snapshot of the recent developments in the domain as well as a useful introduction to many subjects.

The volume contains four tutorials comprising introductory material to *Model-Checking, Theorem Proving, Composition and Abstraction Techniques*, and *Timed Systems* (with UPPAAL).

Three research papers give some more detailed views of High-Level Message Sequence Charts, Industrial Applications of Model-Checking, and the use of Formal Methods in Security.

Finally, four annotated bibliographies give an overview of Infinite State-Space Systems, Testing Transition Systems, Fault-Model-Driven Test Derivation, and Mobile Processes.

The organizers of MOVEP 2000 would like to thank all the contributors for their commitment during the school and for their papers in this volume.

It is a great pleasure for us to be the editors of this *LNCS Tutorials* volume and we hope to meet for the next MOVEP in June 2002.

April 2001   F. Cassez, C. Jard, B. Rozoy and M. Ryan

Program Committee

H. Alla	LAG, Grenoble, F
A. Arnold	LaBRI, Bordeaux, F
E. Brinksma	U. of Twente, NL
A. Cimatti	IRST, Trento, I
J. Esparza	TU. of Munich, D
C. Jard	IRISA, Rennes, F
K. G. Larsen	BRICS-Aalborg, DK
F. Maraninchi	UJF & Verimag, Grenoble, F
S. Merz	U. of Munich, D
A. Petit	LSV, Cachan, F
A. Petrenko	CRIM, Montréal, CA
O. Roux	IRCCyN, Nantes, F
B. Rozoy	LRI, Orsay, F
J. Rushby	SRI, USA
M. Ryan	U. of Birmingham, UK
D. Sangiorgi	INRIA, Sophia-Antipolis, F
P.-Y. Schobbens	U. of Namur, B
R. Valette	LAAS-CNRS, Toulouse, F
M. Wonham	U. of Toronto, CA

Organizing Committee

Franck Cassez	IRCCyN/CNRS, Nantes
Claude Jard	IRISA/CNRS, Rennes
Brigitte Rozoy	LRI, Orsay
Mark Ryan	U. of Birmingham

Local Arrangements

Patricia Galloyer	IRCCyN, Nantes
Marie-Noëlle Georgeault	IRISA, Rennes
Nicole Labaronne	IRCCyN, Nantes

MOVEP 2000 Sponsors

CNRS, INRIA, France Telecom, Ville de Nantes, Conseil Régional des Pays de la Loire, Conseil Général de Loire Atlantique, Université de Nantes, Université de Rennes 1, Ecole Centrale de Nantes, EEC.

Contents

Tutorials and Papers

Model Checking: A Tutorial Overview

Stephan Merz

Institut für Informatik, Universität München
merz@informatik.uni-muenchen.de

Abstract. We survey principles of model checking techniques for the automatic analysis of reactive systems. The use of model checking is exemplified by an analysis of the Needham-Schroeder public key protocol. We then formally define transition systems, temporal logic, ω-automata, and their relationship. Basic model checking algorithms for linear- and branching-time temporal logics are defined, followed by an introduction to symbolic model checking and partial-order reduction techniques. The paper ends with a list of references to some more advanced topics.

1 Introduction

Computerized systems pervade more and more our everyday lives. We rely on digital controllers to supervise critical functions of cars, airplanes, and industrial plants. Digital switching technology has replaced analog components in the telecommunication industry, and security protocols enable e-commerce applications and privacy. Where important investments or even human lives are at risk, quality assurance for the underlying hardware and software components becomes paramount, and this requires formal models that describe the relevant part of the systems at an adequate level of abstraction. The systems we are focussing on are assumed to maintain an ongoing interaction with their environment (e.g., the controlled system or other components of a communication network) and are therefore called *reactive systems* [60,94]. Traditional models that describe computer programs as computing some result from given input values are inadequate for the description of reactive systems. Instead, the behavior of reactive systems is usually modelled by transition systems.

The term model checking designates a collection of techniques for the automatic analysis of reactive systems. Subtle errors in the design of safety-critical systems that often elude conventional simulation and testing techniques can be (and have been) found in this way. Because it has been proven cost-effective and integrates well with conventional design methods, model checking is being adopted as a standard procedure for the quality assurance of reactive systems.

The inputs to a model checker are a (usually finite-state) description of the system to be analysed and a number of properties, often expressed as formulas of temporal logic, that are expected to hold of the system. The model checker either confirms that the properties hold or reports that they are violated. In the latter case, it provides a counter-example: a run that violates the property. Such a run can provide valuable feedback and points to design errors. In practice, this view turns out to be somewhat idealized: quite frequently, available resources

F. Cassez et al. (Eds.): MOVEP 2000, LNCS 2067, pp. 3–38, 2001.
© Springer-Verlag Berlin Heidelberg 2001

only permit to analyse a rather coarse model of the system. A positive verdict from the model checker is then of limited value because bugs may well be hidden by the simplifications that had to be applied to the model. On the other hand, counter-examples may be due to modelling artefacts and no longer correspond to actual system runs. In any case, one should keep in mind that the object of analysis is always an *abstract model* of the system. Standard procedures such as code reviews are necessary to ensure that the abstract model adequately reflects the behavior of the concrete system in order for the properties of interest to be established or falsified. Model checkers can be of some help in this validation task because it is possible to perform "sanity checks", for example to ensure that certain runs are indeed possible or that the model is free of deadlocks.

This paper is intended as a tutorial overview of some of the fundamental principles of model checking, based on a necessarily subjective selection of the large body of model checking literature. We begin with a case study in section 2 where the application of model checking is considered from a user's point of view. Section 3 reviews transition systems, temporal logics, and automata-theoretic techniques that underly some approaches to model checking. Section 4 introduces basic model checking algorithms for linear-time and branching-time logics. Finally, section 5 collects some rather sketchy references to more advanced topics. Much more material can be found in other contributions to this volume and in the textbooks and survey papers [27,28,69,97,124] on the subject. The paper contains many references to the relevant literature, in the hope that this survey can also serve as an annotated bibliography.

2   Analysis of a Cryptographic Protocol

2.1   Description of the Protocol

Let us first consider, by way of example, the analysis of a public-key authentication protocol suggested by Needham and Schroeder [104] using the model checker SPIN [65]. Two agents A(lice) and B(ob) try to establish a common secret over an insecure channel in such a way that both are convinced of each other's presence and no intruder can get hold of the secret without breaking the underlying encryption algorithm. This is one of the fundamental problems in cryptography: for example, a shared secret could be used to generate a session key for subsequent communication between the agents.

The protocol is pictorially represented in Fig. 1.[1] It requires the exchange of three messages between the participating agents. Notation such as $\langle M \rangle_C$ denotes that message M is encrypted using agent C's public key. Throughout, we assume the underlying encryption algorithm to be secure and the private keys of the honest agents to be uncompromised. Therefore, only agent C can decrypt $\langle M \rangle_C$ to learn M.

---

[1] The original protocol includes communication between the agents and a central key server to distribute the public keys of the agents. We concentrate on the core authentication protocol, assuming all public keys to be known to all agents.

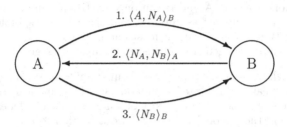

Fig. 1. Needham-Schroeder public-key protocol.

1. Alice initiates the protocol by generating a random number N_A and sending the message $\langle A, N_A \rangle_B$ to Bob (numbers such as N_A are called *nonces* in cryptographic jargon, indicating that they should be used only once by any honest agent). The first component of the message informs Bob of the identity of the initiator. The second component represents "one half" of the secret.
2. Bob similarly generates a nonce N_B and responds with the message $\langle N_A, N_B \rangle_A$. The presence of the nonce N_A generated in the first step, which only Bob could have decrypted, convinces Alice of the authenticity of the message. She therefore accepts the pair $\langle N_A, N_B \rangle$ as the common secret.
3. Finally, Alice responds with the message $\langle N_B \rangle_B$. By the same argument as above, Bob concludes that this message must originate with Alice, and therefore also accepts $\langle N_A, N_B \rangle$ as the common secret.

We assume all messages to be sent over an insecure medium. Attackers may intercept messages, store them, and perhaps replay them later. They may also participate in ordinary runs of the protocol, initiate runs or respond to runs initiated by honest agents, who need not be aware of their partners' true identity. However, even an attacker can only decrypt messages that were encrypted with his own public key.

The protocol contains a severe flaw, and the reader is invited to find it before continuing. The error was discovered some 17 years after the protocol was first published, using model checking technology [91].

2.2   A Promela Model

We represent the protocol in PROMELA ("protocol meta language"), the input language for the SPIN model checker.[2] In order to make the analysis feasible, we make a number of simplifying assumptions:

- We consider a network of only three agents: A, B, and I(ntruder).

---

[2] The full code is available from the author.

– The honest agents A and B can only participate in one protocol run each.
  Agent A can only act as initiator, and agent B as responder. It follows that
  A and B need to generate at most one nonce.
– The memory of agent I is limited to a single message.

Although the protocol is very small, our simplifications are quite typical of the
analysis of "real-world" systems via model checking: models are usually required
to be finite-state, and the complexity of analysis typically depends exponentially
on the size of those models. (Esparza's contribution to this volume surveys the
state of the art concerning model checking techniques for infinite-state models.)
Of course, our assumptions imply that certain errors such as "confusion" that
could arise when multiple runs of the protocol interfere will go undetected in our
model. This explains why model checking is considered a debugging rather than
a verification technique. When no errors have been found on a small model, one
can consider somewhat less stringent restrictions, as far as available resources
permit. In any case, it is important to clearly identify the assumptions that
underly the system model in order to assess the coverage of the analysis.

With these caveats, it is quite straightforward to write a model for the honest agents A and B from the informal description of section 2.1. PROMELA is a
guarded-command language with C-like syntax; it provides primitives for message channels and operations for sending and receiving messages. We first declare
an enumeration type that contains symbolic constants to make the model more
readable. Because one nonce suffices for each agent, we simply assume that these
have been precomputed and refer to them by symbolic names.

```
mtype = { ok, err, msg1, msg2, msg3, keyA, keyB, keyI,
          agentA, agentB, agentI, nonceA, nonceB, nonceI };
```

We represent encrypted messages as records that contain a key and two data
entries. Decryption can then be modelled as pattern-matching on the key entry.

```
typedef Crypt { mtype key, data1, data2 };
```

The network is modelled as a single message channel shared by all three
agents. For simplicity, we assume synchronous communication on the network,
indicated by a buffer length of 0; this does not affect the possible communication
patterns but helps to reduce the size of the model. A message on the network
is modelled as a triple consisting of an identification tag (the message number),
the intended receiver (which the intruder is free to ignore), and an "encrypted"
message body.

```
chan network = [0] of { mtype,   /* msg# */
                        mtype,   /* receiver */
                        Crypt };
```

Figure 2 contains the PROMELA code[3] for agent A. Initially, a partner (either
B or I) is chosen nondeterministically for the subsequent run (the token :: introduces the different alternatives of nondeterministic selection), and its public

---

[3] In actual PROMELA, record formation is not available as a primitive operation, but
must be simulated by a series of assignments.

```
mtype partnerA;
mtype statusA = err;

active proctype Alice() {
  mtype  pkey, pnonce;
  Crypt  data;

  if /* choose a partner for this run */
  :: partnerA = agentB; pkey = keyB;
  :: partnerA = agentI; pkey = keyI;
  fi;
  network ! (msg1, partnerA, Crypt{pkey, agentA, nonceA});

  network ? (msg2, agentA, data);
  (data.key == keyA) && (data.info1 == nonceA);
  pnonce = data.info2;

  network ! (msg3, partnerA, Crypt{pkey, pnonce, 0});
  statusA = ok;
}
```

Fig. 2. PROMELA code for agent A.

key is looked up. A message of type 1 is then sent to the chosen partner, after which agent A waits for a message of type 2 intended for her to arrive on the network. She verifies that the message body is encrypted with her key and that it contains the nonce sent in the first message. (PROMELA allows Boolean conditions to appear as statements; such a statement blocks if the condition is found to be false.) If so, she extracts the partner's nonce, responds with a message of type 3, and declares success. (The variable statusA will be used later to express correctness statements about the model.)

The code for agent B is similar, exchanging sending and reception of messages.

In contrast, the intruder cannot be modelled using a fixed protocol—the purpose of the analysis is to let SPIN find the attack if one exists at all. Instead, agent I is modelled highly nondeterministically: we describe the actions that are possible at any given state and let SPIN choose among them. The overall structure of the code shown in Fig. 3 is an infinite loop that offers a choice between receiving and sending of messages on the network.

The first alternative models the reception or interception of a message (the "don't care" variable "_" reflects the fact that the intruder need not respect the intended recipient of a message). The message body may be stored in the variable intercepted, even if it cannot be decrypted. If, moreover, the message has been encrypted for agent I, it can be analyzed to extract nonces; since the model is based on a fixed set of nonces, it is enough to set Boolean flags for nonces that the intruder has learnt so far.

```
bool   knows_nonceA, knows_nonceB;

active proctype Intruder() {
  mtype msg, recpt;
  Crypt data, intercepted;
  do
  :: network ? (msg, _, data) ->
     if /* perhaps store the message */
     :: intercepted = data;
     :: skip;
     fi;
     if /* record newly learnt nonces */
     :: (data.key == keyI) ->
        if
        :: (data.info1 == nonceA) || (data.info2 == nonceA)
           -> knows_nonceA = true;
        :: else -> skip;
        fi;
        /* similar for knows_nonceB */
     :: else -> skip;
     fi;
  :: /* Replay or send a message */
     if /* choose message type */
     :: msg = msg1;
     :: msg = msg2;
     :: msg = msg3;
     fi;
     if /* choose recipient */
     :: recpt = agentA;
     :: recpt = agentB;
     fi;
     if /* replay intercepted message or assemble it */
     :: data = intercepted;
     :: if
        :: data.info1 = agentA;
        :: data.info1 = agentB;
        :: data.info1 = agentI;
        :: knows_nonceA -> data.info1 = nonceA;
        :: knows_nonceB -> data.info1 = nonceB;
        :: data.info1 = nonceI;
        fi;
        /* similar for data.info2 and data.key */
     fi;
     network ! (msg, recpt, data);
  od;
}
```

Fig. 3. PROMELA code for agent I.

The second alternative represents agent I sending a message. There are two subcases: either replay a previously intercepted message or construct a new message from the information learnt so far. Note that we allow arbitrary ("type-correct") entries for the unencrypted fields of a message. Of course, most of the resulting combinations can be immediately recognized as inappropriate by the honest agents. Our model therefore contains many deadlocks, which we ignore during the following analysis.

2.3   Model Checking the Protocol

The purpose of the protocol is to ensure mutual authentication (of honest agents) while maintaining secrecy. In other words, whenever both A and B have successfully completed a run of the protocol, then A should believe her partner to be B if and only if B believes to talk to A. Moreover, if A successfully completes a run with B then the intruder should not have learnt A's nonce, and similarly for B. These properties are can be expressed in temporal logic (cf. section 3.2) as follows:

$$\mathbf{G}(statusA = ok \wedge statusB = ok \implies$$
$$(partnerA = agentB \Leftrightarrow partnerB = agentA))$$
$$\mathbf{G}(statusA = ok \wedge partnerA = agentB \implies \neg knows\_nonceA)$$
$$\mathbf{G}(statusB = ok \wedge partnerB = agentA \implies \neg knows\_nonceB)$$

We present SPIN with the model of the protocol and the first formula. In a fraction of a second, SPIN declares the property violated and outputs a run that contains the attack. The run is visualized as a message sequence chart, shown in Fig. 4: Alice initiates a protocol run with Intruder who in turn (but masquerading as A) starts a run with Bob, using the nonce received in the first message. Bob replies with a message of type 2 that contains both A's and B's nonces, encrypted for A. Although agent I cannot decrypt that message itself, it forwards it to A. Unsuspecting, Alice finds her nonce, returns the second nonce to her partner I, and declares success. This time, agent I can decrypt the message, extracts B's nonce and sends it to B who is also satisfied. As a result, we have reached a state where A correctly believes to have completed a run with I, but B is fooled into believing to talk to A. The same counterexample will be produced when analysing the third formula, whereas the second formula is declared to hold of the model.

The counterexample produced by SPIN makes it easy to trace the error in the protocol to a lack of explicitness in the second message: the presence of the expected nonce is not sufficient to prove the origin of the message. To avoid the attack, the second message should therefore be replaced with $\langle B, N_A, N_B \rangle$. After this modification, SPIN confirms that all three formulas hold of the model—which of course does not prove the correctness of the protocol (see, e.g., [106] for work on the formal verification of cryptographic protocols using interactive theorem proving).

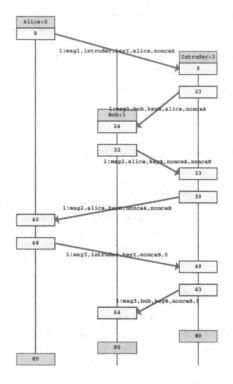

Fig. 4. Message sequence chart visualizing the attack.

3   Systems and Properties

Reactive systems can be broadly classified as *distributed* systems whose sub-components are spatially separated and *concurrent* systems that share resources such as processors and memories. Distributed systems communicate by *message passing*, whereas concurrent systems may use *shared variables*. Concurrent processes may share a common clock and execute in lock-step (*time-synchronous* systems, typical for hardware verification problems) or operate asynchronously, sharing a common processor. In the latter case, one will typically assume *fairness conditions* that ensure processes that could execute are eventually scheduled for execution. A common framework for the representation of these different kinds of systems is provided by the concept of *transition systems*. Properties of (runs of) transition systems are conveniently expressed in temporal logic.

3.1 Transition Systems

Definition 1. *A transition system* $\mathcal{T} = (S, I, \mathcal{A}, \delta)$ *is given by a set S of states, a non-empty subset $I \subseteq S$ of* initial *states, a set $\mathcal{A}$ of actions, and a total transition relation $\delta \subseteq S \times \mathcal{A} \times S$ (that is, we require that for every state $s \in S$ there exist $A \in \mathcal{A}$ and $t \in S$ such that $(s, A, t) \in \delta$).*

An action $A \in \mathcal{A}$ is called enabled *at state $s \in S$ iff $(s, A, t) \in \delta$ holds for some $t \in S$.*

A run *of $\mathcal{T}$ is an infinite sequence $\rho = s_0 s_1 \ldots$ of states $s_i \in S$ such that $s_0 \in I$ and for all $i \in \mathbb{N}$, $(s_i, A_i, s_{i+1}) \in \delta$ holds for some $A_i \in \mathcal{A}$.*

A transition system specifies the allowed evolutions of the system: starting from some initial state, the system evolves by performing actions that take the system to a new state. Slightly different definitions of transition systems abound in the literature. For example, actions are sometimes not explicitly identified. We have assumed the transition relation to be total in order to simplify some of the definitions below. Totality can be ensured by including a *stuttering action* that does not change the state; only the stuttering action is enabled in deadlock or quiescent states. Definition 1 is often augmented by fairness conditions, see section 4.2. Some papers use the term *Kripke structure* instead of transition system, in honor of the logician Saul A. Kripke who used transition systems to define the semantics of modal logics [78].

In practice, reactive systems are described using modelling languages, including (pseudo) programming languages such as PROMELA, but also process algebras or Petri nets. The operational semantics of these formalisms is conveniently defined in terms of transition systems. However, the transition system that corresponds to such a description is typically of size exponential in the length of the description. For example, the state space of a shared-variable program is the product of the variable domains. Modelling languages and their associated model checkers are usually optimized for particular kinds of systems such as synchronous shared-variable programs or asynchronous communication protocols. In particular, for systems composed of several processes it is advantageous to exploit the process structure and avoid the explicit construction of a single transition system that represents the joint behavior of processes. This will be further explored in section 4.4.

3.2 Properties and Temporal Logic

Given a transition system $\mathcal{T}$, we can ask questions such as the following:

- Are any "undesired" states reachable in $\mathcal{T}$, such as states that represent a deadlock, a violation of mutual exclusion etc.?
- Are there runs of $\mathcal{T}$ such that, from some point onwards, some "desired" state is never reached or some action never executed? Such runs may represent livelocks where, for example, some process is prevented from entering its critical section, although other components of the system may still make progress.

- Is some initial system state of $\mathcal{T}$ reachable from every state? In other words, can the system be reset?

Temporal logic [45,79,94,95,117] is a convenient language to formally express such properties. Let us first consider temporal logic of linear time whose formulas express properties of runs of transition systems. Assume given a denumerable set $\mathcal{V}$ of atomic propositions, which represent properties of individual states.

Definition 2. *Formulas of propositional temporal logic* **PTL** *of linear time are inductively defined as follows:*

- *Every atomic proposition $v \in \mathcal{V}$ is a formula.*
- *Boolean combinations of formulas are formulas.*
- *If φ and ψ are formulas then so are $\mathbf{X}\,\varphi$ ("next φ") and $\varphi\,\mathbf{U}\,\psi$ ("φ until ψ").*

PTL formulas are interpreted over *behaviors*, that is, ω-sequences of states. We assume that atomic propositions $v \in \mathcal{V}$ can be evaluated at states $s \in S$ and write $s(\mathcal{V})$ to denote the set of propositions true at state s. For a behavior $\sigma = s_0 s_1 \ldots$, we let σ_i denote the state s_i and $\sigma|_i$ the suffix $s_i s_{i+1} \ldots$ of σ.

Definition 3. *The relation $\sigma \models \varphi$ ("φ holds of σ") is inductively defined as follows:*

- $\sigma \models v$ *(for $v \in \mathcal{V}$) iff $v \in \sigma_0(\mathcal{V})$.*
- *The semantics of boolean combinations is defined as usual.*
- $\sigma \models \mathbf{X}\,\varphi$ *iff $\sigma|_1 \models \varphi$.*
- $\sigma \models \varphi\,\mathbf{U}\,\psi$ *iff for some $k \geq 0$, $\sigma|_k \models \psi$ and $\sigma|_j \models \varphi$ holds for all $0 \leq j < k$.*

Other useful **PTL** formulas can be introduced as abbreviations: $\mathbf{F}\,\varphi$ (*"finally φ"*, *"eventually φ"*) is defined as **true** $\mathbf{U}\,\varphi$; it asserts that φ holds of some suffix. The dual formula $\mathbf{G}\,\varphi \equiv \neg\,\mathbf{F}\,\neg\varphi$ (*"globally φ"*, *"always φ"*) requires φ to hold of all suffixes. The formula $\varphi\,\mathbf{W}\,\psi$ (*"φ waits for ψ"*, *"φ unless ψ"*) is defined as $(\varphi\,\mathbf{U}\,\psi) \vee \mathbf{G}\,\varphi$ and requires φ to hold for as long as ψ does not hold; unlike $\varphi\,\mathbf{U}\,\psi$, it does not require ψ to become true eventually.

The following formulas are examples for typical correctness assertions about a two-process resource manager. We assume req_i and $owns_i$ to be atomic propositions true when process i has requested the resource or when it owns the resource.

$\mathbf{G}\,\neg(owns_1 \wedge owns_2)$: It is never the case that both processes own the resource. In general, properties of the form $\mathbf{G}\,p$, for non-temporal formulas p, express *system invariants*.

$\mathbf{G}(req_1 \implies \mathbf{F}\,owns_1)$: Whenever process 1 has requested the resource, it will eventually obtain it. Formulas of this form are often called *response properties* [93].

$\mathbf{G}\,\mathbf{F}(req_1 \wedge \neg(owns_1 \vee owns_2)) \implies \mathbf{G}\,\mathbf{F}\,owns_1$: If it is infinitely often the case that process 1 has requested the resource when the resource is free, then process 1 infinitely often owns the resource. This formula expresses a (strong) fairness condition for process 1.

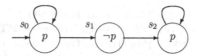

Fig. 5. A transition system $\mathcal{T}$ such that $\mathcal{T} \models \mathbf{F}\,\mathbf{G}\,p$ but $\mathcal{T} \not\models \mathbf{AF}\,\mathbf{AG}\,p$.

$\mathbf{G}(req_1 \wedge req_2 \implies (\neg owns_2\ \mathbf{W}\ (owns_2\ \mathbf{W}\ (\neg owns_2\ \mathbf{W}\ owns_1))))$:
Whenever both processes compete for the resource, process 2 will be granted the resource at most once before it is granted to process 1. This property, known as "1-bounded overtaking", is an example for a *precedence property*. It is best understood as asserting the existence of four, possibly empty or right-open, intervals that satisfy the respective conditions.

PTL formulas assert properties of single behaviors, but we are interested in *system validity*: we say that formula φ holds of $\mathcal{T}$ (written $\mathcal{T} \models \varphi$) if φ holds of all runs of $\mathcal{T}$. In this sense, **PTL** formulas express *correctness properties* of a system. The existence of a run satisfying a certain property cannot be expressed in **PTL**. Such *possibility properties* are the domain of branching-time logics such as the logic **CTL** (*computation tree logic* [25]).

Definition 4. *Formulas of propositional* **CTL** *are inductively defined as follows:*

 - *Every atomic proposition $v \in \mathcal{V}$ is a formula.*
 - *Boolean combinations of formulas are formulas.*
 - *If φ and ψ are formulas then* $\mathbf{EX}\,\varphi$, $\mathbf{EG}\,\varphi$, *and* $\varphi\,\mathbf{EU}\,\psi$ *are formulas.*

CTL formulas are interpreted at the states of a transition system. A *path* in $\mathcal{T}$ is an ω-sequence $\sigma = s_0 s_1 \ldots$ of states related by δ; it is an *s-path* if $s = s_0$.

Definition 5. *The relation* $\mathcal{T}, s \models \varphi$ *is inductively defined as follows:*

 - $\mathcal{T}, s \models v$ *(for $v \in \mathcal{V}$) iff $v \in s(\mathcal{V})$.*
 - *The semantics of boolean combinations is defined as usual.*
 - $\mathcal{T}, s \models \mathbf{EX}\,\varphi$ *iff there exists an s-path $s_0 s_1 \ldots$ such that $\mathcal{T}, s_1 \models \varphi$.*
 - $\mathcal{T}, s \models \mathbf{EG}\,\varphi$ *iff there is an s-path $s_0 s_1 \ldots$ such that $\mathcal{T}, s_i \models \varphi$ holds for all i.*
 - $\mathcal{T}, s \models \varphi\,\mathbf{EU}\,\psi$ *iff there exist an s-path $s_0 s_1 \ldots$ and $k \geq 0$ such that $\mathcal{T}, s_k \models \psi$ and $\mathcal{T}, s_j \models \varphi$ holds for all $0 \leq j < k$.*

Derived **CTL**-formulas include $\mathbf{EF}\,\varphi \equiv \mathbf{true}\,\mathbf{EU}\,\varphi$, $\mathbf{AX}\,\varphi \equiv \neg\,\mathbf{EX}\,\neg\varphi$, and $\mathbf{AG}\,\varphi \equiv \neg\,\mathbf{EF}\,\neg\varphi$. For example, the formula $\mathbf{AG}\,\neg(owns_1 \wedge owns_2)$ expresses mutual exclusion for the two-process resource manager, whereas $\mathbf{AG}(req_1 \implies \mathbf{EF}\,owns_1)$ asserts that whenever process 1 requests the resource, it *can* eventually obtain the resource, although there may be executions that do not honor the request. The formula $\mathbf{AG}\,\mathbf{EF}\,init$ (for a suitable predicate $init$) asserts that the system is resettable.

System validity for **CTL**-formulas is defined by $\mathcal{T} \models \varphi$ if $\mathcal{T}, s \models \varphi$ holds for all initial states s of $\mathcal{T}$. The expressiveness of **PTL** and **CTL** can be compared by analyzing which properties of transition systems can be formulated. It turns out that neither logic subsumes the other one [84,41,43]: whereas **PTL** is clearly incapable of expressing possibility properties, fairness properties cannot be stated in **CTL**. More specifically, there is no **CTL** formula that is system valid iff the **PTL** formula $\mathbf{F}\,\mathbf{G}\,\varphi$ is. In particular, it does not correspond to $\mathbf{AF}\,\mathbf{AG}\,\varphi$, as shown in Fig. 5: every run of the transition system $\mathcal{T}$ satisfies $\mathbf{F}\,\mathbf{G}\,p$ (either it stays in state s_0 forever or it ends in state s_2), but $\mathcal{T}, s_0 \not\models \mathbf{AF}\,\mathbf{AG}\,p$ (for the run that stays in state s_0 there is always the possibility to move to state s_1).

Extensions and variations. The lack of expressiveness of **CTL** is due to the requirement that path quantifiers (**E**, **A**) and temporal operators (**X**, **G**, **U**) alternate. The logic **CTL*** [41,43] removes this restriction and (strictly) subsumes both **PTL** and **CTL**. For example, the **CTL*** formula $\mathbf{AFG}\,p$ is system valid iff the **PTL** formula $\mathbf{F}\,\mathbf{G}\,p$ is.

The *propositional μ-calculus* [77], also known as μ**TL**, allows properties to be defined as smallest or greatest fixed points, generalizing recursive characterizations of temporal operators such as

$$\mathbf{EG}\,\varphi \;\equiv\; \varphi \wedge \mathbf{EX}\,\mathbf{EG}\,\varphi$$

It strictly subsumes the logic **CTL***. For example, the formula $\nu X.\varphi \wedge \mathbf{AX}\,\mathbf{AX}\,X$ asserts that φ holds at every state with even distance from the current state.

Alternating-time temporal logic [6] refines the path quantifiers of branching time temporal logics by allowing references to different processes (or agents) of a reactive system. One can, for example, assert that the resource manager can ensure mutual exclusion between the clients, or that the manager and client 1 can cooperate to prevent client 2 to access the resource.

3.3 ω-Automata

We have seen how to interpret temporal logic formulas over transition systems. On the other hand, one can construct a finite automaton that represents the models of a given **PTL** formula. This close connection between temporal logic and automata is the basis for **PTL** decision procedures and model checking algorithms because many properties of finite automata are decidable, even when applied to ω-words. The theory of automata over infinite words and trees was initiated by Büchi [19], Muller [101], and Rabin [110]. We present some of its basic elements; for more comprehensive expositions see the excellent survey articles by Thomas [120,121].

Definition 6. *A Büchi automaton $\mathcal{B} = (Q, I, \delta, F)$ over an alphabet Σ is given by a finite set Q of locations[4], a non-empty set $I \subseteq Q$ of initial locations, a transition relation $\delta \subseteq Q \times \Sigma \times Q$, and a set $F \subseteq Q$ of accepting locations.*

---

[4] We use the term *locations* rather than the conventional *states* to avoid confusion with the states of transition systems and temporal logic.

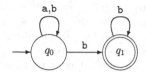

Fig. 6. A Büchi automaton.

A run *of* $\mathcal{B}$ *over an* ω*-word* $w = a_0 a_1 \ldots \in \Sigma^\omega$ *is an infinite sequence* $\rho = q_0 q_1 \ldots$ *of locations* $q_i \in Q$ *such that* $q_0 \in I$ *and* $(q_i, a_i, q_{i+1}) \in \delta$ *holds for all* $i \in \mathbb{N}$. *The run* ρ *is* accepting *iff there exists some* $q \in F$ *such that* $q_i = q$ *holds for infinitely many* $i \in \mathbb{N}$.

The language $\mathcal{L}(\mathcal{B}) \subseteq \Sigma^\omega$ *is the set of* ω*-words for which there exists some* accepting run ρ *of* $\mathcal{B}$. *A language* $L \subseteq \Sigma^\omega$ *is called* ω*-regular iff* $L = \mathcal{L}(\mathcal{B})$ *for some Büchi automaton* $\mathcal{B}$.

Büchi automata are presented just as ordinary (non-deterministic) finite automata over finite words [68]. The notion of "final locations", which obviously does not apply to ω-words, is replaced by the requirement that a run passes infinitely often through an accepting location. Figure 6 shows a two-location Büchi automaton with initial location q_0 and accepting location q_1 whose language is the set of ω-words over $\{a, b\}$ that contain only finitely many a's.

Many properties of classical finite automata carry over to Büchi automata. For example, the emptiness problem is decidable.

Theorem 1. *For a Büchi automaton* $\mathcal{B}$ *with* n *locations, it is decidable in time* $O(n)$ *whether* $\mathcal{L}(\mathcal{B}) = \emptyset$.

Proof. Because Q is finite, $\mathcal{L}(\mathcal{B}) \neq \emptyset$ iff there exist locations $q_0 \in I$, $q \in F$ and finite words $x \in \Sigma^*$ and $y \in \Sigma^+$ such that $q_0 \overset{x}{\Rightarrow} q$ and $q \overset{y}{\Rightarrow} q$ (where $q \overset{w}{\Rightarrow} q'$ means that there is a path in $\mathcal{B}$ from location q to q' labelled with w). The existence of such paths can be decided in linear time using the Tarjan-Paige algorithm [119] that enumerates the strongly connected components of $\mathcal{B}$ reachable from locations in I, and checking whether some SCC contains some accepting location. $\qquad\Box$

Observe that the construction used in the proof of theorem 1 implies that an ω-regular language is non-empty iff it contains some word of the form xy^ω where $x \in \Sigma^*$ and $y \in \Sigma^+$.

Unlike the case of standard finite automata, deterministic Büchi automata are strictly weaker than non-deterministic ones. For example, there is no deterministic Büchi automaton that accepts the same language as the automaton $\mathcal{B}$ of Fig. 6. Intuitively, the reason is that $\mathcal{B}$ uses unbounded non-determinism to "guess" when it has seen the last input a (for a rigorous proof see e.g. [120]). It is therefore impossible to prove closure of the class of ω-regular languages under complement in the standard way (first construct a deterministic Büchi automaton equivalent to the initial one, then complement the set of accepting locations). Nevertheless, Büchi [19] has shown that the complement of an ω-regular language is again ω-regular. His proof relied on combinatorial arguments (Ramsey's theorem) and was non-constructive. A succession of papers has replaced this argument with explicit constructions, culminating in the following result due to Safra [111] of essentially optimal complexity; Thomas [121,122] explains different strategies for proving closure under complement.

Proposition 1. *For a Büchi automaton $\mathcal{B}$ with n locations over alphabet Σ there is a Büchi automaton $\overline{\mathcal{B}}$ with $2^{O(n \log n)}$ locations such that $\mathcal{L}(\overline{\mathcal{B}}) = \Sigma^{\omega} \setminus \mathcal{L}(\mathcal{B})$.*

Other types of ω-automata have also been considered. *Generalized Büchi automata* define the acceptance condition by a (finite) set $\mathcal{F} = \{F_1, \ldots, F_n\}$ of sets of locations [126]. A run is accepting if some location from every F_i is visited infinitely often. Using a counter modulo n, it is not difficult to simulate a generalized Büchi automaton by a standard one. The algorithm for checking nonemptiness can be adapted by searching some strongly connected component that contains some location from every F_i. *Muller automata* also specify the acceptance condition as a set $\mathcal{F}$ of set of locations; a run is accepting if the set of locations that appears infinitely often is an element of $\mathcal{F}$. Rabin and Streett automata use pairs of sets of locations to define even more elaborate acceptance conditions, such as requiring that if locations in a set $R \subseteq Q$ are visited infinitely often then there are also infinitely many visits to locations in another set $G \subseteq Q$. Streett automata can be exponentially more succinct than Büchi automata, and deterministic Rabin and Streett automata are at the heart of Safra's proof. It is also possible to place acceptance conditions on the transitions rather than the locations [7,36].

Alternating automata [102] present a more radical departure from the format of Büchi automata and have attracted considerable interest in recent years. The basic idea is to allow the automaton to make a transition from one location to several successor locations that are simultaneously active. One way to define such a relation is to let $\delta(q, a)$ be a positive Boolean formula with the locations as atomic propositions. For example,

$$\delta(q_1, a) \quad = \quad (q_2 \wedge q_3) \vee q_4$$

specifies that whenever location q_1 is active and input symbol $a \in \Sigma$ is read, the automaton moves to locations q_2 and q_3 in parallel, or to location q_4. Runs of alternating automata are no longer infinite sequences, but rather infinite trees or dags of locations. Although they also define the class of ω-regular languages, alternating automata can be exponentially more succinct than Büchi automata, due to their inherent parallelism. On the other hand, checking for nonemptiness is normally of exponential complexity.

3.4   Temporal Logic and Automata

We can consider a behavior as an ω-word over the alphabet $2^{\mathcal{V}}$, identifying a system state s and the set $s(\mathcal{V})$ of atomic propositions that s satisfies. From

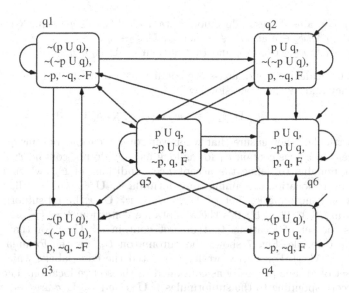

Fig. 7. Büchi automaton for $F \equiv (p \ \mathbf{U} \ q) \vee (\neg p \ \mathbf{U} \ q)$.

this perspective, **PTL** formulas and ω-automata are two different formalisms to describe ω-words, and it is interesting to compare their expressiveness. For example, the Büchi automaton of Fig. 6 can be identified with the **PTL** formula **F G** b.

We outline a construction of a generalized Büchi automaton $\mathcal{B}_\varphi$ for a given **PTL** formula φ such that $\mathcal{B}_\varphi$ accepts precisely those runs over which φ holds. In view of the high complexity of complementation (cf. Prop. 1), the construction is not defined by induction on the structure of φ but is based on a "global" construction that considers all subformulas of φ simultaneously. The *Fischer-Ladner closure* $\mathcal{C}(\varphi)$ of formula φ is the set of subformulas of φ and their complements, identifying $\neg\neg\psi$ and ψ. The locations of $\mathcal{B}_\varphi$ are subsets of $\mathcal{C}(\varphi)$, with the intuition that an accepting run of $\mathcal{B}_\varphi$ from location q satisfies the formulas in q. More precisely, the locations q of $\mathcal{B}_\varphi$ are all subsets of $\mathcal{C}(\varphi)$ that satisfy the following *healthiness conditions*:

- For all $\psi \in \mathcal{C}(\varphi)$, either $\psi \in q$ or $\neg\psi \in q$, but not both.
- If $\psi_1 \vee \psi_2 \in \mathcal{C}(\varphi)$ then $\psi_1 \vee \psi_2 \in q$ iff $\psi_1 \in q$ or $\psi_2 \in q$.
- Conditions for other boolean combinations are similar.
- If $\psi_1 \ \mathbf{U} \ \psi_2 \in q$, then $\psi_2 \in q$ or $\psi_1 \in q$.
- If $\psi_1 \ \mathbf{U} \ \psi_2 \in \mathcal{C}(\varphi) \setminus q$, then $\psi_2 \notin q$.

The initial locations of $\mathcal{B}_\varphi$ are those locations containing φ. The transition relation δ of $\mathcal{B}_\varphi$ is defined such that $(q, s, q') \in \delta$ iff all of the following conditions hold:

- $s = q \cap \mathcal{V}$ is the set of atomic propositions that appear in $\mathcal{V}$; these must obviously be satisfied immediately by any run starting in q.

- q' contains ψ (resp., does not contain ψ) if $\mathbf{X}\,\psi \in q$ (resp., $\mathbf{X}\,\psi \in \mathcal{C}(\varphi) \setminus q$).
- If $\psi_1\,\mathbf{U}\,\psi_2 \in q$ and $\psi_2 \notin q$ then $\psi_1\,\mathbf{U}\,\psi_2 \in q'$.
- If $\psi_1\,\mathbf{U}\,\psi_2 \in \mathcal{C}(\varphi) \setminus q$ and $\psi_1 \in q$ then $\psi_1\,\mathbf{U}\,\psi_2 \notin q'$.

The healthiness and next-state conditions are justified by propositional consistency and by the "recursion law"

$$\psi_1\,\mathbf{U}\,\psi_2 \;\equiv\; \psi_2 \vee (\psi_1 \wedge \mathbf{X}(\psi_1\,\mathbf{U}\,\psi_2))$$

In particular, they ensure that whenever some location contains $\psi_1\,\mathbf{U}\,\psi_2$, subsequent locations contain ψ_1 for as long as they do not contain ψ_2.

It remains to define the acceptance conditions of $\mathcal{B}_\varphi$, which must ensure that every location containing some formula $\psi_1\,\mathbf{U}\,\psi_2$ will be followed by some location containing ψ_2. Let $\psi_1^1\,\mathbf{U}\,\psi_2^1, \ldots, \psi_1^k\,\mathbf{U}\,\psi_2^k$ be all subformulas of this form in $\mathcal{C}(\varphi)$. Then $\mathcal{B}_\varphi$ has the acceptance condition $\mathcal{F} = \{F_1, \ldots, F_k\}$ where F_i is the set of locations that do not contain $\psi_1^i\,\mathbf{U}\,\psi_2^i$ or that contain ψ_2^i. As an example, Fig. 7 shows the automaton $\mathcal{B}_F$ for the formula $F \equiv (p\,\mathbf{U}\,q) \vee (\neg p\,\mathbf{U}\,q)$. For clarity, we have omitted the edge labels, which are simply the set of atomic propositions contained in the source location. The acceptance sets corresponding to the subformulas $p\,\mathbf{U}\,q$ and $\neg p\,\mathbf{U}\,q$ are $\{q_1, q_3, q_4, q_5, q_6\}$ and $\{q_1, q_2, q_3, q_5, q_6\}$. For example, they ensure that no accepting run remains forever in location q_2.

This construction, which is very similar to a tableau construction [128], implies the existence of a Büchi automaton that accepts precisely the models of any given **PTL** formula. The following proposition is due to [87,126].

Proposition 2. *For every **PTL** formula φ of length n there exists a Büchi automaton $\mathcal{B}_\varphi$ with $2^{O(n)}$ locations that accepts precisely the behaviors of which φ holds.*

Combining proposition 2 and theorem 1, it follows that the satisfiability problem for **PTL** is solvable in exponential time by checking whether $\mathcal{L}(\mathcal{B}_\varphi) = \emptyset$; in fact, Sistla and Clarke [114] have shown that the **PTL** satisfiability problem is PSPACE-complete. Note that the above construction invariably produces a Büchi automaton $\mathcal{B}_\varphi$ whose size is exponential in the length of the formula φ. Constructions that try to avoid this exponential blow-up [56,38,36] are the basis for actual implementations.

On the other hand, it is not the case that every ω-regular language can be defined by a **PTL** formula: Kamp [74] has shown that **PTL** formulas can define exactly the same behaviors as first-order logic formulas of the *monadic theory of linear orders*, that is, formulas built from $=$, $<$, and unary predicates $P_v(x)$, for $v \in \mathcal{V}$, interpreted over the natural numbers, see also [54]. This fragment of first-order logic is known to define the set of *star-free* ω-regular languages, a result due to McNaughton and Papert [98,121]. For example, the set of behaviors such that proposition p is true at the even positions (and may be true or false elsewhere) is not **PTL**-definable [128]. To attain the level of expressiveness of ω-regular languages (which, by Büchi's theorem, is that of the monadic second order theory of linear orders), **PTL** can be augmented by so-called "automaton operators" [128], by fixed-point formulas [117] or by quantification over atomic propositions. Unfortunately, the satisfiability problem for some of these logics is of non-elementary complexity; moreover, few applications seem to require the added expressiveness. Nevertheless, such a decision procedure has been implemented in MONA [76] and performs surprisingly well on practical examples.

Automata for other temporal logics. Automata-theoretic characterizations of branching-time logics [80] are based on tree automata [120,121], which again define a notion of regular tree languages. Alternating automata allow for a rather uniform presentation of decision procedures for linear-time, branching-time, and alternating-time temporal logics [103,125,82], based on different restrictions on the automaton format. An essentially equivalent approach that does not mention automata can be formulated in terms of logical games [118]. In particular, winning strategies replace the traditional presentation of counter-examples; this can give better feedback to the user who can then explore different scenarios that violate a property. The model checkers Truth [85] and CWB-NC [31] are based on these concepts.

4   Algorithms for Model Checking

Given a transition system $\mathcal{T}$ and a formula φ, the model checking problem is to decide whether $\mathcal{T} \models \varphi$ holds or not. If not, the model checker should provide an explanation why, in the form of a counterexample (i.e., a run of $\mathcal{T}$ that violates φ). For this to be feasible, $\mathcal{T}$ is usually required to be finite-state.

In accordance with the two parameters of the model checking problem ($\mathcal{T}$ and φ), there are two basic strategies when designing a model checking algorithm: "global" algorithms recurse on the structure of φ and evaluate each of its subformulas over all of $\mathcal{T}$. "Local" algorithms, in contrast, explore only parts of the state space of $\mathcal{T}$, but check all subformulas of φ in the process. The choice between global and local model checking algorithms does not affect the worst-case complexity of model checking algorithms, but the average behavior on practical examples can differ greatly. Observe that local algorithms may even be able to find errors of infinite-state systems; this is also true for global algorithms that represent the state space of $\mathcal{T}$ in an implicit form, as considered in section 4.3. Traditionally, **PTL** model checking has been based on the local approach, while model checkers for **CTL** and other branching-time logics have used global algorithms.

4.1   Local PTL Model Checking

The model checking problem for **PTL** can be restated as follows: given $\mathcal{T}$ and φ, does there exist a run of $\mathcal{T}$ that does not satisfy φ? This is a refinement of the satisfiability problem considered in section 3.4: instead of asking whether $\mathcal{L}(\mathcal{B}_{\neg\varphi}) = \emptyset$, we now ask whether the language defined by the product of $\mathcal{T}$ and $\mathcal{B}_{\neg\varphi}$ is empty or not.

Formally, assume given a finite transition system $\mathcal{T} = (S, I, \mathcal{A}, \delta_{\mathcal{T}})$ and a Büchi automaton $\mathcal{B}_{\neg\varphi} = (Q, J, \delta_{\mathcal{B}}, F)$ that accepts precisely those behaviors

```
dfs(boolean search_cycle) {
    p = top(stack);
    foreach (q in successors(p)) {
        if (search_cycle and (q == seed))
            report acceptance cycle and exit;
        if ((q, search_cycle) not in visited) {
            push q onto stack;
            enter (q, search_cycle) into visited;
            dfs(search_cycle);
            if (not search_cycle and (q is accepting)) {
                seed = q; dfs(true);
    } } }
    pop(stack);
}
// initialization
stack = emptystack(); visited = emptyset(); seed = nil;
foreach initial pair p {
    push p onto stack;
    enter (p, false) into visited;
    dfs(false)
}
```

Fig. 8. On-the-fly **PTL** model checking algorithm.

that do not satisfy φ. The model checking algorithm operates on pairs (s, q) of system states and automaton locations. A pair (s_0, q_0) is *initial* if $s_0 \in I$ and $q_0 \in J$ are initial for $\mathcal{T}$ and $\mathcal{B}_{\neg\varphi}$, respectively. A pair (s', q') is a *successor* of (s, q) if both $(s, A, s') \in \delta_{\mathcal{T}}$ (for some $A \in \mathcal{A}$) and $(q, s(\mathcal{V}), q') \in \delta_B$ hold: $\mathcal{T}$ and $\mathcal{B}_{\neg\varphi}$ make joint transitions, the input for $\mathcal{B}_{\neg\varphi}$ being determined by the values of the atomic propositions at the current system state. A pair (s, q) is *accepting* if $q \in F$ is an accepting automaton location; recall that $\mathcal{T}$ does not define an accepting condition. In particular, we assume any fairness conditions to be expressed as part of the formula φ.

As in the proof of theorem 1, $\mathcal{T}$ and $\mathcal{B}_{\neg\varphi}$ admit a joint execution iff there is some accepting pair that is reachable from some initial pair and from itself. The model checking algorithm shown in Fig. 8 is due to Courcoubetis et al [34]. It is called an "on-the-fly" algorithm because the exploration of reachable pairs is interleaved with the search for acceptance cycles. The algorithm maintains a stack of pairs whose successors need to be explored (resulting in a depth-first search) and a set of pairs that have already been visited. Starting from the initial pairs, the procedure dfs generates reachable pairs until some accepting pair is found. At this point, the search switches to cycle search mode (indicated by the boolean parameter search_cycle) and tries to find a path that leads back to the accepting pair. Pairs that have already been encountered in the current search mode are not explored further. Courcoubetis et al. [34] have shown that the algorithm will find some acceptance cycle if one exists, although it is not guaranteed to find all cycles (even if the search were continued instead of exiting).

When an acceptance cycle is found, the sequence of system states contained in the stack represents a run of $\mathcal{T}$ that violates formula φ and can be displayed to the user as a counter-example. Observe that the algorithm of Fig. 8 needs to store only the path back from the current pair back to the initial pair that it started from, and the set of visited pairs. In particular, it does not have to construct the entire product automaton. Of course, when no acceptance cycle is found (and the system is declared error-free), all reachable pairs will have to be explored eventually. However, state exploration stops as soon as an error has been detected. This can be an important practical advantage: the state space of a correct system is constrained by its invariants, which are usually broken when errors are introduced. It is therefore quite common for buggy systems to have many more reachable states, and resources could easily be exhausted if all of them had to be explored.

For large models, storing the set of visited pairs may become a problem. If one is willing to trade complete coverage for the ability to analyze systems that would otherwise be unmanageable, one can instead maintain a set of *hash codes* of visited pairs, possibly using several hashing functions [66].

The model checking algorithm of Fig. 8 has time complexity linear in the product of the sizes of $\mathcal{T}$ and of $\mathcal{B}_{\neg\varphi}$; by proposition 2 the latter can be exponential in the size of φ. However, correctness assertions are often rather short, and as we mentioned in section 3.1, the size of $\mathcal{T}$ can be exponential in the size of the description input to the model checker. Therefore, in practice the size of the transition system is the limiting factor. Given current technology, the analysis of systems on the order of 10^6–10^7 reachable states is feasible. Techniques that try to overcome this limit are described in section 4.4.

4.2   Global CTL Model Checking

Let us now consider global model checking algorithms for the logic **CTL**. By $[\![\psi]\!]_{\mathcal{T}}$ (for a **CTL** formula ψ) we denote the set of states s of $\mathcal{T}$ such that $\mathcal{T}, s \models \psi$. The model checking problem can then be rephrased as deciding whether $I \subseteq [\![\varphi]\!]_{\mathcal{T}}$ holds. The satisfaction sets $[\![\psi]\!]_{\mathcal{T}}$ can be computed by induction on the structure of ψ, as follows:

$$[\![v]\!]_{\mathcal{T}} = \{s : v \in s(\mathcal{V})\} \quad (\text{for } v \in \mathcal{V})$$

$$[\![\neg\psi]\!]_{\mathcal{T}} = S \setminus [\![\psi]\!]_{\mathcal{T}}$$

$$[\![\psi_1 \vee \psi_2]\!]_{\mathcal{T}} = [\![\psi_1]\!]_{\mathcal{T}} \cup [\![\psi_2]\!]_{\mathcal{T}}$$

$$[\![\mathbf{EX}\,\psi]\!]_{\mathcal{T}} = \delta^{-1}([\![\psi]\!]_{\mathcal{T}}) \;\; = \;\; \{s : t \in [\![\psi]\!]_{\mathcal{T}} \text{ for some } A, t \text{ s.t. } (s, A, t) \in \delta\}$$

$$[\![\mathbf{EG}\,\psi]\!]_{\mathcal{T}} = gfp(\lambda X.[\![\psi]\!]_{\mathcal{T}} \cap \delta^{-1}(X))$$

$$[\![\psi_1\,\mathbf{EU}\,\psi_2]\!]_{\mathcal{T}} = lfp(\lambda X.[\![\psi_2]\!]_{\mathcal{T}} \cup ([\![\psi_1]\!]_{\mathcal{T}} \cap \delta^{-1}(X)))$$

where $lfp(f)$ and $gfp(f)$, for a function $f : 2^S \to 2^S$, denote the least and greatest fixed points of f. (These fixed points exist and can be computed effectively because S is finite.) The clauses for the **EG** and **EU** connectives are justified from the recursive characterizations

$$\mathbf{EG}\,\psi \equiv \psi \wedge \mathbf{EX}\,\mathbf{EG}\,\psi$$

$$\psi_1\,\mathbf{EU}\,\psi_2 \equiv \psi_2 \vee (\psi_1 \wedge \mathbf{EX}(\psi_1\,\mathbf{EU}\,\psi_2))$$

The clause for **EU** calls for the computation of a least fixed point. Intuitively, this is because ψ_2 has to become true eventually, and thus the unfolding
of the fixed point must eventually terminate. On the other hand, the greatest
fixed point is required in the computation of $[\![\mathbf{EG}\,\psi]\!]$ because ψ has to hold ar-
bitrarily far down the path. Observe that the least fixed point of the function
corresponding to **EG** ψ is the empty set, whereas the greatest fixed point in the
case of **EU** computes $[\![\psi_1\ \mathbf{EW}\ \psi_2]\!]$.

For an implementation, we need to be able to efficiently calculate the *in-
verse image* function δ^{-1}. Sets $[\![\psi]\!]_{\mathcal{T}}$ that have already been computed can be
memorized in order to avoid recomputation of common subformulas. In order to
assess the complexity of the algorithm, first note that computation of the fixed
points is at most cubic in $|S|$ (if the computation has not stabilized, at least one
state is added to or removed from the current approximation per iteration, and
every iteration may need to search the entire set of transitions, which may be
quadratic in $|S|$). Second, there are as many recursive calls as φ has subformulas,
so the overall complexity is linear in the length of φ and cubic in $|S|$.

Clarke, Emerson, and Sistla [29] have proposed a less naive algorithm whose
complexity is linear in the product of the sizes of the formula and the model.
For formulas ψ_1 **EU** ψ_2, the idea is to apply backward breadth-first search. For
EG ψ, first the model is restricted to states satisfying ψ (which have already been
computed recursively), and the strongly connected components of this restricted
graph are enumerated. The set $[\![\mathbf{EG}\,\psi]\!]_{\mathcal{T}}$ consists of all states of the restricted
model from which some SCC can be reached; these states are again found using
breadth-first search.

Because fairness assumptions can not be formulated in **CTL**, they must
be specified as part of the model, and the model checking algorithm needs to
be adapted accordingly. For example, the SMV model checker [97] allows to
specify fairness constraints via **CTL** formulas. We define fair variants $\mathbf{EG}_f$ and
$\mathbf{EU}_f$ of the **CTL** operators whose semantics is as in definition 5, except that
quantifiers are restricted to fair paths, i.e., paths that contain infinitely many
states satisfying the constraints. Let us call a state s *fair* iff there is some fair s-
path; this is the case iff $\mathcal{T}, s \models \mathbf{EG}_f$ **true** holds. It is easy to see that $\psi_1\ \mathbf{EU}_f\ \psi_2$
is equivalent to ψ_1 **EU** $(\psi_2 \wedge \mathbf{EG}_f$ **true**$)$, hence we need only define an algorithm
to compute $[\![\mathbf{EG}_f\,\psi]\!]_{\mathcal{T}}$. The algorithm of Clarke, Emerson, and Sistla can be
modified by restricting to those SCCs that for each fairness constraint ζ_i contain
some state satisfying ζ_i. The complexity of fair **CTL** model checking is thus
still linear in the sizes of the formula and the model. For more information
on different kinds of fairness constraints and their associated model checking
algorithms see [42,44,81].

A global model checking algorithm for the branching-time fixed point logic
μ**TL** can be defined along the same lines. The complexity is then of the order
$|\varphi| \cdot |S|^{qd(\varphi)}$ where $qd(\varphi)$ denotes the nesting depth of the fixed point operators in
the formula φ. However, Emerson and Lei [44] observed that the computation of
fixed points can be optimized for blocks of fixed point operators of the same type,
resulting in a complexity of order $|\varphi| \cdot |S|^{ad(\varphi)}$ where $ad(\varphi)$ is the alternation
depth of fixed point operators of different type in φ. In particular, the complexity
of model checking *alternation-free* μ**TL** is the same as for **CTL** [42,32].

4.3 Symbolic Model Checking

The ability to analyze systems of relevant size using model checking requires efficient data structures to represent objects such as transition systems and sets of system states. Any finite-state system can be encoded using a set $\{b_1, \ldots, b_n\}$ of binary variables, just as ordinary data types of programming languages are represented in binary form on a digital computer. Sets of states, for example the set of initial states, can then be represented as propositional formulas over $\{b_1, \ldots, b_n\}$, and sets of pairs of states, such as the pairs (s, t) related by δ (for some action) can be represented as propositional formulas over $\{b_1, \ldots, b_n, b_1', \ldots, b_n'\}$ where the unprimed variables represent the pre-state s and the primed variables represent the post-state t. The size of the representing formula depends on the structure of the represented set rather than on its size: for example, the empty set and the set of all states are represented by **false** and **true**, both of size 1. For this reason, such representations are often called *symbolic*, and model checking algorithms that work on symbolic representations are called *symbolic model checking* techniques [20,97].

Binary decision diagrams [16,18] (more precisely, reduced ordered BDDs) are a data structure for the symbolic representation of sets that have become very popular for model checking because they offer the following features:

- Every boolean function has a unique, canonical BDD representation. If sharing of BDD nodes is enforced, equality of two functions can be decided in constant time by checking for pointer equality.
- Boolean operations such as negation, conjunction, implication etc. can be implemented with complexity proportional to the product of the inputs.
- Projection (quantification over one or several boolean variables) is easily implemented; its complexity is exponential in the worst case but tends to be well behaved in practice.

BDDs can be understood as compact representations of ordered decision trees. For example, Fig. 9 shows a decision tree for the formula

$$(x_1 \wedge y_1) \vee ((x_1 \vee y_1) \wedge (x_0 \wedge y_0))$$

which is the characteristic function for the carry bit produced by an addition of the two-bit numbers $x_1 x_0$ and $y_1 y_0$. To find the result for a given input, follow the path labelled with the bit values for each of the inputs. The label of the leaf indicates the value of the function. The tree is ordered because the variables appear in the same order along every branch.

The decision tree of Fig. 9 contains many redundancies. For example, the values of y_0 and y_1 are irrelevant if x_0 and x_1 are both 0. Similarly, y_0 is irrelevant in case x_0 is 0 and x_1 is 1. The redundancies can be removed by combining isomorphic subtrees (producing a directed acyclic graph from the tree) and eliminating nodes with identical subtrees. In our example, we obtain the BDD shown on the left-hand side of Fig. 10, where the leaf labelled 0 and all edges leading into it have been deleted for clarity. In an actual implementation, all BDD nodes that have been allocated are kept in a hash table indexed by the top variable and the two sub-BDDs, in order to avoid identical BDDs to be created twice.

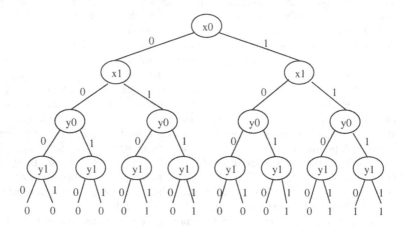

Fig. 9. Ordered decision tree for 2-bit carry.

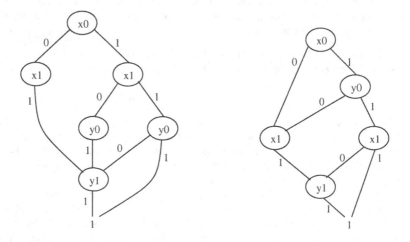

Fig. 10. BDDs for carry from 2-bit adder.

This ensures that two BDDs are functionally equivalent if and only if they are identical.

For a fixed variable ordering the BDD representing any given propositional formula is uniquely determined (and equivalent formulas are represented by the same BDD), but BDD sizes can vary greatly for different variable orderings. For example, the right-hand side of Fig. 10 shows a BDD for the same formula as before, but with the variable ordering x_0, y_0, x_1, y_1. When considering the carry for n-bit addition, the BDD sizes for the variable ordering $x_0, \ldots, x_{n-1}, y_0, \ldots, y_{n-1}$ grow exponentially with n, whereas they grow only linearly for the ordering $x_0, y_0, \ldots, x_{n-1}, y_{n-1}$. It is usually a good heuristic to group "dependent" variables closely together [53,47]. In general, however, the problem of finding an optimal variable ordering is NP-hard [17], and existing BDD libraries offer automatic reordering strategies based on steepest-ascent heuristics [51,10]. There are also functions (such as multiplication) for which no variable ordering can avoid exponential growth. This is also a problem when representing queues, frequently necessary for the analysis of communication protocols, and special-purpose data structures have been suggested [13,57].

Given two BDDs f and g (w.r.t. some fixed variable ordering) the BDD that corresponds to Boolean combinations such as $f \wedge g$, $f \vee g$ etc. can be constructed as follows:

- If f and g are both terminal BDDs (0 or 1), return the terminal BDD for the result of applying the operation.
- Otherwise, let v be the smaller of the variables at the root of f and g. Recursively apply the operation to the sub-BDDs that correspond to v being 0 and 1 (often called the "co-factors" of f and g for variable v). The results l and r correspond to the left- and right-hand branches of the result BDD. If $l = r$, return l, otherwise return a BDD with top variable v and children l and r.

When recursive calls to this "apply" function are memorized in a hash table, the number of subproblems to be solved is at most the number of pairs of nodes in f and g. Assuming perfect hashing, the complexity is therefore linear in the product of the sizes of f and g.

Observing that existential quantification over propositional variables can be computed as

$$(\exists v : f) \quad \equiv \quad f|_{v=0} \vee f|_{v=1}$$

the computation of a BDD corresponding to the quantified formula can be reduced to calculating co-factors and disjunction, and in fact quantification over a set of variables can be performed in a single pass over the BDD.

Symbolic **CTL** *model checking.* The naive **CTL** model checking algorithm of section 4.2 is straightforward to implement based on a BDD representation of the transition system $\mathcal{T}$. It computes BDDs for the sets $[\![\psi]\!]_{\mathcal{T}}$; in particular, the inverse image $\delta^{-1}(X)$ of a set X that is represented as a BDD is computed as the BDD

$$\exists b'_1, \ldots, b'_n : \delta \wedge X'$$

where X' is a copy of X in which all variables have been primed, and $b'_1, \ldots, b'_n$ are all the primed variables. Naive computation of fixed points is also very simple using BDDs because equality of BDDs can be decided in constant time.

It is interesting to compare the complexity of this BDD-based algorithm with that of explicit-state **CTL** model checking: Because the representation of the transition relation using BDDs can be exponentially more succinct than an explicit enumeration, the symbolic algorithm has exponential worst-case complexity in terms of the BDD sizes for the transition relation. First, the number of iterations required for the calculation of the fixed points may be exponential in the number of the input variables, and secondly, the computation of the inverse image may produce BDDs exponential in the size of their inputs. In practice, however, the number of iterations required for stabilization is often quite small, and the inverse image operation is well-behaved. This holds especially for hardware verification problems of "regular" structure and with short data paths. (A precise definition of "regular" is, however, very difficult.) For this class of problems, symbolic model checking has been successfully applied to the analysis of systems with 10^{100} states and more [30]. The main problem is then to find a variable ordering that yields a small representation of the transition system.

Symbolic model checking for other logics. The approach used for symbolic **CTL** model checking extends basically unchanged for propositional μ**TL**. An extension for the richer *relational μ-calculus* [105] has been described by Burch et al. [20] and implemented in the model checker μcke [12].

Symbolic model checking for **PTL** has been considered in [24,112]. The basic idea is to represent each formula in $\mathcal{C}(\varphi)$ by a boolean variable and to define the transition relation and acceptance condition of $\mathcal{B}_{\neg\varphi}$ in terms of these variables rather than constructing the automaton explicitly.

Bounded model checking. Although symbolic model checking has traditionally been associated with BDDs, other representations of boolean functions have also attracted interest. A recent example is the *bounded model checking* technique described in [11]. It relies on the observation that state sequences of fixed length, say k, can be represented using k copies of the variables used to represent a single state. The set of fixed-length sequences that represent terminating or looping runs of a given finite-state transition system $\mathcal{T}$ can therefore be encoded by formulas of (non-temporal) propositional logic, as well as the semantics of **PTL** formulas φ over such sequences. For any given length k, the existence of a state sequence of length k that represents a run of $\mathcal{T}$ satisfying φ can thus be reduced to the satisfiability of a certain propositional formula, which can be decided using efficient algorithms such as Stålmarck's algorithm [115] or SATO [130]. On the other hand, the *small model property* of **PTL** (which follows from the tableau-based decision procedure discussed in section 3.4) implies that there is a run of $\mathcal{T}$ satisfying φ if and only if there is some such run that can be represented by a sequence of length at most $|S| \cdot 2^{|\varphi|}$. A model checking algorithm is therefore obtained by enumerating all finite executions up to this bound.

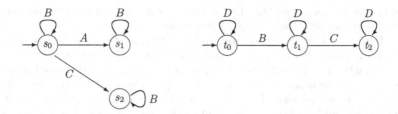

Fig. 11. Transition systems for two processes.

4.4 Partial-Order Reductions

Whereas symbolic model checking derives its power from efficient data structures for the representation and manipulation of large sets of sufficiently regular structure, algorithms based on explicit state enumeration can be improved if only a fraction of the reachable pairs need to be explored. This idea has been applied most successfully in the case of asynchronous systems that are composed of concurrent processes with relatively little interaction. The full transition system has as its runs all possible interleavings of the actions of the individual processes. For many properties, however, the relative order of concurrent actions is irrelevant, and it suffices to consider only a few sequentializations. More sophisticated models than simple interleaving-based representations have been considered in concurrency theory. In particular, *Mazurkiewicz traces* model runs as partial orders of events. Reduction techniques that take advantage of the commutativity of actions are therefore often called *partial-order reductions*, although the analogy to Mazurkiewicz traces is usually rather superficial.

The main problem in the design of a practical algorithm is to detect when two actions commute, given only the "local" knowledge available at a given system state. For example, consider the transition systems for two processes represented in Fig. 11. The left-hand process has a choice between executing actions A and C, whereas the right-hand process must perform action B before action C. Assuming that processes synchronize on common actions, action C is disabled at the global state (s_0, t_0), whereas A, B, and D could be performed. Moreover, all these actions commute at state (s_0, t_0). In particular, A and B can be executed in either order, resulting in the global state (s_1, t_1). However, it would be an error to conclude that only the successors of state (s_0, t_0) with respect to action A need be considered, because action C can then never be taken. The lesson is that actions that are currently disabled must nevertheless be taken into account when constructing a reduced state space.

There is also a danger of prematurely stopping the state exploration because actions are delayed forever along a loop. For an extreme example, consider again the transition systems of Fig. 11 at the global state (s_0, t_0). The local action D of the right-hand process is certainly independent of all other actions. The only successor with respect to that action is again state (s_0, t_0). A naive modification of the model checking algorithm of Fig. 8 would stop generating further states at that point, which is obviously inadequate.

Partial-order reduction algorithms [123,58,67,48,108] differ in how these problems are dealt with in order to arrive at a reasonably efficient algorithm that is adequate for the given task. The general idea is to approximate the semantic notion of commutativity of actions using syntactic criteria. For example, for a language based on shared variables, two actions of different processes are certainly independent if they do not update the same variable. For message passing communication, send and receive operations over the same channel are independent at those states where the channel is neither empty nor full. Second, the formula φ being analysed must be taken into account: call an action A *visible* for φ if A may change the value of a variable that occurs in φ. Holzmann and Peled [67] define an action to be *safe* if it is not visible and if it is provably independent (with the help of syntactic criteria) of all actions of different processes, even if these actions are currently disabled. The depth-first search algorithm shown in figure 8 can then be modified so that only successor states are considered for some process that can only perform safe actions at the current state. Consideration of the actions of other processes is thus delayed. However, the delayed actions must be considered before a loop is completed. This rather simple heuristic can already lead to substantial savings and carries almost no overhead because the set of safe actions can be determined statically.

More elaborate reduction techniques are considered, for example, in [58,107, 124]. There is always a tradeoff between the potential effectiveness of a reduction method and the overhead involved in computing a sufficient set of actions that must be explored at a given state. Moreover, the effectiveness of partial-order reductions in general depends on the structure of the system: while they are useless for tightly synchronized systems, they may dramatically reduce the numbers of states and transitions explored during model checking for loosely coupled, asynchronous systems.

5   Further Topics

We conclude this survey with brief references to some more advanced topics in the context of model checking. Several of these issues are addressed in detail in other contributions to this volume.

Abstraction. Although techniques such as symbolic model checking and partial-order reduction attempt to battle the infamous state explosion problem, the size of systems that can be analysed using model checking remains relatively limited: even astronomical numbers such as 10^{100} states are generated by systems with a few hundred bits, which is a far cry from realistic hardware or software systems. Model checking must therefore be performed on rather abstract models. It is often advocated that model checking be applied to high-level designs during the early stages of system development because the payoff of finding bugs at that level is high whereas the costs are low. For example, Lilius and Paltor [88] describe a tool for model checking UML state machine diagrams [14], and model checking of system specifications of similar degrees of abstraction has been considered in [5,52].

When the analysis of big models cannot be avoided, it is rarely necessary to consider them in full detail in order to verify or falsify some given property. This idea can be formalized as an abstraction function (or relation) that induces some abstract system model such that the property holds of the original, "concrete" model if it can be proven for the abstract model. (Dually, abstractions can be set up such that failure of the property in the abstract model implies failure in the concrete model.) In general, the appropriate abstraction relation depends on the application and has to be defined by the user. Abstraction-based approaches are therefore not entirely automatic "push-button" methods in the same way that standard model checking is. Given a concrete model and an abstraction relation, one can either attempt to construct the abstract model using techniques of abstract interpretation [35] or verify the correctness of a proposed abstract model using theorem proving. There is a large body of literature on abstraction techniques, including [26,37,89,90,99].

A particularly attractive way of presenting abstractions is in the form of *predicate abstractions* where predicates of interest at the concrete level are mapped to Boolean variables at the abstract level. The abstract models can then be presented as *verification diagrams*, which are intuitively meaningful to system designers and can be used to (interactively) verify systems of arbitrary complexity [39,92,113,75,22].

For restricted classes of systems, it may be possible to apply fixed abstraction mappings (an example is provided by parameterized systems with simple communication patterns [9]) and thus obtain completely automatic methods. Valmari, in his contribution to this volume, also considers a fixed notion of abstraction that is amenable to full automation.

Symmetry reductions. Informal correctness arguments are often simplified by appealing to some form of symmetry in the system. For examples, components may be replicated in a regular manner, or data may be processed such that permuting individual values does not affect the overall behavior. More formally, a transition system $\mathcal{T}$ is said to be invariant under a permutation π of its states and actions if $(s, A, t) \in \delta$ iff $(\pi(s), \pi(A), \pi(t)) \in \delta$ and $s \in I$ iff $\pi(s) \in I$ holds for all states s, t and all actions A. $\mathcal{T}$ is invariant under a group G of permutations if it is invariant under every permutation in the group. Such a group G induces an equivalence relation on the set of states defined by $s \sim t$ iff $t = \pi(s)$ for some $\pi \in G$. Provided the properties are also insensitive to the permutations in G, one can check the quotient of $\mathcal{T}$ under $\sim$ and obtain a system that can be much smaller [116,23,70,71].

Infinite-state systems. The extension of model checking techniques to infinite-state systems with sufficiently regular state spaces has been an area of active research in recent years [21,49,50,100]. See Esparza's contribution to this volume for more details.

Parameterized systems. One is often interested in the properties of a family of finite-state systems that differ in some parameter such as the number of processes. Although individual members of the family can be analyzed using standard model checking techniques, the verification of the entire family requires additional considerations. A natural idea is to perform standard model checking for fixed parameter values and then establish correctness for arbitrary parameter values by induction. In some cases, even the induction step can be justified by model checking. For example, Browne et al. [15] suggest to model check a two-process system, and to establish a bisimulation relation between two-process and n-process systems, ensuring that formulas expressed in a suitable logic cannot distinguish between them. This approach has been extended in [83,127] by using a finite-state process I that acts as an invariant in that the composition of I with another process is again bisimilar to I. Because both I and the individual processes are finite-state, this can be accomplished using (a variation of) standard model checking. Related techniques are described in [46,55].

Compositional verification. The effects of state explosion can be mitigated when the overall verification effort can be subdivided by considering the components of a complex system one at a time. As in the case of abstraction, compositional reasoning normally requires additional input from the user who must specify appropriate properties to be verified of the individual components. The main problem is that components cannot necessarily be expected to function correctly in arbitrary environments, because their design relies on properties of the system the components are expected to be part of. Thus, corresponding assumptions have to be introduced in the statement of the components' correctness properties. Early work on compositional verification [8,109] required components to form a hierarchy with respect to their dependency. In general, however, every component is part of every other component's environment, and circular dependencies among components are to be expected. More recently, different formulations of assumption-commitment specifications have been studied [1,33,96] that can accomodate circular dependencies, based on a form of computational induction. A collection of papers on compositional methods for specification and verification is contained in [40]. Model checking algorithms for modular verification are described, among others, in [59,73,72].

Real-time systems. Whereas temporal logics such as **PTL** and **CTL** only formalize the relative ordering of states and events, many systems require assertions about quantitative aspects of time, and adequate formal models such as timed automata [2] or timed transition systems [62] and logics [4] have been proposed. Algorithms for the reachability and model checking problems for such models include [3,63,64]. In general, the complexity for the verification of real-time and hybrid systems is much higher than for untimed systems, and tools such as KRONOS [129], UPPAAL [86] or HYTECH [61] are restricted to relatively small systems. See the contribution by Larsen and Pettersson to this volume for a more comprehensive presentation of the state of the art in model checking techniques for real-time systems.

References

1. Martín Abadi and Leslie Lamport. Conjoining specifications. *ACM Transactions on Programming Languages and Systems*, 17(3):507–534, May 1995.
2. R. Alur. Timed automata. In *Verification of Digital and Hybrid Systems*, NATO ASI Series. Springer-Verlag, 1998.
3. R. Alur, C. Courcoubetis, and D. Dill. Model-checking for real-time systems. In *5th Ann. IEEE Symp. on Logics in Computer Science*, pages 414–425. IEEE Press, 1990.
4. R. Alur and T. A. Henzinger. Logics and models of real time: a survey. In *Real Time: Theory in Practice*, volume 600 of *Lecture Notes in Computer Science*, pages 74–106. Springer-Verlag, 1992.
5. R. Alur, G. J. Holzmann, and D. Peled. An analyzer for message sequence charts. In B. Steffen and T. Margaria, editors, *Tools and Constructions for the Analysis of Systems (TACAS'96)*, volume 1055 of *Lecture Notes in Computer Science*, pages 35–48, Passau, Germany, 1996. Springer-Verlag. See also http://cm.bell-labs.com/cm/cs/what/ubet/index.html.
6. Rajeev Alur, Thomas A. Henzinger, and Orna Kupferman. Alternating-time temporal logic. In *38th IEEE Symposium on Foundations of Computer Science*, pages 100–109. IEEE Press, October 1997.
7. A. Anuchitanukul. *Synthesis of Reactive Programs*. PhD thesis, Stanford University, 1995.
8. H. Barringer, R. Kuiper, and A. Pnueli. Now you may compose temporal logic specifications. In *16th ACM Symp. on Theory of Computing*, pages 51–63. ACM Press, 1984.
9. K. Baukus, S. Bensalem, Y. Lakhnech, and K. Stahl. Abstracting WS1S systems to verify parameterized networks. In S. Graf and M. Schwartzbach, editors, *Tools and Algorithms for the Construction and Analysis of Systems (TACAS 2000)*, volume 1785 of *Lecture Notes in Computer Science*, pages 188–203. Springer-Verlag, 2000.
10. J. Bern, C. Meinel, and A. Slobodová. Global rebuilding of BDDs – avoiding the memory requirement maxima. In P. Wolper, editor, *7th Workshop on Computer Aided Verification (CAV'95)*, volume 939 of *Lecture Notes in Computer Science*, pages 4–15. Springer-Verlag, 1995.
11. A. Biere, A. Cimatti, M. Fujita, and Y. Zhu. Symbolic model checking using SAT procedures instead of BDDs. In *36th ACM/IEEE Design Automation Conference (DAC'99)*, 1999.
12. Armin Biere. *Effiziente Modellprüfung des μ-Kalküls mit binären Entscheidungsdiagrammen*. PhD thesis, Univ. Karlsruhe, Germany, 1997.
13. B. Boigelot and P. Godefroid. Symbolic verification of communication protocols with infinite state spaces using QDDs. In R. Alur and T. Henzinger, editors, *8th Workshop on Computer-Aided Verification (CAV'96)*, volume 1102 of *Lecture Notes in Computer Science*, pages 1–12. Springer-Verlag, 1996.
14. G. Booch, J. Rumbaugh, and I. Jacobson. *Unified Modelling Language: User Guide*. Addison Wesley, 1999.
15. M. C. Browne, E. M. Clarke, and O. Grumberg. Reasoning about networks with many identical finite-state processes. *Information and Computation*, 81:13–31, 1989.
16. R. E. Bryant. Graph-based algorithms for boolean function manipulation. *IEEE Transactions on Computers*, C-35(8):677–691, 1986.

17. R. E. Bryant. On the complexity of VLSI implementations and graph representations of boolean functions with application to integer multiplication. *IEEE Trans. on Computers*, 40(2):205–213, 1991.

18. R. E. Bryant. Symbolic boolean manipulations with ordered binary decision diagrams. *ACM Computing Surveys*, 24(3):293–317, 1992.

19. J. R. Büchi. On a decision method in restricted second-order arithmetics. In *International Congress on Logic, Method and Philosophy of Science*, pages 1–12. Stanford University Press, 1962.

20. J. R. Burch, E. M. Clarke, K. L. McMillan, D. Dill, and L. J. Hwang. Symbolic model checking: 10^{20} states and beyond. *Information and Computation*, 98(2):142–170, 1992.

21. O. Burkart and J. Esparza. More infinite results. *Electronic Notes in Theoretical Computer Science*, 6, 1997. http://www.elsevier.nl/locate/entcs/volume6.html.

22. Dominique Cansell, Dominique Méry, and Stephan Merz. Predicate diagrams for the verification of reactive systems. In *2nd Intl. Conf. on Integrated Formal Methods (IFM 2000)*, Lecture Notes in Computer Science, Dagstuhl, Germany, November 2000. Springer-Verlag. To appear.

23. E. M. Clarke, T. Filkorn, and S. Jha. Exploiting symmetry in temporal logic model checking. In C. Courcoubetis, editor, *5th Workshop on Computer-Aided Verification (CAV'93)*, volume 697 of *Lecture Notes in Computer Science*, Elounda, Crete, 1993. Springer-Verlag.

24. E. M. Clarke, O. Grumberg, and K. Hamaguchi. Another look at LTL model checking. *Formal Methods in System Design*, 10:47–71, 1997.

25. Edmund M. Clarke and E. Allen Emerson. Synthesis of synchronization skeletons for branching time temporal logic. In *Workshop on Logic of Programs*, volume 131 of *Lecture Notes in Computer Science*, Yorktown Heights, N.Y., 1981. Springer-Verlag.

26. Edmund M. Clarke, Orna Grumberg, and David E. Long. Model checking and abstraction. *ACM Transactions on Programming Languages and Systems*, 16(5):1512–1542, September 1994.

27. Edmund M. Clarke, Orna Grumberg, and Doron Peled. *Model Checking*. MIT Press, Cambridge, MA, 1999.

28. Edmund M. Clarke and Holger Schlingloff. Model checking. In A. Voronkov, editor, *Handbook of Automated Deduction*. Elsevier, 2000. To appear.

29. E.M. Clarke, E.A. Emerson, and A.P. Sistla. Automatic verification of finite-state concurrent systems using temporal logic specifications. *ACM Transactions on Programming Languages and Systems*, 8(2):244–263, 1986.

30. E.M. Clarke, O. Grumberg, H. Hiraishi, S. Jha, D.E. Long, K.L. McMillan, and L.A. Ness. Verification of the Futurebus+ cache coherence protocol. In D. Agnew, L. Claesen, and R. Camposano, editors, *IFIP Conference on Computer Hardware Description Languages and their Applications*, pages 5–20, Ottawa, Canada, 1993. Elsevier Science Publishers B.V.

31. R. Cleaveland and S. Sims. Generic tools for verifying concurrent systems. *Science of Computer Programming*, 2000. See also http://www.cs.sunysb.edu/~cwb/.

32. R. Cleaveland and B. Steffen. A linear-time model-checking algorithm for the alternation-free modal μ-calculus. *Formal Methods in System Design*, 2:121–147, 1993.

33. P. Collette. An explanatory presentation of composition rules for assumption-commitment specifications. *Information Processing Letters*, 50(1):31–35, 1994.

34. C. Courcoubetis, M. Vardi, P. Wolper, and M. Yannakakis. Memory-efficient algorithms for the verification of temporal properties. *Formal methods in system design*, 1:275–288, 1992.

35. Patrick Cousot and Radhia Cousot. Abstract interpretation: A unified lattice model for static analysis of programs by construction or approximation of fixpoints. In *4th ACM Symposium on Principles of Programming Languages*, pages 238–252, Los Angeles, California, 1977. ACM Press.

36. J.-M. Couvreur. On-the-fly verification of linear temporal logic. In J.M. Wing, J. Woodcock, and J. Davies, editors, *FM'99 – Formal Methods*, volume 1708 of *Lecture Notes in Computer Science*, pages 253–271, Toulouse, France, 1999. Springer-Verlag.

37. Dennis Dams, Orna Grumberg, and Rob Gerth. Abstract interpretation of reactive systems: Abstractions preserving ∀CTL*, ∃CTL* and CTL*. In Ernst-Rüdiger Olderog, editor, *Programming Concepts, Methods, and Calculi (PRO-COMET '94)*, pages 561–581, Amsterdam, 1994. North Holland/Elsevier.

38. M. Daniele, F. Giunchiglia, and M. Vardi. Improved automata generation for linear temporal logic. In *Computer Aided Verification (CAV'99)*, volume 1633 of *Lecture Notes in Computer Science*, pages 249–260, Trento, Italy, 1999. Springer-Verlag.

39. Luca de Alfaro, Zohar Manna, Henny B. Sipma, and Tomás Uribe. Visual verification of reactive systems. In Ed Brinksma, editor, *Tools and Algorithms for the Construction and Analysis of Systems (TACAS'97)*, volume 1217 of *Lecture Notes in Computer Science*, pages 334–350. Springer-Verlag, 1997.

40. W.-P. de Roever, H. Langmaack, and A. Pnueli, editors. *Compositionality: The Significant Difference*, volume 1536 of *Lecture Notes in Computer Science*. Springer-Verlag, 1998.

41. E. A. Emerson and J. Y. Halpern. "sometimes" and "not never" revisited: on branching time vs. linear time. *Journal of the ACM*, 33:151–178, 1986.

42. E. A. Emerson, C. S. Jutla, and A. P. Sistla. On model checking for fragments of μ-calculus. In C. Courcoubetis, editor, *5th Workshop on Computer-Aided Verification (CAV'93)*, volume 697 of *Lecture Notes in Computer Science*. Springer-Verlag, 1993.

43. E. A. Emerson and C. L. Lei. Modalities for model checking: Branching time strikes back. In *12th Symp. on Principles of Programming Languages (POPL'85)*, New Orleans, 1985. ACM Press.

44. E. A. Emerson and C. L. Lei. Efficient model checking in fragments of the propositional μ-calculus. In *1st Symp. on Logic in Computer Science*, Boston, Mass., 1986. IEEE Press.

45. E. Allen Emerson. *Handbook of theoretical computer science*, chapter Temporal and modal logic, pages 997–1071. Elsevier Science Publishers B.V., 1990.

46. E. Allen Emerson and Kedar S. Namjoshi. Automatic verification of parameterized synchronous systems. In R. Alur and T. Henzinger, editors, *8th International Conference on Computer Aided Verification (CAV'96)*, Lecture Notes in Computer Science. Springer-Verlag, 1996.

47. R. Enders, T. Filkorn, and D. Taubner. Generating BDDs for symbolic model checking. *Distributed Computing*, 6:155–164, 1993.

48. J. Esparza. Model checking using net unfoldings. *Science of Computer Programming*, 23:151–195, 1994.

49. J. Esparza. Decidability of model-checking for infinite-state concurrent systems. *Acta Informatica*, 34:85–107, 1997.

50. J. Esparza, A. Finkel, and R. Mayr. On the verification of broadcast protocols. In *14th IEEE Symposium on Logic in Computer Science*, pages 352–359, Trento, Italy, 1999. IEEE Press.

51. E. Felt, G. York, R. Brayton, and A. S. Vincentelli. Dynamic variable reordering for BDD minimization. In *European Design Automation Conference*, pages 130–135, 1993.

52. T. Firley, U. Goltz, M. Huhn, K. Diethers, and T. Gehrke. Timed sequence diagrams and tool-based analysis – a case study. In R. France and B. Rumpe, editors, *2nd Intl. Conference on the Unified Modelling Language (UML'99)*, volume 1723 of *Lecture Notes in Computer Science*, pages 645–660. Springer-Verlag, 1999.

53. H. Fuji, G. Oomoto, and C. Hori. Interleaving based variable ordering methods for binary decision diagrams. In *Intl. Conf. on Computer Aided Design (ICCAD'93)*. IEEE Press, 1993.

54. D. Gabbay, I. Hodkinson, and M. Reynolds. *Temporal Logic: Mathematical Foundations and Computational Aspects*, volume 1. Clarendon Press, Oxford, UK, 1994.

55. S. M. German and A. P. Sistla. Reasoning about systems with many processes. *Journal of the ACM*, 39:675–735, 1992.

56. R. Gerth, D. Peled, M. Vardi, and P. Wolper. Simple on-the-fly automatic verification of linear temporal logic. In *Protocol Specification, Testing, and Verification*, pages 3–18, Warsaw, Poland, 1995. Chapman & Hall.

57. P. Godefroid and D. E. Long. Symbolic protocol verification with queue BDDs. In *11th Ann. IEEE Symp. on Logic in Computer Science (LICS'96)*, New Brunswick, NJ, 1996. IEEE Press.

58. P. Godefroid and P. Wolper. A partial approach to model checking. *Information and Computation*, 110(2):305–326, 1994.

59. Orna Grumberg and David E. Long. Model checking and modular verification. *ACM Transactions on Programming Languages and Systems*, 16(3):843–871, May 1994.

60. David Harel and Amir Pnueli. On the development of reactive systems. In K. R. Apt, editor, *Logics and Models of Concurrent Systems*, volume F13 of *NATO ASI Series*, pages 477–498. Springer-Verlag, 1985.

61. T. A. Henzinger, P.-H. Ho, and H. Wong-Toi. HyTech: A model checker for hybrid systems. *Software Tools for Technology Transfer*, 1:110–122, 1997.

62. T. A. Henzinger, Z. Manna, and A. Pnueli. Temporal proof methodologies for timed transition systems. *Information and Computation*, 112:273–337, 1994.

63. Thomas A. Henzinger, Orna Kupferman, and Moshe Y. Vardi. A space-efficient on-the-fly algorithm for real-time model checking. In *7th International Conference on Concurrency Theory (CONCUR 1996)*, volume 1119 of *Lecture Notes in Computer Science*, pages 514–529. Springer-Verlag, 1996.

64. Thomas A. Henzinger, Xavier Nicollin, Joseph Sifakis, and Sergio Yovin. Symbolic model checking for real-time systems. *Information and Computation*, 111:193–244, 1994.

65. Gerard Holzmann. The Spin model checker. *IEEE Trans. on Software Engineering*, 23(5):279–295, may 1997.

66. Gerard Holzmann. An analysis of bitstate hashing. *Formal Methods in System Design*, November 1998.

67. Gerard Holzmann and Doron Peled. An improvement in formal verification. In *IFIP WG 6.1 Conference on Formal Description Techniques*, pages 197–214, Bern, Switzerland, 1994. Chapman & Hall.

68. John E. Hopcroft and Jeffrey D. Ullman. *Introduction to automata theory, languages, and computation.* Addison-Wesley, Reading, Mass., 1979.
69. Michael Huth and Mark D. Ryan. *Logic in Computer Science.* Cambridge University Press, Cambridge, U.K., 2000.
70. C. N. Ip and D. Dill. Better verification through symmetry. In *11th Intl. Symp. on Computer Hardware Description Languages and their Applications*, pages 87–100. North Holland, 1993.
71. C. N. Ip and D. Dill. Verifying systems with replicated components in Murphi. In *Intl. Conference on Computer-Aided Verification (CAV'96)*, Lecture Notes in Computer Science. Springer-Verlag, 1996.
72. Bernhard Josko. Verifying the correctness of AADL modules using model checking. In J. W. de Bakker, W.-P. de Roever, and G. Rozenberg, editors, *Stepwise Refinement of Distributed Systems: Models, Formalisms, Correctness*, volume 430 of *Lecture Notes in Computer Science*, pages 386–400. Springer-Verlag, Berlin, 1989.
73. Bernhard Josko. *Modular Specification and Verification of Reactive Systems.* PhD thesis, Univ. Oldenburg, Fachbereich Informatik, April 1993.
74. H. W. Kamp. *Tense Logic and the Theory of Linear Order.* PhD thesis, Univ. of California at Los Angeles, 1968.
75. Yonit Kesten and Amir Pnueli. Verifying liveness by augmented abstraction. In *Annual Conference of the European Association for Computer Science Logic (CSL'99)*, Lecture Notes in Computer Science, Madrid, 1999. Springer-Verlag.
76. Nils Klarlund. Mona & Fido: The logic-automaton connection in practice. In *Computer Science Logic, CSL '97*, volume 1414 of *LNCS*, pages 311–326, Aarhus, Denmark, 1998.
77. Dexter Kozen. Results on the propositional mu-calculus. *Theoretical Computer Science*, 27:333–354, 1983.
78. Saul A. Kripke. Semantical considerations on modal logic. *Acta Philosophica Fennica*, 16:83–94, 1963.
79. Fred Kröger. *Temporal Logic of Programs*, volume 8 of *EATCS Monographs on Theoretical Computer Science*. Springer-Verlag, Berlin, 1987.
80. O. Kupferman, M. Vardi, and P. Wolper. An automata-theoretic approach to branching-time model checking. In *6th Intl. Conf. on Computer-Aided Verification (CAV'94)*, Lecture Notes in Computer Science. Springer-Verlag, 1994. Full version (1999) available at http://www.cs.rice.edu/~vardi/papers/.
81. O. Kupferman and M. Y. Vardi. Verification of fair transition systems. In R. Alur and T. Henzinger, editors, *8th Workshop on Computer-Aided Verification (CAV'96)*, volume 1102 of *Lecture Notes in Computer Science*, pages 372–382. Springer-Verlag, 1996.
82. Orna Kupferman and Moshe Y. Vardi. Weak alternating automata are not so weak. In *5th Israeli Symposium on Theory of Computing and Systems*, pages 147–158. IEEE Press, 1997.
83. R. P. Kurshan and K. L. McMillan. A structural induction theorem for processes. In *8th Ann. ACM Symp. on Principles of Distributed Computing.* ACM Press, 1989.
84. Leslie Lamport. 'sometime' is sometimes 'not never'. In *Proc. 7th Ann. Symp. on Princ. of Prog. Lang. (POPL'80)*, pages 174–185. ACM SIGACT-SIGPLAN, January 1980.

85. M. Lange, M. Leucker, T. Noll, and S. Tobies. Truth – a verification platform for concurrent systems. In *Tool Support for System Specification, Development, and Verification*, Advances in Computing Science. Springer-Verlag Wien New York, 1999.

86. K. Larsen, P. Petterson, and W. Yi. Uppaal in a nutshell. *Software Tools for Technology Transfer*, 1, 1997.

87. Orna Lichtenstein, Amir Pnueli, and Lenore Zuck. The glory of the past. In Rohit Parikh, editor, *Logics of Programs*, volume 193 of *Lecture Notes in Computer Science*, pages 196–218, Berlin, June 1985. Springer-Verlag.

88. J. Lilius and I. P. Paltor. Formalising UML state machines for model checking. In R. France and B. Rumpe, editors, *UML'99 – Beyond the Standard*, volume 1723 of *Lecture Notes in Computer Science*. Springer-Verlag, 1999.

89. Claire Loiseaux, Susanne Graf, Joseph Sifakis, Ahmed Bouajjani, and Saddek Bensalem. Property preserving abstractions for the verification of concurrent systems. *Formal Methods in System Design*, 6:11–44, 1995. A preliminary version appeared as Spectre technical report RTC40, Grenoble, France, 1993.

90. D. E. Long. *Model checking, Abstraction and Compositional Verification*. PhD thesis, CMU School of Computer Science, 1993. CMU-CS-93-178.

91. Gavin Lowe. Breaking and fixing the Needham-Schroeder public key protocol using FDR. In *Tools and Algorithms for the Construction and Analysis of Systems (TACAS'96)*, volume 1055 of *Lecture Notes in Computer Science*, pages 147–166. Springer-Verlag, 1996.

92. Z. Manna, A. Browne, H.B. Sipma, and T.E. Uribe. Visual abstractions for temporal verification. In A. Haeberer, editor, *AMAST'98*, volume 1548 of *Lecture Notes in Computer Science*, pages 28–41. Springer-Verlag, 1998.

93. Zohar Manna and Amir Pnueli. A hierarchy of temporal properties. In *9th. ACM Symposium on Principles of Distributed Computing*, pages 377–408. ACM, 1990.

94. Zohar Manna and Amir Pnueli. *The temporal logic of reactive and concurrent systems—Specification*. Springer-Verlag, New York, 1992.

95. Zohar Manna and Amir Pnueli. *The temporal logic of reactive and concurrent systems—Safety properties*. Springer-Verlag, New York, 1995.

96. Kenneth L. McMillan. A compositional rule for hardware design refinement. In O. Grumberg, editor, *9th International Conference on Computer Aided Verification (CAV'97)*, volume 1254 of *Lecture Notes in Computer Science*, pages 24–35, Haifa, Israel, 1997. Springer-Verlag.

97. K.L. McMillan. *Symbolic Model Checking*. Kluwer Academic Publishers, 1993.

98. R. McNaughton and S. Papert. *Counter-Free Automata*. MIT Press, Cambridge, Mass., 1971.

99. Stephan Merz. Rules for abstraction. In R. K. Shyamasundar and K. Ueda, editors, *Advances in Computing Science—ASIAN'97*, volume 1345 of *Lecture Notes in Computer Science*, pages 32–45, Kathmandu, Nepal, December 1997. Springer-Verlag.

100. Faron Moller. Infinite results. In U. Montanari and V. Sassone, editors, *7th International Conference on Concurrency Theory (CONCUR'96)*, volume 1119 of *Lecture Notes in Computer Science*, pages 195–216, Pisa, Italy, 1996. Springer-Verlag.

101. D. E. Muller. Infinite sequences and finite machines. In *Switching Circuit Theory and Logical Design: Fourth Annual Symposium*, pages 3–16, New York, 1963. IEEE Press.

102. D. E. Muller, A. Saoudi, and P. E. Schupp. Alternating automata, the weak monadic theory of the tree and its complexity. In *13th ICALP*, volume 226 of *Lecture Notes in Computer Science*, pages 275–283. Springer-Verlag, 1986.

103. D.E. Muller, A. Saoudi, and P.E. Schupp. Weak alternating automata give a simple explanation of why most temporal and dynamic logics are decidable in exponential time. In *3rd IEEE Symposium on Logic in Computer Science*, pages 422–427. IEEE Press, 1988.

104. Roger Needham and Michael Schroeder. Using encryption for authentication in large networks of computers. *Communications of the ACM*, 21(12):993–999, 1978.

105. D. M. Park. Finiteness is mu-ineffable. Theory of Computation Report 3, University of Warwick, 1974.

106. Lawrence C. Paulson. Proving security protocols correct. In *14th IEEE Symposium on Logic in Computer Science*, pages 370–383, Trento, Italy, 1999. IEEE Press.

107. D. Peled. Combining partial order reductions with on-the-fly model-checking. *Formal Methods in System Design*, 8(1):39–64, 1996.

108. W. Penczek, R. Gerth, and R. Kuiper. Partial order reductions preserving simulations. Submitted for publication, 1999.

109. Amir Pnueli. In transition from global to modular temporal reasoning about programs. In K. R. Apt, editor, *Logics and Models of Concurrent Systems*, volume F 13 of *ASI*, pages 123–144. Springer-Verlag, Berlin, 1985.

110. M. O. Rabin. Decidability of second-order theories and automata on infinite trees. *Transactions of the American Mathematical Society*, 141:1–35, 1969.

111. Shmuel Safra. On the complexity of ω-automata. In *29th IEEE Symposium on Foundations of Computer Science*, pages 319–327. IEEE Press, 1988.

112. Klaus Schneider. Yet another look at LTL model checking. In *IFIP Advanced Research Working Conference on Correct Hardware Design and Verification Methods (CHARME'99)*, Lecture Notes in Computer Science, Bad Herrenalb, Germany, 1999.

113. H.B. Sipma, T.E. Uribe, and Z. Manna. Deductive model checking. In *8th International Conference on Computer-Aided Verification*, volume 1102 of *Lecture Notes in Computer Science*, pages 208–219, New Brunswick, N.J., 1996. Springer-Verlag.

114. A.P. Sistla and E.M. Clarke. The complexity of propositional linear temporal logic. *Journal of the ACM*, 32:733–749, 1985.

115. G. Stålmarck. A system for determining propositional logic theorems by applying values and rules to triplets that are generated from a formula. Swedish Patent No. 467076 (1992), US Patent No. 5 276 897 (1994), European Patent No. 0404 454 (1995).

116. P. H. Starke. Reachability analysis of Petri nets using symmetries. *Syst. Anal. Model. Simul.*, 8:293–303, 1991.

117. Colin Stirling. *Handbook of Logic in Computer Science*, volume 2, chapter Modal and temporal logics, pages 477–563. Oxford Science Publications, Clarendon Press, Oxford, 1992.

118. Colin Stirling. Bisimulation, model checking, and other games. Mathfit instructional meeting on games and computation, 1997. Available at http://www.dcs.ed.ac.uk/home/cps/.

119. R. E. Tarjan. Depth first search and linear graph algorithms. *SIAM Journal of Computing*, 1:146–160, 1972.

120. Wolfgang Thomas. Automata on infinite objects. In Jan van Leeuwen, editor, *Handbook of Theoretical Computer Science, volume B: Formal Models and Semantics*, pages 133–194. Elsevier, Amsterdam, 1990.
121. Wolfgang Thomas. Languages, automata, and logic. In G. Rozenberg and A. Salomaa, editors, *Handbook of Formal Language Theory*, volume III, pages 389–455. Springer-Verlag, New York, 1997.
122. Wolfgang Thomas. Complementation of Büchi automata revisited. In J. Karhumäki, editor, *Jewels are Forever, Contributions on Theoretical Computer Science in Honor of Arto Salomaa*, pages 109–122. Springer-Verlag, 2000.
123. A. Valmari. A stubborn attack on state explosion. In *2nd International Workshop on Computer Aided Verification*, volume 531 of *Lecture Notes in Computer Science*, pages 156–165, Rutgers, June 1990. Springer-Verlag.
124. A. Valmari. The state explosion problem. In *Lectures on Petri Nets I: Basic Models*, volume 1491 of *Lecture Notes in Computer Science*, pages 429–528. Springer-Verlag, 1998.
125. Moshe Y. Vardi. Alternating automata and program verification. In *Computer Science Today*, volume 1000 of *Lecture Notes in Computer Science*, pages 471–485. Springer-Verlag, 1995.
126. M.Y. Vardi and P. Wolper. Reasoning about infinite computations. *Information and Computation*, 115(1):1–37, 1994.
127. P. Wolper and V. Lovinfosse. Verifying properties of large sets of processes with network invariants. In J. Sifakis, editor, *Intl. Workshop on Automatic Verification Methods for Finite State Systems*, volume 407 of *Lecture Notes in Computer Science*. Springer-Verlag, 1989.
128. Pierre Wolper. Temporal logic can be more expressive. *Information and Control*, 56:72–93, 1983.
129. S. Yovine. Kronos: A verification tool for real-time systems. *Software Tools for Technology Transfer*, 1, 1997.
130. H. Zhang. Sato: An efficient propositional prover. In *Intl. Conf. on Automated Deduction (CADE'97)*, number 1249 in Lecture Notes in Computer Science, pages 272–275. Springer-Verlag, 1997.

Theorem Proving for Verification*

John Rushby

Computer Science Laboratory
SRI International
333 Ravenswood Avenue
Menlo Park, CA 94025, USA
rushby@csl.sri.com

Abstract. The challenges in using theorem proving for verification of parallel systems are to achieve adequate automation, and to allow human guidance to be expressed in terms of the system under examination rather than the mechanisms of the prover. This paper provides an overview of techniques that address these challenges.

1   Introduction

Formal verification is accomplished by constructing a mathematical model of the computer program, hardware, or system concerned, and then using calculation to determine whether the model satisfies desired properties. This is exactly analogous to the ways in which mathematical modeling and calculation are used to validate the structural design of a bridge, say, or the aerodynamic properties of a wing. However, the appropriate mathematics for modeling computer systems is formal logic, and calculation is accomplished by formal deduction—which has far higher computational complexity (indeed, many questions are algorithmically undecidable) than solvers for the partial differential equations used to model many physical phenomena. Consequently, formal calculation often requires recourse to human guidance or to simplified models.

Formal deduction by human-guided theorem proving (i.e., interactive proof checking) can, in principle, verify any correct design, but doing so may require unreasonable amounts of effort, time, or skill. On the other hand, the models employed with automated methods such as model checking may be so simplified or "downscaled" that their verification does not necessarily guarantee that the property concerned will hold of the actual system. Mechanization of formal deduction in support of verification must therefore strike a delicate balance between the extent and the form of human guidance required, the heuristic and algorithmic automation provided, and the convenience and fidelity of the modeling supported.

---

* This research was supported by DARPA through USAF Rome Laboratory Contract F30602-96-C-0204 and USAF Electronic Systems Center Contract F19628-96-C-0006.

F. Cassez et al. (Eds.): MOVEP 2000, LNCS 2067, pp. 39–57, 2001.

In the following sections I briefly sketch some of the main issues in theorem proving for formal verification, particularly for parallel processes, and outline the choices made in the PVS and SAL verification systems [3,20].[1]

2   Choice of Logic and Language

Formal verification requires a formal model of the system concerned (usually, a model of its assumed environment is required also), and descriptions of the properties to be examined. When theorem proving provides the means of calculation, both of these models are constructed as formal specifications in a single specification language. Necessary "background" knowledge of the domain is also specified in the same language and verification is accomplished by showing that the required properties are entailed by the other elements of the specification:

$$background + environment + system \vdash requirement.$$

One of the most fundamental choices in this approach to verification is that of the logic on which to base the specification language. There is a tradeoff, at least in theory, between expressiveness of the logic and the automation that can be provided for it. Thus, most classical theorem proving research focusses on standard first-order logic because it can be semi-decided by resolution. In practice, however, the difficulties in performing formal verification are dominated by the need to deal effectively with interpreted theories such as arithmetic and datatypes, where resolution offers little help. Thus, restriction to standard first-order logic provides few benefits, while imposing an impoverished notational foundation on the specification language.

The discipline of strong typing is at least as beneficial in specification as in programming, and it is also very convenient to be able to supply functions as arguments to other functions (e.g., to parameterize a sorting function with respect to the sorting criterion) and to be able to quantify over functions (e.g., to specify what it means for a sorting criterion to be well-founded). Higher-order logic provides both these benefits, together with an adequate treatment of set theory, and is the foundation for several popular specification languages, including PVS, where the type system is further extended with predicate subtypes and dependent types. Some of the conveniences and benefits of these choices are illustrated in [22].

Although some of the problems in theorem proving for higher-order logic are harder than for first-order (e.g., matching is undecidable), this is of little practical moment: instances of higher-order problems that arise in practice are usually in some easy fragment. The difficulties that dominate practical verification concern the treatment of interpreted theories, selection and instantiation of axioms and lemmas, and case-splitting—and these are essentially the same in all frameworks. The core capabilities required to perform these are outlined in the next section.

---

[1] These systems are the work of my colleagues at SRI, most notably Sam Owre and N. Shankar.

3   Basic Mechanization

As noted above, practical verification problems demand the ability to deal effectively with (sub)formulas involving equality and uninterpreted functions, real and integer linear arithmetic, abstract datatypes (such as lists and trees), and combinations of these. The following formulas illustrate some of these (the symbol $\supset$ denotes implication, and formulas are implicitly universally quantified in their free variables).

Equality: $x = y \wedge f(f(f(x))) = f(x) \supset f(f(f(f(f(y))))) = f(x)$.
Linear Arithmetic: $x \le y \wedge x \le 1 - y \wedge 2 \times x \ge 1 \supset F(4 \times x) = F(2)$.
Datatypes: $\mathrm{car}(\mathrm{cons}(a, b)) = a$.
Combination: $x \le \mathrm{car}(a) \supset \mathrm{car}(a) \ge \mathrm{car}(\mathrm{cons}(x, b))$.

The first-order (i.e., quantified) forms of these theories are decidable individually, but their combination is not. Experience shows that the most effective way to deal with this difficulty is to decide the unquantified combination, and to handle quantifier instantiation separately by heuristic or interactive means. Algorithms for deciding unquantified combinations of suitable theories were introduced by Shostak [28] and by Nelson and Oppen [19]; equality with uninterpreted functions is decided by the method of congruence closure [26], while linear arithmetic can be decided by several methods, including loop residue [27] and SUP-INF [25]. PVS uses methods based on those of Shostak [8].

Rewriting is another capability that is crucial to effective verification: it can be used to expand definitions and automatically to locate and instantiate appropriate lemmas or axioms. Although some theories can be decided by rewriting whenever any rule applies, most verification problems demand more controlled application. Suitable heuristics are those that rewrite a conditional rule only when its condition can first be discharged (or, equivalently, when it can be decided which case of a top-level if-then-else applies in an unconditional rule). Thus, the following rewrite rule would be applied in contexts containing $factorial(n)$ where n is known to be zero or is known to be nonzero, but not otherwise:

$$factorial(n : nat) \stackrel{\mathrm{def}}{=} \text{if } n = 0 \text{ then } 1 \text{ else } n \times factorial(n - 1).$$

Such heuristics require use of decision procedures during rewriting, together with recursive application of the rewriter, so that the integration between the rewriter and decision procedures becomes a critical element in the overall performance of the theorem prover. Forward chaining is another mechanism for invoking suitable lemmas and axioms automatically and, like rewriting, is most effective when integrated with decision procedures.

Propositional calculus must also be decided efficiently, so procedures based on BDDs (ordered binary decision diagrams) or on the Davis-Putnam or Stålmark methods are attractive ([12] provides references to all of these and describes an interesting new method). However, it is seldom that the best approach is to expand everything out and then call a propositional satisfiability procedure on the (usually huge) result: rather, intelligent case analysis (that avoids the unnecessary work of dealing repeatedly with similar subgoals) is what is required, so that propositional calculus is another capability that must be integrated with rewriting and decision procedures. That integration then forms the core mechanization that supports the remaining parts of the theorem prover.

Those remaining parts consist of interactive and tactical guidance having the goal of reducing the overall problem to decidable subproblems as quickly as possible. Given the core mechanization described above, the tasks left to interactive human guidance are selecting the rules and definitions to make available to the rewriter, explicitly invoking lemmas and axioms not having the form of rewrite (or forward chaining) rules, suggesting instantiations for quantified variables, and guiding case analysis where necessary. Systematic patterns of interactions can be captured as macros or, more powerfully, as programs (having the ability to adjust their control flow according to the formulas of the theorem being proved and the outcome of other proof steps): such "tactic" or "strategy" languages provide a convenient way for developers and users to extend the capabilities of the core mechanization. First introduced in the LCF system [10] (whose "metalanguage" became the programming language ML), such languages and extension capabilities are found in many verification systems, including PVS.

4   The Challenge of Human Guidance

The mechanisms described above are present to some degree in all theorem provers that have proved effective for verification problems.[2] These provers can be quite productive for skilled users, but still are insufficiently automatic for general use. The main barrier to greater automation is quantifier instantiation: heuristic instantiation too often guesses incorrectly and sends the proof down a wrong path.[3] It seems that some combination of proof search (shades of resolution!) and exploitation of decision procedures can significantly improve quantifier elimination (PVS includes experimental capabilities of this sort), but that some human guidance will always be required for verification problems of any substance. The design challenge then becomes one of choosing the most effective and acceptable form to present this guidance.

Theorem provers currently require guidance to be presented in their terms: an interactive theorem prover such as PVS requires the user to suggest case-splits, lemmas, and so on during the course of a proof; a noninteractive prover such as ACL2 receives human guidance through the selection and ordering of the lemmas it is invited to prove. Neither of these forms of guidance seems acceptable to nonspecialists: they wish to provide guidance in terms of the *system design* (its properties and structure), not in terms of its proof. The example of model

---

[2] These differ primarily in their choice of logic—ACL2 [16] uses an unquantified and untyped first order logic—and in the extent to which they employ decision procedures—those of the HOL [11] tradition generally eschew them.

[3] Unquantified logics such as ACL2 avoid the problem of instantiation, but instead must use induction (arguably a harder problem) in similar situations.

checking is instructive here: models must often be significantly downscaled to be acceptable to a model checker, yet this form of "guidance" does seem acceptable to nonspecialists—presumably because it directly concerns, and is conducted in terms of, the design. I return to this topic in Section 7, but need first to discuss the additional issues raised by parallel processes.

5 Verifying Parallel Processes

Theorem provers operate on specification languages that are basically logics: models of computation are not built-in but must be constructed on the resources of the specification logic concerned. The construction can be chosen to suit the application: for some purposes, sequential programs are best modeled function-ally, while for others a Hoare-style axiomatic treatment may be preferred. Par-allel programs can also be modeled in a variety of ways—for example, as state machines or process algebras. To make things concrete, I will focus on their representation as state machines, and will concentrate on safety properties.

In this representation, a parallel program is modeled as a nondeterministic automaton over a possibly infinite set of states. Given set of states S, initiality predicate I on S, and transition relation T on S, a predicate P on S is *inductive* for $\mathcal{S} = (S, I, T)$ if

$$I(s) \supset P(s) \tag{1}$$

and

$$P(s) \wedge T(s, t) \supset P(t). \tag{2}$$

The *reachable states* are those characterized by the smallest (ordered by implica-tion) inductive predicate R on $\mathcal{S}$. A predicate G is an *invariant* or *safety property* if it is larger than R (i.e., includes all reachable states). Since the focus here is on safety (as opposed to liveness) properties, we need not be concerned with the acceptance criterion on the automaton $\mathcal{S}$.

Using theorem proving, the usual way to establish that a predicate G is in-variant to show that it is inductive—i.e., we attempt to prove the verification conditions (1) and (2) with G substituted for P. Unfortunately, most safety prop-erties are not inductive, and must be strengthened (i.e., replaced by a smaller property) to make them so. Typically, this is done by conjoining additional pred-icates in an incremental fashion, so that G is replaced by

$$G_{\wedge}^i = G \wedge G_1 \wedge \cdots \wedge G_i \tag{3}$$

until an inductive $G_{\wedge}^m$ is found. This process can be made systematic, but is always tedious. In one well-known example, 57 such strengthenings were required to verify a bounded retransmission communications protocol [14]; each G_{i+1} was discovered by inspecting a failed proof for inductiveness of $G_{\wedge}^i$, and the process consumed several weeks.

Some improvements can be made in this process: static analysis [4] and automated calculations of (approximations to) fixpoints of weakest preconditions or strongest postconditions [7] can discover many useful invariants that can be used to seed the process as $G_1, \ldots, G_i$. Nonetheless, the transformation of a desired safety property into a provably inductive invariant remains the most difficult and costly element in verification of parallel programs using theorem proving. One of the chief attractions to model checking is that it calculates reachability directly and thereby eliminates the need to strengthen proposed invariants to make them inductive. The drawbacks to model checking are that the system must have a finite (and fairly small—typically less than about 2^{300}) number of states, and must be represented in a very concrete form (e.g., no uninterpreted functions).

6   Abstraction

A very attractive idea is to combine theorem proving and model checking in a way that preserves their advantages while each compensates for the deficiencies of the other. Abstraction provides a bridge between the two methods: we construct a simpler model of the system that can be model checked, and use theorem proving to establish that the simpler model is a property-preserving abstraction of the original system [18]. If S_c, I_c, T_c, P_c and S_a, I_a, T_a, P_a represent the concrete (i.e., original) stateset, initiality predicate, transition relation, and desired invariant, and their abstract counterparts, respectively, and $\phi : S_c \to S_a$ is the abstraction function, then the proof obligations that must be discharged are the following.

Initiality simulation: $I_c(s) \supset I_a(\phi(s))$,
Transition simulation: $T_c(s,t) \supset T_a(\phi(s), \phi(t))$,
Safety Preservation: $P_a(\phi(s)) \supset P_c(s)$, and
Abstract Invariant: $I_a(s) \supset \mathrm{AG}(T_a, P_a)(s)$, where AG is the "globally always" modality of CTL.

The first three can be discharged by theorem proving, and the last by model checking. Here, model checking the reduced model does verify the original, because the other proof obligations ensure that the reduced model is a property-preserving abstraction of the original. The necessary integration of theorem proving and model checking can be cleanly handled by using the mechanisms of a model checker to provide a decision procedure for the finite fragment of a μ-calculus (quantified Boolean logic extended with fixpoint operators or $\square$ and $\diamond$ modalities) [21]. Such μ-calculi can be specified within higher-order logic and are sufficiently expressive to define CTL model checking.

The drawback to this approach is that discharging the transition simulation proof obligation usually requires auxiliary invariants: in the bounded retransmission example cited earlier, 45 invariants were required to discharge this obligation. An exciting way to reduce this burden is described in the next section.

7   Automated Abstraction

Instead of constructing a downscaled system model by hand and then proving that it is, indeed, a property-preserving abstraction, an alternative approach is to *calculate* a reduced system description that has this property by construction. Given an abstraction function relating the original and abstracted state spaces, a verification condition can be generated for each pair of abstract states that specifies the conditions under which no transition is required between those states in the abstracted system description (the condition is that there is no transition between any pair of original states that map to those abstract states). If this verification condition can be proved (using automatic proof procedures), then the transition can be omitted from the abstracted system description; if not, then it is conservative to include the transition. For the bounded retransmission protocol, this approach is able to compute automatically an abstracted system description suitable for model checking [5].

A particularly useful form of abstraction is *predicate abstraction*, in which predicates on the concrete state are abstracted to Boolean values [23]. The abstraction function is then defined implicitly in terms of the list of predicates to be abstracted, and the abstracted system can be constructed by a very efficient method [24]. This approach is available as a standard command in PVS and also is able to verify the bounded retransmission protocol automatically in a few seconds.

One of the great attractions of approaches based on automated abstraction is that they make very effective use of fully automated theorem proving: instead of requiring the theorem prover to tackle one big theorem (the desired invariant), they instead invoke it on large numbers of smaller problems (the verification conditions that construct the abstracted system). Not only are these problems smaller and simpler (making the automation more likely to succeed), but it is not catastrophic if the automation sometimes fails to prove true verification conditions: the only penalty is that the abstraction will be more conservative than necessary—but it may still be good enough.

When an automatically constructed abstraction is *not* good enough (i.e., when model checking fails to verify the abstracted property because the abstracted system is insufficiently precise), it is sometimes possible to use the counterexample trace to help refine the abstraction. In other cases, auxiliary invariants may be required—and the combination of automated abstraction and model checking can sometimes be used in a recursive fashion to help develop these. The idea is to construct an even simpler abstraction than the one desired, and then use a model checker to calculate the reachable states of that abstraction (most model checkers can do this). The reachable states characterize the strongest invariant of that abstraction; their concretization (the inverse of abstraction) is an invariant—and plausibly a strong one—of the original system. An invariant discovered in this way can often be strengthened further by a few iterations of a strongest postcondition computation. This approach suggests iterated application of these techniques (one abstraction is used to calculate an invariant that helps calculate another abstraction, and so on), which in turn suggests a blackboard architecture in which a common intermediate representation is used to accumulate useful properties and abstractions of a design in a form that many different tools can both use and contribute to. A common intermediate representation also provides a way to support many source notations without inordinate cost. Verification systems that explore this approach include SAL [3], which is under development at SRI, and InVeSt [6], which is a collaboration between Verimag and SRI (InVeSt is built on PVS and is being integrated with SAL). Other experiments using related methods have been reported recently [1, 9].

The great benefit of these approaches is that human guidance to the process of iterated abstraction and model checking is conducted in terms of properties related to the design: the user suggests predicates to be abstracted, examines counterexample traces or derived invariants, and suggests new predicates. Theorem proving is a central element in the mechanization, but is fully automated and conducted behind the scenes.

8   Summary

Verification using theorem proving has two great advantages over algorithmic methods such as model checking: it can deal with unbounded or infinite systems, and it can support highly expressive, yet abstract, specifications of system models and properties. Its disadvantages are that it generally requires extensive human guidance, and that guidance is expressed in terms of the operation of the theorem prover, rather than in terms of the problem. Powerful automation, including extensive use of decision procedures and integration with model checking through automated abstraction, promises to overcome these disadvantages.

Opportunities for further research include new decision procedures and new ways to exploit decision procedures (e.g., abstracting to WS1S [2]), returning counterexamples from failed proof attempts, improved methods for generating and strengthening invariants, and new methods for integrating the techniques of theorem proving with those of model checking and reachability analysis.

Acknowledgment. My colleague N. Shankar is the source of most of the ideas described here, and also provided helpful comments that improved their presentation.

References

Papers on formal methods and automated verification by SRI authors can generally be found at http://www.csl.sri.com/fm-papers.html.

[1] Parosh Aziz Abdulla, Aurore Annichini, Saddek Bensalem, Ahmed Bouajjani, Peter Habermehl, and Yassine Lakhnech. Verification of infinite-state systems by combining abstraction and reachability analysis. In Halbwachs and Peled [13], pages 146–159.

[2] Kai Baukus, Saddek Bensalem, Yassine Lakhnech, and Karsten Stahl. Abstracting WS1S systems to verify parameterized networks. In Susanne Graf and Michael Schwartzbach, editors, *Tools and Algorithms for the Construction and Analysis of Systems (TACAS 2000)*, pages 188–203, Berlin, Germany, March 2000.

[3] Saddek Bensalem, Vijay Ganesh, Yassine Lakhnech, Cesar Muñoz, Sam Owre, Harald Rueß, John Rushby, Vlad Rusu, Hassen Saïdi, N. Shankar, Eli Singerman, and Ashish Tiwari. An overview of SAL. In C. Michael Holloway, editor, *LFM 2000: Fifth NASA Langley Formal Methods Workshop*, NASA Langley Research Center, Hampton, VA, June 2000. To appear.

[4] Saddek Bensalem and Yassine Lakhnech. Automatic generation of invariants. *Formal Methods in Systems Design*, 15(1):75–92, July 1999.

[5] Saddek Bensalem, Yassine Lakhnech, and Sam Owre. Computing abstractions of infinite state systems compositionally and automatically. In Hu and Vardi [15], pages 319–331.

[6] Saddek Bensalem, Yassine Lakhnech, and Sam Owre. InVeSt: A tool for the verification of invariants. In Hu and Vardi [15], pages 505–510.

[7] Nikolaj Bjørner, I. Anca Browne, and Zohar Manna. Automatic generation of invariants and intermediate assertions. *Theoretical Computer Science*, 173(1):49–87, 1997.

[8] David Cyrluk, Patrick Lincoln, and N. Shankar. On Shostak's decision procedure for combinations of theories. In M. A. McRobbie and J. K. Slaney, editors, *Automated Deduction—CADE-13*, Volume 1104 of Springer-Verlag *Lecture Notes in Artificial Intelligence*, pages 463–477, New Brunswick, NJ, July/August 1996.

[9] Satyaki Das, David L. Dill, and Seungjoon Park. Experience with predicate abstraction. In Halbwachs and Peled [13], pages 160–171.

[10] M. Gordon, R. Milner, and C. Wadsworth. *Edinburgh LCF: A Mechanized Logic of Computation*, volume 78 of *Lecture Notes in Computer Science*. Springer-Verlag, 1979.

[11] M. J. C. Gordon and T. F. Melham, editors. *Introduction to HOL: A Theorem Proving Environment for Higher-Order Logic*. Cambridge University Press, Cambridge, UK, 1993.

[12] Jan Friso Groote and Joost P. Warners. The propositional formula checker Heer-Hugo. *Journal of Automated Reasoning*, 24(1–2):101–125, February 2000.

[13] Nicolas Halbwachs and Doron Peled, editors. *Computer-Aided Verification, CAV '99*, Volume 1633 of Springer-Verlag *Lecture Notes in Computer Science*, Trento, Italy, July 1999.

[14] Klaus Havelund and N. Shankar. Experiments in theorem proving and model checking for protocol verification. In *Formal Methods Europe FME '96*, Volume 1051 of Springer-Verlag *Lecture Notes in Computer Science*, pages 662–681, Oxford, UK, March 1996.

[15] Alan J. Hu and Moshe Y. Vardi, editors. *Computer-Aided Verification, CAV '98*, Volume 1427 of Springer-Verlag *Lecture Notes in Computer Science*, Vancouver, Canada, June 1998.

[16] Matt Kaufmann, Panagiotis Manolios, and J Strother Moore. *Computer-Aided Reasoning: An Approach*, volume 3 of *Advances in Formal Methods*. Kluwer, 2000.

[17] Leslie Lamport. A new solution of Dijkstra's concurrent programming problem. *Communications of the ACM*, 17(8):453–455, August 1974.

[18] C. Loiseaux, S. Graf, J. Sifakis, A. Bouajjani, and S. Bensalem. Property preserving abstractions for the verification of concurrent systems. *Formal Methods in System Design*, 6:11–44, 1995.

[19] G. Nelson and D. C. Oppen. Simplification by cooperating decision procedures. *ACM Transactions on Programming Languages and Systems*, 1(2):245–257, 1979.

[20] Sam Owre, John Rushby, Natarajan Shankar, and Friedrich von Henke. Formal verification for fault-tolerant architectures: Prolegomena to the design of PVS. *IEEE Transactions on Software Engineering*, 21(2):107–125, February 1995.

[21] S. Rajan, N. Shankar, and M.K. Srivas. An integration of model-checking with automated proof checking. In Pierre Wolper, editor, *Computer-Aided Verification, CAV '95*, Volume 939 of Springer-Verlag *Lecture Notes in Computer Science*, pages 84–97, Liege, Belgium, June 1995.

[22] John Rushby, Sam Owre, and N. Shankar. Subtypes for specifications: Predicate subtyping in PVS. *IEEE Transactions on Software Engineering*, 24(9):709–720, September 1998.

[23] Hassen Saïdi and Susanne Graf. Construction of abstract state graphs with PVS. In Orna Grumberg, editor, *Computer-Aided Verification, CAV '97*, Volume 1254 of Springer-Verlag *Lecture Notes in Computer Science*, pages 72–83, Haifa, Israel, June 1997.

[24] Hassen Saïdi and N. Shankar. Abstract and model check while you prove. In Halbwachs and Peled [13], pages 443–454.

[25] Robert E. Shostak. On the SUP-INF method for proving Presburger formulas. *Journal of the ACM*, 24(4):529–543, October 1977.

[26] Robert E. Shostak. An algorithm for reasoning about equality. *Communications of the ACM*, 21(7):583–585, July 1978.

[27] Robert E. Shostak. Deciding linear inequalities by computing loop residues. *Journal of the ACM*, 28(4):769–779, October 1981.

[28] Robert E. Shostak. Deciding combinations of theories. *Journal of the ACM*, 31(1):1–12, January 1984.

A   Example: Bakery

This appendix uses Lamport's well-known "Bakery" Algorithm [17] for distributed mutual exclusion to illustrate some of the topics outlined in the body of the paper. The specifications and verifications presented here use PVS, but I do not provide an introduction to PVS: I hope the material is fairly self-explanatory, but those who would like to understand more can obtain the PVS system, its manuals, and its tutorials from `http://pvs.csl.sri.com`. The PVS files for the specifications and proofs used here are available from `http://www.csl.sri.com/~rushby/movep2k.html`.

The Bakery Algorithm is intended to ensure mutual exclusion among a collection of concurrent processes. The algorithm resembles the queuing discipline in a bakery or deli, where a machine dispenses tickets printed with numbers that increase monotonically; each customer desiring service takes a ticket and the unserved customer with the lowest number is served. The algorithm employs this basic idea without needing the centralized ticket dispenser: a process desiring to enter its critical section sets its counter (which takes the role of the ticket) to be one greater than that of any other process. The process whose counter is least may enter its critical section; on leaving the critical section, it sets its counter back to zero. The property we would like to verify for this algorithm is mutual exclusion: at most one process is in its critical section at any time.

In constructing a formal model for this system, we must make some choices about the level of detail that should be considered. The algorithm uses shared memory and is sensitive to the exact "memory model" used: for example, what is the value obtained by a process that reads the counter of another process simultaneously with that process updating it? It requires judgment to select a suitable level of detail in constructing the formal model. If we wish to examine the mutual exclusion property of a particular implementation of the algorithm, we will need to consider the memory model employed—which could be quite challenging. Instead (or at first), we may prefer to focus on the behavior of the algorithm in an ideal environment with sequentially consistent memory.

For example purposes, I will use an interleaving model of concurrency (where there are no simultaneous accesses) and limit attention to the case of just two processes. And although each process will perform activities other than merely execute the Bakery Algorithm, I will abstract these details away and assume that each process is always in one of three "phases":

idle: performing work outside its critical section,
trying: to enter its critical section, or
critical: performing work inside its critical section.

Each process has a system state comprising two values:

- The value of its counter, recorded in the variables `t1` or `t2` (for Process 1 and 2, respectively) which is a natural number, and
- The phase it is in, recorded in its "program counter," `pc1` or `pc2` respectively, which can take values `idle`, `trying`, `critical`.

The algorithm can then be specified by the following transitions in a Unity-like notation.

```
Type
    phase: enum {idle, trying, critical};
    counter: nat;
Var
    pc1, pc2: phase;
    t1, t2: counter;
Initially
    t1 := 0;        t2 := 0;
    pc1 := idle;    pc2 := idle;
Rules
    pc1 = idle ==>  t1 := t2+1; pc1 := trying;
    pc2 = idle ==>  t2 := t1+1; pc2 := trying;

    pc1 = trying & (t1 < t2 | t2 = 0) ==> pc1 := critical;
    pc2 = trying & (t1 > t2 | t1 = 0) ==> pc2 := critical;

    pc1 = critical ==> t1 := 0;    pc1 := idle;
    pc2 = critical ==> t2 := 0;    pc2 := idle;

    else ==> do nothing;
Invariant
    NOT (pc1=critical & pc2=critical);
```

There is a peculiarity of this specification that a process that *can* make a move *must* do so (e.g., an idle process must go to its trying phase). I have introduced this peculiarity in order to provoke outcomes that help me illustrate certain points during the analysis.

Observe that the algorithm has infinite state: the counters can increase without bound. If we wish to analyze the algorithm using finite state methods, we must fix the maximum counter value and then take some special action if an attempt is made to increase a counter beyond that value—but then we are modeling a modified algorithm. Although we cannot verify the original algorithm by model checking the downscaled version, we may be able to find bugs by this means. It is generally worthwhile to debug a design to the extent possible using inexpensive techniques such as typechecking, animation, simulation, and model checking on downscaled models, before undertaking more expensive analyses such as proof. Once we have established some confidence that the mutual exclusion property is true for the downscaled algorithm using model checking and other inexpensive methods, we can attempt to verify it for unbounded counters by theorem proving using PVS.

PVS is a *logic*, it does not have a notion of state, nor of programs, built in, so the specification must embed the transition relation semantics directly—as in the following specification.

```
bakery: THEORY
BEGIN

phase : TYPE = {idle, trying, critical}
state: TYPE = [# pc1, pc2: phase, t1,t2: nat #]
s, pre, post: VAR state

P1_transition(pre, post): bool =
 IF pre'pc1 = idle
   THEN post = pre WITH [(t1) := pre't2 + 1, (pc1) := trying]
 ELSIF pre'pc1 = trying AND (pre't2 = 0 OR pre't1 < pre't2)
   THEN post = pre WITH [(pc1) := critical]
 ELSIF pre'pc1 = critical
   THEN post = pre WITH [(t1) := 0, (pc1) := idle]
 ELSE post = pre
 ENDIF

P2_transition(pre, post): bool =
 IF pre'pc2 = idle
   THEN post = pre WITH [(t2) := pre't1 + 1, (pc2) := trying]
 ELSIF pre'pc2 = trying AND (pre't1 = 0 OR pre't1 > pre't2)
   THEN post = pre WITH [(pc2) := critical]
 ELSIF pre'pc2 = critical
   THEN post = pre WITH [(t2) := 0, (pc2) := idle]
 ELSE post = pre
 ENDIF

transitions(pre, post): bool =
  P1_transition(pre, post) OR P2_transition(pre, post)

init(s): bool = s'pc1 = idle AND s'pc2 = idle
                AND s't1 = 0 AND s't2 = 0

safe(s): bool = NOT(s'pc1 = critical AND s'pc2 = critical)
```

In this PVS specification, the notation [# ... #] is a record type constructor and the backquote indicates access to the fields of a record. The WITH construct is used to "update" record or array values.

We desire to show that the predicate safe is an invariant. In the next section we will attempt to do this by proving that it is inductive.

A.1   Inductive Invariance Proof

We begin by specifying what it means for predicate INV to be an inductive invariant of a transition relation R with initiality predicate INIT, and then establish as our first_try the goal of proving that safe is an inductive invariant of the algorithm.

```
INV, INIT: var pred[state]

R: VAR pred[[state,state]]

inductive_invariant(INV, INIT, R): bool =
 FORALL s: INIT(s) => INV(s)
  AND FORALL pre,post: INV(pre) AND R(pre,post) => INV(post)

first_try: LEMMA inductive_invariant(safe, init, transitions)
```

If we start the PVS theorem prover on this goal, we will be presented with the following *sequent*.

```
first_try :
  |-------
{1}    inductive_invariant(safe, init, transitions)
Rule?
```

The proof commands (EXPAND "inductive_invariant") and (GROUND) open up the definition of inductive_invariant and split it into cases. We are then presented with the first of the two cases.

```
This yields  2 subgoals:
first_try.1 :
  |-------
{1}    FORALL s: init(s) => safe(s)
```

This is discharged by the proof command (GRIND), which expands definitions and performs obvious deductions, and we are then presented with the remaining subgoal.

```
This completes the proof of first_try.1.
first_try.2 :
  |-------
{1}    FORALL pre, post:
          safe(pre) AND transitions(pre, post) => safe(post)
```

The commands (SKOSIMP), (EXPAND "transitions"), and (GROUND) eliminate the quantification and split transitions into separate cases for Processes 1 and 2.

```
first_try.2.1 :
{-1}  P1_transition(pre!1, post!1)
[-2]  safe(pre!1)
  |-------
[1]   safe(post!1)
```

A PVS sequent such as this is true if the conjunction of formulas above the "turnstile" line |------- implies the disjunction of formulas below. The numbers serve simply to label the formulas; those enclosed in curly braces highlight formulas that are changed from the previous sequent.

The commands (EXPAND "P1_transition") and (GROUND) split the proof into four cases according to the kind of step made by the process. The first one is discharged by (GRIND), but the second is not and we are presented with the following sequent.

```
first_try.2.1.2 :
[-1]  pre!1't2 = 0
{-2}  trying?(pre!1'pc1)
[-3]  post!1 = pre!1 WITH [(pc1) := critical]
[-4]  safe(pre!1)
{-5}  critical?(pre!1'pc2)
   |-------
```

When there are no formulas below the line, a sequent can only be true if there is a contradiction among those above the line.

Here, Process 1 enters its critical section (Formula -3) because Process 2's counter is zero (Formula -1)—but Process 2 is already in its critical section (Formula -5). This situation is impossible because Process 2 must have incremented its counter (making it nonzero) when it entered its **trying** phase. But contemplation, or experimentation with the prover, shows that this fact is not provable from the information provided. The same holds for the other unprovable subgoals. The problem is not that **safe** is untrue, but that it is not *inductive*: it does not provide a strong enough antecedent to support the proof of its own invariance.

The solution is to prove a stronger property than the one we are really interested in: we strengthen the desired invariant by conjoining some additional clauses.

```
strong_safe(s): bool = safe(s)
   AND ((s'pc1 = trying OR s'pc1 = critical) => s't1 /= 0)
   AND ((s'pc2 = trying OR s'pc2 = critical) => s't2 /= 0)

second_try: LEMMA
      inductive_invariant(strong_safe, init, transitions)
```

Rerunning the proof developed so far, we find that the strengthened invariant deals with the case we just examined, and the symmetric case for Processor 2, but its proof still produces two unproved subgoals. The first of these is the following.

```
second_try.2 :
{-1}  trying?(pre!1'pc1)
{-2}  pre!1't1 < pre!1't2
{-3}  post!1 = pre!1 WITH [(pc1) := critical]
{-4}  critical?(pre!1'pc2)
   |-------
{1}   (pre!1't1 = 0)
```

The situation here is that Process 1 is entering its critical section (Formula -3) even though Process 2 is already in its critical section (Formula -4). But this cannot happen, because Formula 1 indicates that Process 1 has a nonzero counter (formulas below the line are the negations of their equivalents above the line), so that Process 2 must have had the smaller counter when it entered—thereby contradicting Formula -2. Again we need to strengthen the invariant to carry along this fact.

```
inductive_safe(s):bool = strong_safe(s)
 AND ((s'pc1 = critical AND s'pc2 = trying) => s't1 < s't2)
 AND ((s'pc2 = critical AND s'pc1 = trying) => s't1 > s't2)

third_try: LEMMA
      inductive_invariant(inductive_safe, init, transitions)
```

Finally, we have an invariant that is inductive—and is proved with (GRIND).

A.2   Proof by Manual Abstraction and Model Checking

It does not matter to the operation of algorithm what the actual values of the counters are: all that matters is whether or not each of them is zero, and whether one is less than the other. We can use Booleans to represent these relations and can construct an abstracted specification that operates on this abstracted representation. We begin by introducing the abstracted (finite) state type (whose field names indicate their intended interpretation), the abstraction function abst from concrete to abstract states, and the abstracted safety property.

```
abstract_state: TYPE =
  [# pc1, pc2: phase, t1_is_0, t2_is_0, t1_lt_t2: bool #]

as, a_pre, a_post: VAR abstract_state

abst(s): abstract_state =
  (# pc1 := s'pc1,
     pc2 := s'pc2,
     t1_is_0 := s't1 = 0,
     t2_is_0 := s't2 = 0,
     t1_lt_t2 := s't1 < s't2 #)

a_safe(as): bool =
  NOT (as'pc1 = critical AND as'pc2 = critical)
```

Then we specify the abstracted algorithm in terms of its initiality predicate

```
a_init(as): bool =
  as'pc1 = idle AND as'pc2 = idle
    AND as't1_is_0 AND as't2_is_0
```

and its transition relation.

```
a_P1_transition(a_pre, a_post): bool =
 IF a_pre'pc1 = idle
   THEN a_post = a_pre WITH [(t1_is_0) := false,
                             (t1_lt_t2) := false,
                             (pc1) := trying]
 ELSIF a_pre'pc1 = trying
         AND (a_pre't2_is_0 OR a_pre't1_lt_t2)
   THEN a_post = a_pre WITH [(pc1) := critical]
 ELSIF a_pre'pc1 = critical
   THEN a_post = a_pre WITH [(t1_is_0) := true,
                             (t1_lt_t2) := NOT a_pre't2_is_0,
                             (pc1) := idle]
 ELSE a_post = a_pre
ENDIF

a_P2_transition(a_pre, a_post): bool =
 IF a_pre'pc2 = idle
   THEN a_post = a_pre WITH [(t2_is_0) := false,
                             (t1_lt_t2) := true,
                             (pc2) := trying]
 ELSIF a_pre'pc2 = trying
         AND (a_pre't1_is_0 OR NOT a_pre't1_lt_t2)
   THEN a_post = a_pre WITH [(pc2) := critical]
 ELSIF a_pre'pc2 = critical
   THEN a_post = a_pre WITH [(t2_is_0) := true,
                             (t1_lt_t2) := false,
                             (pc2) := idle]
 ELSE a_post = a_pre
ENDIF

a_trans(a_pre, a_post): bool = a_P1_transition(a_pre, a_post)
                           OR a_P2_transition(a_pre, a_post)
```

Next, we state (without justification) the four verification conditions from Section 6 that are sufficient to establish that safe is an invariant using the abstraction function abst.

```
init_simulation: THEOREM init(s) IMPLIES a_init(abst(s))

trans_simulation: THEOREM
   transitions(pre, post) IMPLIES a_trans(abst(pre), abst(post))

safety_preserved: THEOREM a_safe(abst(s)) IMPLIES safe(s)

abs_invariant_ctl: THEOREM
   a_init(as) IMPLIES AG(a_trans, a_safe)(as)
```

The conditions init_simulation and safety_preserved are proved by (GRIND), and abs_invariant_ctl is proved by (MODEL-CHECK) (which calls the PVS model checker).

However, `trans_simulation` results in two unproved cases; the first is shown below.

```
trans_simulation.2.6.1 :
[-1]   post!1 = pre!1
{-2}   idle?(pre!1'pc1)
  |-------
{1}    critical?(pre!1'pc2)
[2]    pre!1't1 = 0
[3]    pre!1't1 > pre!1't2
{4}    idle?(pre!1'pc2)
{5}    pre!1't1 < pre!1't2
```

The problem here is that when the two counters are equal but nonzero, the concrete algorithm drops through to the **ELSE** case and requires the pre and post states to be the same—whereas in the abstracted algorithm, this situation can satisfy the condition for Process 2 to enter its critical section. This is because `NOT t1_lt_t2` abstracts `t1 >= t2` rather than `t1 > t2`. However, this situation can never arise, because each counter is always incremented to be strictly greater than the other. We can establish this fact as an invariant that is proved with (`GRIND`).

```
not_eq(s): bool = s't1 = s't2 => s't1 = 0

extra: LEMMA inductive_invariant(not_eq, init, transitions)
```

A modified version of the verification condition for simulation (stated here without justification) allows us to use a known invariant to establish it.

```
strong_trans_simulation: THEOREM
   inductive_invariant(not_eq, init, transitions)
     AND not_eq(pre) AND not_eq(post)
     AND transitions(pre, post)
       IMPLIES a_trans(abst(pre), abst(post))
```

This modified verification condition is discharged by the following proof.

```
(SKOSIMP)
(EXPAND "transitions")
(GROUND)
(("1" (EXPAND "P1_transition")
      (APPLY (THEN (GROUND) (GRIND))))
 ("2" (EXPAND "P2_transition")
      (APPLY (THEN (GROUND) (GRIND))))))
```

A.3   Proof by Automated Abstraction and Model Checking

We have seen that proof by inductive invariance requires several strengthenings of the desired invariant to obtain one that is inductive, and that justification of a manually constructed abstraction also requires an auxiliary invariant. However, the PVS mechanism for automatic construction of abstractions succeeds without further assistance. We first state the desired safety property as a CTL formula over the original (infinite state) system.

```
auto_abstract: THEOREM
    init(s) IMPLIES AG(transitions, safe)(s)
```

Then we instruct PVS to abstract the resulting sequent on the predicates t1=0, t2=0, and t1 < t2 and to model check the resulting finite state system. This is done by the following command.

```
(ABSTRACT-AND-MC
 ( "lambda(s) :s't1=0"
   "lambda(s) :s't2=0"
   "lambda(s) :s't1 < s't2 "))
```

PVS constructs the abstracted system (automatically checking 62 verification conditions while doing so) and model checks the result—all in less than 10 seconds on a 500 MHz Pentium.

Composition and Abstraction

Antti Valmari

Tampere University of Technology, Software Systems Laboratory
PO Box 553, FIN-33101 Tampere
FINLAND
ava@cs.tut.fi

Abstract. This article is a tutorial on advanced automated process-algebraic verification of concurrent systems, and it is organised around a case study. The emphasis is on verification methods that rely on the inherent compositionality of process algebras. The fundamental concepts of labelled transition systems, strong bisimilarity, synchronous parallel composition, hiding, renaming, abstraction, CFFD-equivalence and CFFD-preorder are presented as the case study proceeds. The necessity of presenting assumptions about the users of the example system is discussed, and it is shown how CFFD-preorder supports their modelling. The assumptions are essential for the verification of so-called liveness properties. The correctness requirements of the system are stated, presented in linear temporal logic, and distributed to a number of more "localised" requirements. It is shown how they can be checked with the aid of suitably chosen CFFD-abstracted views to the system. The state explosion problem that hampers automatic verification is encountered. Compositional LTS construction, interface specifications and induction are used to solve the problem and, as a result, an infinite family of systems is verified with a limited amount of effort.

1 Introduction

The goal of this article is to introduce some advanced automated process-algebraic verification methods that are based on abstraction and compositionality. The article is organised around a case study: the verification of a demand-driven token-ring mutual exclusion system. The verification methods and their underlying theory are introduced as the case study proceeds.

The article has been primarily intended for potential users of the methods, rather than verification theory researchers or tool developers. Therefore, although the article contains mathematical definitions and theorems, it presents neither proofs nor algorithms, with the exception that the basic reason why a theorem holds is sometimes explained.

Section 2 presents the system and its verification model. The structure of the system is described in Section 2.1, as is also the basic idea of the operation of the system. The system consists of n *servers* and n *clients*. The servers are modelled in Section 2.2 in *ARA Lotos*. "ARA" [37] is an abbreviation for "Advanced Reachability Analysis", and it is the name of the main tool used in the case

F. Cassez et al. (Eds.): MOVEP 2000, LNCS 2067, pp. 58–98, 2001.
© Springer-Verlag Berlin Heidelberg 2001

study. (The other tool that was used is *Ltspar* [19].) "ARA Lotos" is the input language of the tool, and it resembles closely the internationally standardised specification language Lotos [2,13].

A *labelled transition system*, or *LTS* for brevity, is a graph-like representation of the behaviour of a system or its component. The concept is introduced and defined in Section 2.3, where also LTSs that show the behaviours of the servers are shown. Section 2.4 discusses what it means for two LTSs to represent the "same" behaviour, and introduces the important notions of *isomorphism* and *strong bisimilarity* between LTSs.

The clients that use the system are presented in Section 2.5. Special attention is paid to the subtle issue of modelling the *progress properties* of the clients in an adequate way.

The system is put together with the *parallel composition* operator. It and two other useful operators, namely *renaming* and *hiding*, are defined in Section 2.6. Hiding and renaming are presented in a slightly more general form than usually in process-algebraic literature. The section also introduces the notorious *state explosion* phenomenon. The parallel composition operator used in this article is *synchronous*, while real systems are often based on *asynchronous* communication. This apparent incompatibility is discussed and the use of a synchronous operator is justified in Section 2.7. The operator is also compared to two well-known synchronous alternatives, namely the Lotos and CCS [23] parallel composition operators. It is shown that the latter two can be simulated with the operator in this article, so its use does not restrict generality. Also the fact that *interleaving semantics* is used instead of *true parallelism* is discussed a bit.

Section 3 is devoted to the verification of the system. It starts by stating the requirements of the system verbally and in *linear temporal logic* [22], and by transforming them into a total of $\frac{1}{2}n(n+1)$ requirements that refer to at most two clients at a time.

Then, in Section 3.2, process-algebraic *abstraction* is introduced by showing two *reduced* abstract views to the system. It is discussed how the validity of the requirements can be checked from such abstract views. The particular formal notion of abstraction used in this case study is the *CFFD semantics* [40,41]. It is defined and its relevance to the verification of the requirements of the system is discussed in Section 3.3. Special attention is paid to how the properties of *CFFD-preorder* can be taken advantage of in the modelling of the clients. Also, what can and what can not be read from an LTS obtained with the CFFD semantics is discussed. The reason for the name "CFFD" is explained in Section 3.4, where the CFFD semantics is compared to the main semantic model in the famous *CSP* theory [28,4,11]. (The version of CSP semantics described in [3] was not the final one.)

The first of the advanced verification methods introduced in this article, namely *compositional LTS construction*, is presented in Section 3.5. The method is a direct application of the congruence property of many process-algebraic equivalences, and has been in use since [21], or perhaps earlier. Section 3.6 shows how *interface specifications* can be used to improve the compositional method in situations where a subsystem has much more behaviour in isolation than it has in its intended environment. Interface specifications were first presented in [9], and they have not been applied to the CFFD semantics before this article. Finally, *induction* in the style of [44,20,5] is applied to the system in Section 3.7. As a result, the demand-driven token-ring system becomes verified for any $n \geq 2$ with a limited finite amount of effort.

Despite of its length, the case study cannot be used for illustrating all advanced verification methods. Further reading is suggested and other final remarks are made in Section 4.

2   Systems and Their Behaviour

2.1   The Architecture of the Example System

Figure 1 shows the architecture of the example system and the environment where it is used. The system is a ring of n processes $Server_1$, $Server_2$, ... , $Server_n$. Each server has one *client*. The purpose of the system is to act as an arbiter between the clients, so that at most one client at a time can perform some critical activity. The system is thus a distributed mutual exclusion system.

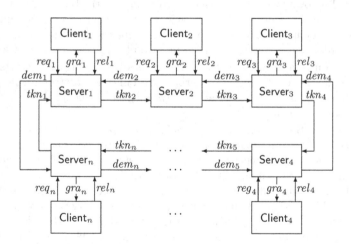

Fig. 1. The architecture of the example system.

When a client wants to perform the critical activity, it requests permission from its server by executing req_i, where i is the number of the client. The server may grant the permission by executing gra_i. After the client has finished with the critical activity, it indicates this to its server by executing rel_i (for "release"), so that the system knows that now some other client can be given the permission.

The ring of servers contains precisely one *token*. A server can grant permission to its client only when it is in possession of the token. If a server needs the token but does not have it, then the server demands it from the previous server in the ring by executing dem_i. Here i is the number of the server that needs the token, and the number of the previous server is $i - 1$, except that the predecessor of Server$_1$ is Server$_n$. If the previous server does not have the token, then it forwards the demand to its predecessor, and so on.

When the demand reaches the server Server$_j$ that has the token, this server (if necessary) first waits until its client is not doing the critical activity. Then it delivers the token to the next server in the ring by executing $tkn_{j \oplus 1}$ (where $n \oplus 1 = 1$, and $x \oplus 1 = x + 1$ when $1 \leq x < n$). The next server forwards the token to its successor either immediately or after first serving its own client. In this way the token eventually propagates to the server who made the original demand.

In order to prevent the system from serving only one client and ignoring the rest, any server that has just served its client gives the token to the next server even if that server has not demanded it. As a consequence, the server can serve its client again only after the token has made a full circle in the ring, and thus all the other clients have had a chance to get service.

2.2   The Servers

Although the description of the system might sound simple, the server is actually difficult to specify precisely. It has to communicate with three other processes: its client, and the previous and the next server in the ring. A message may come from one direction while the server is engaged in an interaction in another direction, and this message may have an effect on the interaction. For instance, while the server is waiting for the token to satisfy a pending demand by the next server, the client may execute req_i, so that the server must serve its client before delivering the token to the next server.

Figure 2 shows ARA Lotos code that specifies a server. The first line declares a new enumerated type that consists of five values, and gives it the name **tkn_status**. The next non-empty line specifies that the name of the process is Server and the actions with which it communicates with the rest of the world are tl, tr, ... , and rel. In the code, tl replaces tkn_i ("l" is a mnemonic for "left") and tr replaces $tkn_{i \oplus 1}$ ("r" for "right"), and similarly with dem. Furthermore, the subscripts of req, gra and rel have been omitted.

The next line declares three local variables t_st, is_req and is_dem. They are used for keeping track of what the server knows about the location of the token, and whether a request by the client or a demand by the next server is pending. The latter two variables are of the type **Bool**, so they may assume the values False and True, and they can be used in conditions as such. The variable t_st is of the type **tkn_status** that has been defined in the first line as the set { t_out, t_dem, t_in, t_down, t_used }. The first two of these values mean that the server does not have the token and has (t_dem) or has not (t_out) requested it. In the last three cases the server has the token, and the client has not started the

```
$sort tkn_status is ( t_out, t_dem, t_in, t_down, t_used )

process Server[ tl, tr, dl, dr, req, gra, rel ](
  t_st : tkn_status, is_req, is_dem : Bool
) :=
  [ ( is_req or is_dem ) and ( t_st == t_out ) ]->
  dl; S[...]( t_dem, is_req, is_dem )
    []
  [ ( t_st == t_dem ) or ( t_st == t_out ) ]->
  tl; S[...]( t_in, is_req, is_dem )
    []
  [ not( is_req ) ]-> req; S[...]( t_st, True, is_dem )
    []
  [ ( t_st == t_in ) and is_req ]->
  gra; S[...]( t_down, is_req, is_dem )
    []
  [ t_st == t_down ]-> rel; S[...]( t_used, False, is_dem )
    []
  dr; S[...]( t_st, is_req, True )
    []
  [ ( t_st == t_used ) ]-> tr; S[...]( t_out, is_req, False )
    []
  [ is_dem and ( t_st == t_in ) and not( is_req ) ]->
  tr; S[...]( t_out, is_req, False )
endproc
```

Fig. 2. A server specified in ARA Lotos.

critical activity (t_in), is performing it (t_down), or has finished it (t_used). The figure does not show the initial values of the variables. Initially is_req and is_dem are False, and t_st is t_in in the server that initially has the token, and t_out in the other servers.

Between the symbols ":=" and "**endproc**" the specification lists eight possible ways the server can make a transition, separated with "[]". The notation "[*cond*]→" specifies a condition *cond* that must hold for the transition to be possible. In the one place where it is missing, the corresponding transition is always enabled. Then comes the name of the action that is executed during the transition, and finally the new values of the local variables are listed in parenthesis. The text "S[...]" is neither ARA Lotos nor ordinary Lotos; it is an abbreviation used only in Figure 2 to make it more readable. In ARA Lotos and ordinary Lotos the string "Server[tl, tr, dl, dr, req, gra, rel]" occurs in its place. It denotes Server calling itself recursively.

For example, the first transition specifies that the server can make a *dl*-transition whenever there is a pending request from the client or from the next server, and token status is t_out. When the transition is made, the token status changes to t_dem, so the transition cannot be made immediately again. The other two local variables retain their values.

As another example, the last two transitions specify that tr can be executed because of two reasons, and in both cases it sets the token status to t_out and marks off any pending demand from the next server. The first reason is that the client has done its critical activity. It implements the requirement that after serving the client, the server pushes the token to the next server even if it has not demanded it. The second reason is that the server has the token, the next server has demanded it, and the client has not. This last conjunct implies that the client is given priority, if both it and the next server need the token at the same time.

Although the basic idea of the server is simple, its design contains many details, and some of them are subtle. It is not easy to convince oneself merely by looking at the code that the server is correct. In the remainder of this article we will verify that it indeed is.

2.3   Labelled Transition Systems

The behaviour of a process-algebraic system can be represented as a *labelled transition system*, abbreviated *LTS*. It is a directed graph whose edges are labelled with action names. The vertices are called *states*, and one of them is distinguished as the *initial state*.[1] The edges together with their labels are called *transitions*.

There are two kinds of actions: the system communicates with its environment by executing *visible actions*, and it can also execute *invisible actions* that the environment cannot directly observe. The set of the names of the visible actions of the system is called the *alphabet*, and it is also considered as a part of the LTS. Invisible actions do not have names. Instead, a special symbol "τ" that is not in the alphabet is used to denote them.

Definition 1. *A* labelled transition system, *abbreviated* LTS, *is a four-tuple* $(S, \Sigma, \Delta, \hat{s})$, *where*

- S *is the set of* states.
- Σ, *also known as the* alphabet, *is the set of* visible actions. *It satisfies* $\tau \notin \Sigma$.
- $\Delta \subseteq S \times (\Sigma \cup \{\tau\}) \times S$ *is the set of transitions.*
- $\hat{s} \in S$ *is the* initial state.

The definition implies that the alphabet contains at least those visible actions that the system can execute, but it can contain more. When we later define parallel composition we will see that the "extra" elements in the alphabet are significant.

In drawings, the states of an LTS are usually denoted with circles, and the initial state is indicated with a small arrow that starts at no state. Any transition

---

[1] Sometimes it is useful to specify more than one initial state, or specify no initial states.

(s, a, s') is represented as an arrow from s to s' with a written somewhere near the arrow. Sometimes an arrow is labelled with several action names; then it represents several transitions between the same states. Unless otherwise specified either in the drawing or in its accompanying text, the alphabet of the LTS is precisely the set of the visible action names that occur as transition labels in the drawing. The names of the states are often considered insignificant, and are omitted in the drawing.

Figure 3 shows the behaviours of the servers as an LTS with two initial states. The initial state of the server that has the token initially is the third state in the top row, and the initial state of the other servers is the second state in the same row. Several easily understandable transition sequences can be found in the figure, such as the *dr-dl-tl-tr*-sequence from the leftmost initial state to itself. In it, the next server demands the token (*dr*), the current server forwards the demand to the previous server in the ring (*dl*), the token arrives from the previous server (*tl*), and is delivered to the next server (*tr*). More complicated behaviour arises if a request from the client is interleaved with the demand by the next server, or if the token arrives unexpectedly. The servers have been designed to treat reasonably all these possibilities.

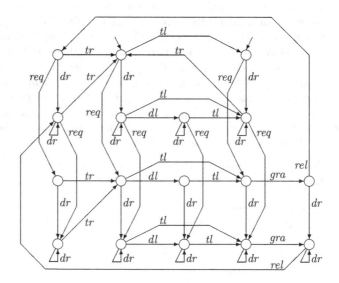

Fig. 3. The LTS of a server that initially has ("/") or has not ("\") the token.

The states in Figure 3 are anonymous, and thus do not make the contents of the local variables t_st, is_req and is_dem explicit. However, the figure has been drawn such that the location of a state reveals the values of the local variables. The value of t_st is t_used in the first column, t_out in the second, and t_dem, t_in and t_down in the third, fourth and last column. The bit is_req is True in precisely the two bottom rows, and is_dem = True in the second row and bottom row.

The "$(s, a, s') \in \Delta$" notation is inconvenient for talking about sequences of transitions. We therefore define a notation where only the first and optionally also the last state are mentioned, and the actions executed along a path from the first to the last state are listed within an arrow symbol. We will also need symbols for the sets of finite and infinite sequences of elements of a given set.

Definition 2. Let $(S, \Sigma, \Delta, \hat{s})$ be an LTS, $s, s' \in S$, $n \geq 0$, and $a_1, a_2, \ldots \in \Sigma \cup \{\tau\}$.

- $s - a_1 a_2 \cdots a_n \rightarrow s'$ if and only if
  $\exists s_0, s_1, \ldots, s_n \in S : s_0 = s \wedge s_n = s' \wedge \forall i \in \{1, 2, \ldots, n\} : (s_{i-1}, a_i, s_i) \in \Delta$.
- $s - a_1 a_2 \cdots a_n \rightarrow$ if and only if $\exists s' : s - a_1 a_2 \cdots a_n \rightarrow s'$.
- $s - a_1 a_2 a_3 \cdots \rightarrow$ if and only if
  $\exists s_0, s_1, s_2, \ldots \in S : s_0 = s \wedge \forall i \in \{1, 2, 3, \ldots\} : (s_{i-1}, a_i, s_i) \in \Delta$.

Let A be a set.

- ε denotes the empty sequence, that is, $a_1 a_2 \cdots a_n = \varepsilon$ whenever $n = 0$.
- A^* is the set of finite sequences of elements of A, that is,
  $A^* = \{ a_1 a_2 \cdots a_n \mid n \geq 0 \wedge a_1 \in A \wedge \cdots \wedge a_n \in A \}$.
- A^ω is the set of infinite sequences of elements of A, that is,
  $A^\omega = \{ a_1 a_2 a_3 \cdots \mid \forall i \in \{1, 2, 3, \ldots\} : a_i \in A \}$.

It follows from the definitions that $s - \varepsilon \rightarrow s$ holds for every $s \in S$.

If $s - a_1 a_2 \cdots a_n \rightarrow s'$ holds for some $a_1, a_2, \ldots, a_n$, then we say that s' is *reachable* from s. The *reachable part* of an LTS is obtained by discarding those states and transitions that are not reachable from the initial state.

Definition 3. Let $P = (S, \Sigma, \Delta, \hat{s})$ be an LTS. The reachable part of P is repa$(P) = (S', \Sigma', \Delta', \hat{s}')$, where

- $S' = \{ s \in S \mid \exists \sigma \in (\Sigma \cup \{\tau\})^* : \hat{s} - \sigma \rightarrow s \}$,
- $\Sigma' = \Sigma$,
- $\Delta' = \Delta \cap (S' \times (\Sigma \cup \{\tau\}) \times S')$, and
- $\hat{s}' = \hat{s}$.

As defined above, the arrow notation does not make explicit the LTS whose transition relation is in question. Therefore, we sometimes decorate the arrow in the same way as the LTS, such as in $s - a \rightarrow' s'$ and $s - a \rightarrow_1 s'$, when the LTSs are P' and P_1.

2.4 "Sameness" of LTSs

The obvious mathematical definition of the equivalence of two LTSs is equality: $(S, \Sigma, \Delta, \hat{s}) = (S', \Sigma', \Delta', \hat{s}')$ if and only if $S = S'$, $\Sigma = \Sigma'$, $\Delta = \Delta'$, and $\hat{s} = \hat{s}'$. However, the names of the states of an LTS are usually considered insignificant in process-algebraic verification, and this definition distinguishes between two

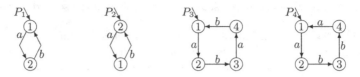

Fig. 4. Four LTSs with varying level of differences.

LTSs that are otherwise the same but happen to use different names for states. For instance, it distinguishes between P_1 and P_2 in Figure 4. In the figure, the names of the states are the numbers drawn within the circles.

What mathematicians usually do in this kind of a situation is to use *isomorphism* instead of equality as the notion of "sameness". Two LTSs are isomorphic, if and only if one can be converted to the other by changing the names of the states.

Definition 4. *Let $P = (S, \Sigma, \Delta, \hat{s})$ and $P' = (S', \Sigma', \Delta', \hat{s}')$ be LTSs.*

- *An* isomorphism *is a bijection (that is, a 1–1 correspondence) $f : S \to S'$ such that $f(\hat{s}) = \hat{s}'$ and $(s_1, a, s_2) \in \Delta \Leftrightarrow (f(s_1), a, f(s_2)) \in \Delta'$.*
- *P and P' are* isomorphic, *denoted $P =_{\mathsf{iso}} P'$, if and only if $\Sigma = \Sigma'$ and there is an isomorphism $f : S \to S'$.*

Although we will use isomorphism of LTSs a couple of times in this article, it is usually considered too strict a notion of "sameness" of LTSs. It unites P_1 and P_2 in Figure 4, but distinguishes between P_1 and P_3. However, the behaviours represented by P_1 and P_3 look the same to an external observer that cannot directly see the state the LTS is in, but sees the actions it makes. On the other hand, P_1 should be distinguished from P_4, because the latter can do two b-actions in a row, but the former cannot.

Strong bisimilarity [23,25] (or just *bisimilarity*) is a relation that is well-suited for comparing LTSs. It unifies the above-mentioned P_1, P_2 and P_3, but distinguishes them from P_4. Its definition resembles the definition of the isomorphism of LTSs, but instead of a bijection f, a binary relation "$\sim$" called *strong bisimulation* is used.

Definition 5. *Let $P = (S, \Sigma, \Delta, \hat{s})$ and $P' = (S', \Sigma', \Delta', \hat{s}')$ be LTSs.*

- *The relation "$\sim$" $\subseteq S \times S'$ is a* strong bisimulation, *if and only if for every $s_1, s_2 \in S$, $s'_1, s'_2 \in S'$ and $a \in \Sigma \cup \{\tau\}$:*
  - *If $s_1 \sim s'_1$ and $(s_1, a, s_2) \in \Delta$, then there is an $s' \in S'$ such that $s_2 \sim s'$ and $(s'_1, a, s') \in \Delta'$.*
  - *If $s_1 \sim s'_1$ and $(s'_1, a, s'_2) \in \Delta'$, then there is an $s \in S$ such that $s \sim s'_2$ and $(s_1, a, s) \in \Delta$.*
- *P and P' are* strongly bisimilar, *denoted $P =_{\mathsf{sb}} P'$, if and only if $\Sigma = \Sigma'$, and there is a strong bisimulation "$\sim$" $\subseteq S \times S'$ such that $\hat{s} \sim \hat{s}'$.*

In Figure 4, the relation "$\sim$" that satisfies $1 \sim 2$, $1 \sim 4$, $2 \sim 1$, $2 \sim 3$ and $x \not\sim y$ in all the remaining cases, is a strong bisimulation between the states of P_2 and the states of P_3, thus $P_2 =_{\mathsf{sb}} P_3$.

If two LTSs are isomorphic, then they are also strongly bisimilar, but the opposite does not always hold. This is because a relation between S and S' is an isomorphism if and only if it is simultaneously a strong bisimulation and a bijection, and $\hat{s} \sim \hat{s}'$.

Now that our relation of "sameness" is no more the equality, we have to be careful that the relation is appropriate for its purpose. Namely, the relation must be an *equivalence*.

Definition 6. *The relation "$=_\times$" is an equivalence, if and only if for every P_1, P_2 and P_3:*

- $P_1 =_\times P_1$ *(reflexivity)*.
- *If $P_1 =_\times P_2$, then $P_2 =_\times P_1$ (symmetry)*.
- *If $P_1 =_\times P_2$ and $P_2 =_\times P_3$, then $P_1 =_\times P_3$ (transitivity)*.

Both isomorphism and strong bisimilarity are equivalences. This holds because if $(S_1, \Sigma_1, \Delta_1, \hat{s}_1)$, $(S_2, \Sigma_2, \Delta_2, \hat{s}_2)$ and $(S_3, \Sigma_3, \Delta_3, \hat{s}_3)$ are LTSs, then

- The identity function $id : S_1 \to S_1 : id(s) = s$ is an isomorphism.
- If $f : S_1 \to S_2$ is an isomorphism, then its inverse function $f^{-1} : S_2 \to S_1$ that satisfies $f^{-1}(f(s_1)) = s_1$ and $f(f^{-1}(s_2)) = s_2$ exists and is an isomorphism.
- If $f : S_1 \to S_2$ and $g : S_2 \to S_3$ are isomorphisms, then $h : S_1 \to S_3 : h(s) = g(f(s))$ is an isomorphism.
- The identity relation "$=_{id}$" $\subseteq S_1 \times S_1 : s =_{id} s' \Leftrightarrow s = s'$ is a strong bisimulation such that $\hat{s}_1 =_{id} \hat{s}_1$.
- If "$\sim$" $\subseteq S_1 \times S_2$ is a strong bisimulation between the states of P_1 and P_2 such that $\hat{s}_1 \sim \hat{s}_2$, then "$\sim^{-1}$" $\subseteq S_2 \times S_1 : s_2 \sim^{-1} s_1 \Leftrightarrow s_1 \sim s_2$ is a strong bisimulation between the states of P_2 and P_1 such that $\hat{s}_2 \sim^{-1} \hat{s}_1$.
- If "$\sim_{12}$" $\subseteq S_1 \times S_2$ and "$\sim_{23}$" $\subseteq S_2 \times S_3$ are strong bisimulations such that $\hat{s}_1 \sim_{12} \hat{s}_2$ and $\hat{s}_2 \sim_{23} \hat{s}_3$, then "$\sim_{13}$" $\subseteq S_1 \times S_3 : s_1 \sim_{13} s_3 \Leftrightarrow \exists s_2 \in S_2 : s_1 \sim_{12} s_2 \wedge s_2 \sim_{23} s_3$ is a strong bisimulation such that $\hat{s}_1 \sim_{13} \hat{s}_3$.

Another important feature that strong bisimilarity shares with isomorphism is that the ability to simulate extends from individual transitions to sequences of transitions of any finite or even infinite length.

Theorem 1. *Let $(S, \Sigma, \Delta, \hat{s})$ and $(S', \Sigma', \Delta', \hat{s}')$ be LTSs, $s_0, s_1, s_2, \ldots \in S$, a_1, $a_2, \ldots \in \Sigma \cup \{\tau\}$, and $s'_0 \in S'$. Assume that $s_0 -a_1\to s_1 -a_2\to \cdots -a_n\to s_n -a_{n+1}\to \cdots$.*

- *If $f : S \to S'$ is an isomorphism, then $f(s_0) -a_1\to' f(s_1) -a_2\to' \cdots -a_n\to' f(s_n) -a_{n+1}\to' \cdots$.*
- *If "$\sim$" $\subseteq S \times S'$ is a strong bisimulation and $s_0 \sim s'_0$, then there are $s'_1, s'_2, \ldots, s'_n, \ldots$ such that $s'_0 -a_1\to' s'_1 -a_2\to' \cdots -a_n\to' s'_n -a_{n+1}\to' \cdots$ and $s_1 \sim s'_1, s_2 \sim s'_2, \ldots, s_n \sim s'_n, \ldots$.*

The claim remains valid if the sequences are ended at the nth state.

An important difference between strong bisimilarity and isomorphism is that strong bisimilarity of an LTS with another LTS depends only on those states and transitions that are reachable from the initial state of the LTS. This is because a strong bisimulation remains a strong bisimulation, when the pairs (s, s') are removed where s or s' is not reachable from the corresponding initial state.

Some above-mentioned and other facts about isomorphism and strong bisimilarity are collected into the following theorem.

Theorem 2. *Let P and Q be LTSs.*

- "$=_{iso}$" *and* "$=_{sb}$" *are equivalences.*
- *If $P =_{iso} Q$, then $P =_{sb} Q$.*
- *$P =_{sb} Q$ if and only if* repa$(P) =_{sb}$ repa(Q).
- *If $P =_{iso} Q$, then* repa$(P) =_{iso}$ repa(Q).

As defined above, strong bisimilarity is a relation between two LTSs. It can, however, be applied also to two states of the same LTS $P = (S, \Sigma, \Delta, \hat{s})$ by defining that s_1 and s_2 are strongly bisimilar, denoted by $s_1 \sim_{sb} s_2$, if and only if $(S, \Sigma, \Delta, s_1) =_{sb} (S, \Sigma, \Delta, s_2)$. The relation "$\sim_{sb}$" is a strong bisimulation between the states of P and the states of P such that $\hat{s} \sim_{sb} \hat{s}$. Furthermore, it is the *largest* such strong bisimulation: If "$\sim$" $\subseteq S \times S$ is a strong bisimulation, then $s \sim s'$ implies $s \sim_{sb} s'$.

If $s \in S$, then let $[[s]] = \{ s' \in S \mid s \sim_{sb} s' \}$, that is, $[[s]]$ is the set of the states of P that are strongly bisimilar to s. For any finite LTS $P = (S, \Sigma, \Delta, \hat{s})$, there is a unique (excluding the naming of states) LTS $P_{min} = (S_{min}, \Sigma, \Delta_{min}, \hat{s}_{min})$ that has as few states as possible, and is strongly bisimilar to P. It is the following:

- $S_{min} = \{ [[s]] \mid s \in S \wedge \exists \sigma \in (\Sigma \cup \{\tau\})^* : \hat{s} -\sigma \rightarrow s \}$.
- $\Delta_{min} = \{ ([[s]], a, [[s']]) \mid [[s]] \in S_{min} \wedge (s, a, s') \in \Delta \}$.
- $\hat{s}_{min} = [[\hat{s}]]$.

To be more precise, $P_{min} =_{sb} P$, and any LTS that is strongly bisimilar to P is either isomorphic to P_{min}, or has more states than P_{min}. A basic property of this construction is that if $(s, a, s') \in \Delta$, then for *every* $s_1 \in [[s]]$ there is $s_1' \in [[s']]$ such that $(s_1, a, s_1') \in \Delta$; this follows directly from the definitions of $[[s]]$ and strong bisimulation. Therefore, the relation "$\sim$" $\subseteq S \times S_{min}$: $(s_1 \sim [[s]] \Leftrightarrow s_1 \in [[s]])$ is a strong bisimulation. The purpose of the condition "$\exists \sigma \in (\Sigma \cup \{\tau\})^* : \hat{s} -\sigma \rightarrow s$" is to restrict P_{min} to the reachable part or, equivalently, avoid unnecessary simulation of the unreachable part of P. Without it, the result would be the smallest possible LTS that simulates every state of P. (The definition of P_{min} is valid even if P is not finite, although then one has to be careful with what is meant by "as few states as possible".)

P_{min} can be constructed rather efficiently with the algorithms presented in [17, 7]. A closely related algorithm can be used for testing whether two finite LTSs $(S_1, \Sigma, \Delta_1, \hat{s}_1)$ and $(S_2, \Sigma, \Delta_2, \hat{s}_2)$ are strongly bisimilar. That algorithm applies the construction of P_{min} to both LTSs simultaneously, such that any $[[s]]$ may contain states from both LTSs. That is, $[[s]] = \{ s' \in S_1 \cup S_2 \mid$ there is a strong bisimulation "$\sim$" such that $s \sim s' \}$. The LTSs are strongly bisimilar if and only if $\hat{s}_1$ and $\hat{s}_2$ end up in the same $[[s]]$.

The minimal LTS that is strongly bisimilar to the servers is shown in Figure 5. Compared to Figure 3, the bottom row and the first state of the second row have disappeared, and some transitions have been re-directed accordingly. This has an intuitive explanation: if there is a pending request from the client or such a request has just been served, then the server will push the token to the next server independently of whether the next server has requested it, so the value of is_dem need not be preserved in those cases.

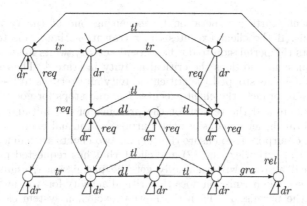

Fig. 5. Minimised version of the servers as an LTS.

2.5   The Clients

Often in process-algebraic verification, the users of a system are not modelled, although, of course, the system is. This is called an *open* model of the system. A *closed* model contains both the system and its users, and it is the norm in most other types of verification. The use of open models is possible in process algebras because of the type of compositionality found in them. We will see in Section 3.5 that the behaviour of any subsystem can be projected to its interface with the rest of the system and then reduced. One possibility is to project the behaviour of the system without the users to its interface with the users. The result shows how arbitrary users would see the system, and is thus often suitable for verification.

In this article, however, there are more clients than we will be able to handle simultaneously. We will, therefore, use projections to one or two clients at a time. For these projections to provide valid information, the remaining clients must be somehow presented at the other side of the interface. For this purpose we will need an adequate model of the clients. Such a model is shown in Figure 6. Since we will have to model almost all clients, it is natural to model them all, that is, use a closed model of the system. That is what we will do.

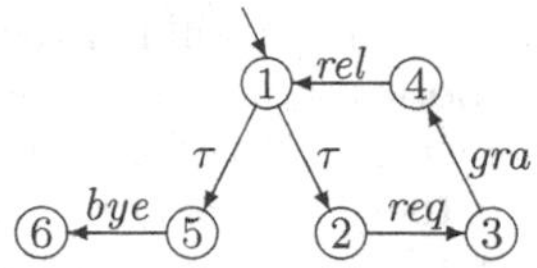

Fig. 6. A client.

A client starts its operation by executing one of the two alternative τ-transitions. If the client executes the τ-transition that leads to state 2, then it requests the permission to do the critical activity, waits in state 3 until it gets the permission, and does the critical activity in state 4. Then it indicates the server that it has stopped the critical activity and returns to its initial state. In the opposite branch, the client executes *bye* and stops for good.

To understand the reason for the presence of the initial τ-transitions and the *bye*-branch, let us consider the purpose of mutual exclusion systems for a while. The purpose is to ensure that (1) no two clients are simultaneously doing their critical activities, and (2) any client that has requested permission to do the critical activity will eventually get the permission. Assume that a client that has got the permission does the critical activity forever, and another client asks for the permission. Then the mutual exclusion system cannot satisfy the specification: if it ever gives the permission to the second client, then it violates (1), and if it does not, it violates (2).

We see that no mutual exclusion system can work correctly unless the clients obey some discipline. If a client has started doing the critical activity — that is, executed *gra* — then it must eventually stop it — that is, execute *rel*. It is also reasonable to require that if it has executed *req*, and *gra* is executable, then it must eventually execute *gra*, because the opposite would mean that it has requested the permission but then refuses to take it when it becomes available. Therefore, to be able to verify the system, we have to assume that the clients follow these rules, and we have to somehow take the assumption into account in the verification process. But we have actually done that (or done as well as can be done in this verification theory): Figure 6 enforces these rules by giving the client no other way to continue after *req* than by executing *gra*, and similarly with *rel* after *gra*.

The *req* action is, however, different. It is up to the client to decide whether it ever wants to ask for the permission. The client must be able to never execute *req* if that is what it wants. The τ-transition from the initial state to state 5 is there to express this possibility. By executing it the client can avoid executing *req*.

The τ-transition from state 1 to state 2 ensures that the client can commit itself to executing *req*. The semantics of interaction in the theory, to be discussed in Sections 2.6 and 2.7, is such that if the *req*-transition started at the initial state, then the server could force the client to execute the τ-transition leading to state 5 by refusing *req* forever. An incorrect server could then do that whenever it is unable to provide service, and thus mask its deficiency.

The *bye*-transition is not really necessary. It makes the interpretation of some of the verification results easier by stating explicitly that the client has decided not to request the permission any more. It would also have been possible to start the *bye*-transition at the initial state and remove state 5 and its adjacent transitions. This would not have given the servers the power to drive the client to state 2 by preventing the execution of the *bye*-transition, because the servers do not interact via *bye*, and thus cannot prevent its execution. However, the environment surrounding both the system and the clients would have got this power. That would not have caused errors to verification results, because in this case there is no such environment. It would, however, have made the results a bit more difficult to read, because the reader would have had to manually apply the piece of information that there will be no processes in addition to the servers and the clients.

The presence of a τ-transition both before the *req*-transition and before the *bye*-transition makes it explicit that it is the client who chooses between requesting and not requesting the permission, and nobody can force it to make one of the choices by preventing the other.

One may wonder whether this model of clients is fully appropriate. Permanent refusal from *req* might seem a bit harsh; would it not be better to refuse for some time and execute *req* again at some later time? After discussing abstract semantic models in Section 3.3 we will see that the model is very appropriate.

2.6 Putting the System Together

All the components of the system and its users have now been specified. They cannot, however, be put together as they are, because they use different action names from those in Figure 1, and the clients share common action names although they have not been intended to communicate directly with each other.

This problem is, of course, easy to solve: the server and client LTSs can be used as models from which LTSs with the same structure but different, appropriate action names are constructed by changing the labels of transitions. In this case visible action names have to be changed to other visible action names, but we will later also need to *hide* visible actions, that is, change them to τ. A general operator that serves both purposes and can even be used to duplicate transitions is defined below.

Definition 7. *Let* $P = (S, \Sigma, \Delta, \hat{s})$ *be an LTS. A binary relation* Φ *is an* action transformer *for* P, *if and only if it satisfies the following conditions:*

- $(\tau, \tau) \in \Phi$.
- *If* $(\tau, a) \in \Phi$, *then* $a = \tau$.
- $\{ a \mid a \neq \tau \wedge \exists b : (a, b) \in \Phi \} = \Sigma$.

If Φ *is an action transformer for* P, *then the LTS* $P\Phi$ *is defined as* $(S, \Sigma', \Delta', \hat{s})$, *where*

- $\Sigma' = \{ b \mid b \neq \tau \wedge \exists a : (a, b) \in \Phi \}$.
- $\Delta' = \{ (s, b, s') \mid \exists a : (s, a, s') \in \Delta \wedge (a, b) \in \Phi \}$.

The first two conditions of the action transformer relation specify that the invisible action symbol τ is transformed to τ and nothing else. The idea is that τ is totally untouchable: it cannot be affected by any operation. The last condition says that in addition to τ, Φ specifies new names for precisely the visible actions of P. Φ may duplicate transitions by specifying more than one new name for a visible action. When an LTS is transformed with the action transformer operator, its set of states and the initial state stay the same. The new alphabet consists of the new names other than τ of the visible actions, and for each transition (s, a, s'), and each b that a is transformed to, there is the transition (s, b, s').

The operator allows the transformation of an action to itself, and the transformation of a visible action to many actions. The simplest example of an action transformer is the *identity action transformer* $\Phi_{\mathsf{id}} = \{(a, a) \mid a \in \Sigma \cup \{\tau\}\}$. It does not change P at all.

The action transformer operator obeys some useful laws.

Theorem 3. *Let P and Q be LTSs, and Φ be an action transformer for P.*

- *If Ψ is an action transformer for $P\Phi$, then $(P\Phi)\Psi = P\Xi$, where*
  $\Xi = \{(a, c) \mid \exists b : (a, b) \in \Phi \wedge (b, c) \in \Psi\}$ *is an action transformer for P.*
- $P\Phi_{\mathsf{id}} = P$.
- *If $P =_{\mathsf{iso}} Q$, then $P\Phi =_{\mathsf{iso}} Q\Phi$.*
- *If $P =_{\mathsf{sb}} Q$, then $P\Phi =_{\mathsf{sb}} Q\Phi$.*

The first of these laws tells how two action transformers can be combined into one. The last two state the non-surprising fact that isomorphism and strong bisimilarity are *congruences* with respect to action transformation.

A more concrete syntax for two special cases of the action transformer is given in the next definition. For convenience, first an operator is defined which converts any binary relation to an action transformer. The resulting transformer inherits from the relation the changes that affect the required alphabet, and specifies no change for τ and the actions that are in the alphabet but are not affected by the relation. The first special case is called the *hiding* operator. It converts explicitly mentioned actions to τ and leaves the rest intact. The second special case can be used to express any action transformer that makes a finite number of changes, and we call it *renaming*. Unlike Φ, neither new operator requires the listing of those visible actions that are not changed. Furthermore, they allow irrelevant visible actions among the actions to be changed, but do nothing with them.

Definition 8. *Let $P = (S, \Sigma, \Delta, \hat{s})$ be an LTS, $A = \{a_1, \ldots, a_n\}$ such that $\tau \notin A$, and let $b_1, \ldots, b_n$ be any action names, X any set, and Φ any binary relation.*

- $\Phi{\downarrow}X = \{(a, b) \mid (a, b) \in \Phi \wedge a \in X - \{\tau\}\} \cup$
  $\qquad \{(a, a) \mid a \in X \wedge \neg\exists b : (a, b) \in \Phi\} \cup \{(\tau, \tau)\}$.
- **hide** A **in** $P = P(\{(a, \tau) \mid a \in A\}{\downarrow}\Sigma)$.
- $P[b_1/a_1, \ldots, b_n/a_n] = P(\{(a_1, b_1), \ldots, (a_n, b_n)\}{\downarrow}\Sigma)$.

The servers and clients of the system can now be represented as

Server_tkn$_1$ =
   Server_tkn$[tkn_1/tl, tkn_2/tr, dem_1/dl, dem_2/dr, req_1/req, gra_1/gra, rel_1/rel]$
Server$_i$ =
   Server$[tkn_i/tl, tkn_{i\oplus1}/tr, dem_i/dl, dem_{i\oplus1}/dr, req_i/req, gra_i/gra, rel_i/rel]$
Client$_i$ = Client$[req_i/req, gra_i/gra, rel_i/rel, bye_i/bye]$.

where "_tkn" refers to the server that has the token initially.

The servers and clients are connected together with the *parallel composition* operator. The state of the parallel composition is a vector consisting of the states of the component processes. The initial state is, of course, the vector that consists of the initial states of the components. The parallel composition has all the visible actions of the components as its visible actions.

Each component can make an invisible transition independently of the other components, and at the level of the composed system the transition appears as an invisible transition. The other components stay where they are during the transition.

Regarding visible transitions, we say that a component is *interested* in a visible action if the action is in its alphabet. A visible transition of the parallel composition consists of simultaneous transitions by one or more components. The transitions of the components must have the same label, and that label is also the label of the joint transition. All components who are interested in the label must participate the transition. This implies that any of these components can postpone or prevent the transition by not being ready for it. All the other participants must then wait or perform some other transition. Again, the transition does not affect the states of those components that are not interested in its label.

Only the states that are reachable from the initial state are taken into account in the parallel composition. In the definition below, this is achieved by using an auxiliary notion of *synchronous product*, and defining the parallel composition to be its reachable part.

Definition 9. *Let* $P_1 = (S_1, \Sigma_1, \Delta_1, \hat{s}_1), \ldots, P_n = (S_n, \Sigma_n, \Delta_n, \hat{s}_n)$ *be LTSs. Their synchronous product is the LTS* $P_1 \times \cdots \times P_n = (S, \Sigma, \Delta, \hat{s})$, *where*

- $S = S_1 \times \cdots \times S_n$
- $\Sigma = \Sigma_1 \cup \cdots \cup \Sigma_n$
- $\hat{s} = \langle \hat{s}_1, \ldots, \hat{s}_n \rangle$
- $(\langle s_1, \ldots, s_n \rangle, \tau, \langle s'_1, \ldots, s'_n \rangle) \in \Delta$, *if and only if there is an* i, $1 \leq i \leq n$, *such that*
  - $(s_i, \tau, s'_i) \in \Delta_i$, *and*
  - $s'_j = s_j$ *whenever* $1 \leq j < i$ *or* $i < j \leq n$.
- $(\langle s_1, \ldots, s_n \rangle, a, \langle s'_1, \ldots, s'_n \rangle) \in \Delta$ *where* $a \in \Sigma$, *if and only if whenever* $1 \leq i \leq n$, *either*
  - $a \in \Sigma_i$ *and* $(s_i, a, s'_i) \in \Delta_i$, *or*
  - $a \notin \Sigma_i$ *and* $s'_i = s_i$.
- Δ *contains no other elements than those generated by the above two rules.*

Their parallel composition *is the LTS* $P_1 \parallel \cdots \parallel P_n = \mathsf{repa}(P_1 \times \cdots \times P_n)$.

Tools that compute parallel compositions do not usually construct the unreachable part at all. This is because the synchronous product is often very much bigger than its reachable part. For instance, the synchronous product corresponding to the 3-server demand-driven token-ring system has $17^3 \cdot 6^3 = 1\,061\,208$ states, whereas only $1\,320$ of them are reachable.

Also the parallel composition obeys some useful laws.

Theorem 4. *Let P, P', P_1, $\ldots$, P_n, Q, and Q' be LTSs, Φ an action transformer for $(P \,\|\, Q)$, and $1 \leq i \leq j \leq n$. Let the alphabets of P and Q be Σ_P and Σ_Q.*

- $P_1 \,\|\, \cdots \,\|\, P_{i-1} \,\|\, (P_i \,\|\, \cdots \,\|\, P_j) \,\|\, P_{j+1} \,\|\, \cdots \,\|\, P_n =_{\mathsf{iso}} P_1 \,\|\, \cdots \,\|\, P_n.$
- $P \,\|\, Q =_{\mathsf{iso}} Q \,\|\, P.$
- *If $P =_{\mathsf{iso}} P'$ and $Q =_{\mathsf{iso}} Q'$, then $P \,\|\, Q =_{\mathsf{iso}} P' \,\|\, Q'$.*
- *If $P =_{\mathsf{sb}} P'$ and $Q =_{\mathsf{sb}} Q'$, then $P \,\|\, Q =_{\mathsf{sb}} P' \,\|\, Q'$.*
- *Assume that for every a, a' and b such that $(a,b) \in \Phi$ and $(a',b) \in \Phi$*
  - $a \in \Sigma_P - \Sigma_Q \Rightarrow b = \tau \vee a' \notin \Sigma_Q,$
  - $a \in \Sigma_Q - \Sigma_P \Rightarrow b = \tau \vee a' \notin \Sigma_P,$ *and*
  - $a \in \Sigma_P \cap \Sigma_Q \Rightarrow b \neq \tau \wedge a' = a.$

  Then $(P \,\|\, Q)\Phi = (P(\Phi{\downarrow}\Sigma_P)) \,\|\, (Q(\Phi{\downarrow}\Sigma_Q)).$

The first law implies that any hierarchical tree of parallel compositions is isomorphic to the flat structure where all components have been connected together in one multi-parameter parallel composition. It also implies that parallel composition is associative, provided that isomorphism is accepted as a strong enough notion of equivalence. Parallel composition is also commutative in the same sense, says the second law.

The next two laws express that isomorphism and strong bisimilarity are congruences also with respect to the parallel composition operator. The laws have been given for the case of two component processes, but they can be extended to any number of components by repeatedly applying the first law.

The fifth law allows the distribution of an action transformer over a parallel composition in certain cases. Its horrible-looking condition is there to ensure that local transitions of P and Q synchronise after the distribution if and only if they synchronise before the distribution.

The n-server demand-driven token-ring system can now be defined as

$$\mathsf{System}_n = \mathsf{Server\_tkn}_1 \,\|\, \mathsf{Client}_1 \,\|\, \mathsf{Server}_2 \,\|\, \mathsf{Client}_2 \,\|\, \cdots \,\|\, \mathsf{Server}_n \,\|\, \mathsf{Client}_n$$

The alphabet of System_n is

$$\Sigma_n^{\mathsf{Sys}} = \{\, tkn_1, \ldots, tkn_n, dem_1, \ldots, dem_n, req_1, \ldots, req_n,$$
$$gra_1, \ldots, gra_n, rel_1, \ldots, rel_n, bye_1, \ldots, bye_n \}$$

The numbers of states and transitions of the system are shown in the second and third column of Table 1.

It can be seen from the table that the size of the system LTS grows very rapidly as a function of n. This phenomenon is very common with parallel composition, and it is called *state explosion*.

Table 1. The size of the LTS of System_n and of $\mathsf{Server\_tkn}_1^{\min} \| \mathsf{Server}_2^{\min} \| \cdots \| \mathsf{Server}_n^{\min}$.

	full system		only min-servers	
n	states	transitions	states	transitions
2	132	298	30	58
3	1 320	4 164	150	402
4	12 320	49 936	680	2 332
5	110 000	544 800	2 900	12 120
6	950 400	5 562 240	11 880	58 560

A part of the state explosion in this system is due to somewhat wasteful modelling. For instance, as was discussed in Section 2.4, Figure 5 could have been used as the model of the servers instead of Figure 3. However, the growth remains exponential even with the most economical modelling. Namely, the token may be in any of the n servers, and any client may have or have not requested the permission independently of the states of the other parts of the system, yielding at least $n2^n$ states. The real growth rate is much faster, as can be seen from the last two columns of Table 1. They act as a lower bound, because they show the size of the LTS of a ring, the servers of which are as in Figure 5, and that has no clients at all.

The lesson to be learnt from the table is that careful modelling helps a lot in keeping the LTS size small, but usually cannot prevent state explosion altogether.

2.7   A Digression on the Parallel Composition Operator

Although the parallel composition operator presented in Definition 9 is very common in the literature (perhaps with the difference that the restriction to the reachable part is sometimes omitted), it deserves some comments.

First, it does not allow *true parallelism.* In reality, transitions that are participated by disjoint sets of component processes may occur simultaneously, but this operator forces them to occur one at a time in an arbitrary order. However, such transitions can be executed in any order, the end result is independent of the order, and it is the same that would have resulted from simultaneous execution. As a consequence, the "one-at-a-time" convention (called *interleaving semantics*) does not affect most of the aspects of systems that people want to verify. There are theories for true parallelism, but they are mathematically complicated. Therefore, many, perhaps the majority of verification researchers use interleaving semantics.

Second, the operator uses *synchronous communication*: processes communicate by executing simultaneously transitions that are labelled with the same action. The operator even allows more than two participants in the same transition. This mode of communication has no clear notions of input and output. There is no buffering between the communicating parties, and the use of the operator leads easily to seemingly superfluous deadlocks where processes wait for synchronisation with each other but with different actions. So it might seem that, say, fifos (first-in first-out queues) would have been a more adequate form of communication.

It has turned out, however, that most, if not all, other modes of communication can reasonably easily be simulated with synchronous communication, whereas simulation in the opposite direction is usually difficult. Input of data is modelled by offering a transition for each possible data value, whereas in the case of output there is a transition only for one value, namely the value that is to be sent. Buffering can be represented by modelling buffers as processes of their own right, such as in Figure 7 that shows a fifo as an LTS. In it, i_1 and i_2 are input actions that are both offered in every state where the fifo is not full, while o_1 and o_2 are output actions, of which at most one is offered at any state.

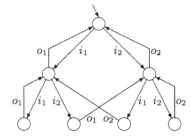

Fig. 7. A fifo of two message types and capacity two.

Although fifos might be less prone to deadlocks than synchronous communication, they have other problems: what happens to the first message in the fifo if the recipient is not willing to read it, and what happens if messages are written to the fifo more frequently than read from it? After these questions have been appropriately answered, the fifo model starts to suffer from unbounded accumulation of messages in fifos, unexpected losses of messages, or deadlocks. Many of the seemingly superfluous deadlocks of synchronous communication would thus not go away when switching over to fifo communication, they would just change shape.

Finally, synchronisation by more than two parties makes it possible to simulate broadcasts, so it is useful.

In conclusion, the use of synchronous communication does not restrict the applicability of the theory as much as it might initially seem.

Third, the operator relies on alphabets for determining which processes synchronise for each action. This makes extra actions in an alphabet significant. This could have been avoided by using some other form of parallel composition. For instance, the main parallel composition operator of Lotos [2] lists explicitly the actions with which the processes synchronise. It looks like this: $P \,|[a_1, \ldots, a_n]|\, Q$.

The Lotos operator can, however, be simulated with our parallel composition and action transformer operators: $P \, |[a_1, \dots, a_n]| \, Q$ behaves in the same way as $(P\Phi \, || \, Q \, || \, \mathbf{stop}_{\{a_1, \dots, a_n\}-(\Sigma_P \cap \Sigma_Q)})\Phi^{-1}$, where

- Σ_P and Σ_Q are the alphabets of P and Q.
- $\mathbf{stop}_X$ is the one-state LTS that has no transitions, and whose alphabet is X.
- $\Phi = [b'_1/b_1, \dots, b'_k/b_k]$, where $\{b_1, \dots, b_k\} = (\Sigma_P \cap \Sigma_Q) - \{a_1, \dots, a_n\}$, and $b'_1, \dots, b'_k$ are new action names, that is, $b'_i \notin \Sigma_P \cup \Sigma_Q \cup \{\tau\} \cup \{a_1, \dots, a_n\}$, and if $i \neq j$, then $b'_i \neq b'_j$.
- $\Phi^{-1} = [b_1/b'_1, \dots, b_k/b'_k]$.

This formula refers to the alphabets. However, if $P = (S_P, \Sigma_P, \Delta_P, \hat{s}_P)$, any set X such that $\tau \notin X$ and $\{ a \mid a \neq \tau \wedge \exists s, s' : (s, a, s') \in \Delta_P \} \subseteq X$ can be used instead of Σ_P without changing anything else than the alphabet of the result, and similarly with Q.

The CCS [23] parallel composition operator can be simulated by taking advantage of the ability of the action transformer operator to duplicate transitions. In CCS, the visible actions are divided to two disjoint sets: "names" like a, and "co-names" like $\bar{a}$. We define that $\bar{\bar{a}} = a$ and $\bar{A} = \{ \bar{a} \mid a \in A \}$. The CCS parallel composition operator "|" takes precisely two operands. Synchronisation occurs when one operand executes a visible action a and the other simultaneously executes $\bar{a}$. The label of the resulting transition of $P \mid Q$ is τ. Furthermore, either operand can do just any action without synchronising with the other operand.[2]

Let $\Sigma = \Sigma_P \cup \Sigma_Q \cup \overline{\Sigma_P} \cup \overline{\Sigma_Q} = \{a_1, \dots, a_n\}$, and let $b_1, \dots, b_n$ and $a'_1, \dots, a'_n$ be different from each other and from all elements of $\Sigma \cup \{\tau\}$. Then $P \mid Q$ behaves like $(((P \, || \, \mathbf{stop}_{\Sigma - \Sigma_P})\Phi_P) \, || \, ((Q \, || \, \mathbf{stop}_{\Sigma - \Sigma_Q})\Phi_Q))\Phi$, where Σ_P and Σ_Q are like above, and

- $\Phi_P = [a'_1/a_1, \dots, a'_n/a_n, b_1/\bar{a}_1, \dots, b_n/\bar{a}_n]$,
- $\Phi_Q = [a_1/a_1, \dots, a_n/a_n, b_1/a_1, \dots, b_n/a_n]$, and
- $\Phi = [a_1/a'_1, \dots, a_n/a'_n, \tau/b_1, \dots, \tau/b_n]$.

Other commonly used parallel composition operators can thus be simulated with our "||". On the other hand, "||" is simple to define and use, is more general than the CCS "|" that allows only two-process synchronisation, and enjoys some useful mathematical properties that the Lotos "|[$\cdots$]|" lacks. Namely, "||" is associative, and if P and Q are *deterministic* (in the sense that if $s -a\to s_1$ and $s -a\to s_2$, then $a \neq \tau$ and $s_1 = s_2$), then also $P \, || \, Q$ is deterministic and $P \, || \, P =_{\mathsf{iso}} P$. These are good reasons for using "||" in our theory.

3   Verification

3.1   Requirements

As was mentioned in Section 2.5, the purpose of the system is to ensure two important properties:

---

[2] This can be prevented with the CCS *restriction* operator $P \backslash L$ that works like $P \, || \, \mathbf{stop}_{L \cup \bar{L}}$.

mutual exclusion: No two clients are simultaneously doing their critical activities.

eventual access: Any client that has requested permission to do the critical activity will eventually get the permission.

To state these properties formally, we define two *state propositions* of Client_i:

- r_i = client i is in state 3.
- g_i = client i is in state 4.

A state proposition is a claim whose truth value depends only on the current state of the system, not on preceding or succeeding states. With these propositions a user of linear temporal logic [22] could formalise the requirements like this ("$\Box$" can be read as "always" and "$\Diamond$" as "eventually"):

mutual exclusion: $\forall i,j \in \{1,2,\dots,n\} : (i \neq j \Rightarrow \Box\neg(\mathsf{g}_i \wedge \mathsf{g}_j))$.
eventual access: $\forall i \in \{1,2,\dots,n\} : \Box(\mathsf{r}_i \Rightarrow \Diamond\mathsf{g}_i)$.

These formulae are difficult to check automatically in their current form, because of the use of the universal quantification "$\forall$". However, the formulae can be interpreted as $\frac{1}{2}n(n+1)$ different propositional linear temporal logic formulae: $\Box\neg(\mathsf{g}_1 \wedge \mathsf{g}_2), \dots, \Box\neg(\mathsf{g}_1 \wedge \mathsf{g}_n), \dots, \Box\neg(\mathsf{g}_{n-1} \wedge \mathsf{g}_n), \Box(\mathsf{r}_1 \Rightarrow \Diamond\mathsf{g}_1), \dots, \Box(\mathsf{r}_n \Rightarrow \Diamond\mathsf{g}_n)$. (Here the $\frac{1}{2}n(n-1)$ formulae of the form $\Box\neg(\mathsf{g}_i \wedge \mathsf{g}_j)$ where $i > j$ were omitted, because they are equivalent to $\Box\neg(\mathsf{g}_j \wedge \mathsf{g}_i)$.) These formulae can be checked from the full LTS of the system with a suitable temporal logic *model checking* tool, provided that the numbers of the states of the clients are preserved in the LTS.

It would be tempting to appeal to the symmetry of the system to reduce further the number of formulae that have to be checked. Unfortunately, although the structure of the system is symmetric, its initial state is not: one server differs from the others in that it has the token. Some properties are sensitive to this difference, such as "if the first request is made by Client_i, then the first permission is given to Client_i". It is true only if Client_i is the one whose server has the token initially. The mutual exclusion and eventual access properties are not sensitive to the initial asymmetry. It is, however, not trivial to see that this is the case, so appealing to it in verification is unsatisfactory at the least.

We shall thus proceed in a different direction.

3.2   Introduction to Abstraction

It is easy to see that the validity of r_i and g_i in a state can be reasoned from the sequence of actions executed so far. It suffices to know which of req_i, gra_i and rel_i has been executed most recently:

- if req_i, then $\mathsf{r}_i = \mathsf{True}$ and $\mathsf{g}_i = \mathsf{False}$,
- if gra_i, then $\mathsf{r}_i = \mathsf{False}$ and $\mathsf{g}_i = \mathsf{True}$,
- if rel_i, then $\mathsf{r}_i = \mathsf{g}_i = \mathsf{False}$.

Also initially $\mathsf{r}_i = \mathsf{g}_i = \mathsf{False}$.

Another important thing is that the mutual exclusion and eventual access properties are *insensitive to stuttering*. That is, their validity depends only on the order in which various combinations of the truth values of the r_i and g_i are obtained; whether a particular combination is valid in 1, 2 or 1 000 000 successive states does not matter. This is not a coincidence. Most, perhaps all, verification researchers agree that in the context of concurrent systems, properties that are sensitive to stuttering are almost always irrelevant.

These facts make it possible to take advantage of process-algebraic *abstraction* in the verification of the mutual exclusion and eventual access properties. The idea is to recognise the actions on which the validity of a formula depends, hide the remaining actions with the hiding operator, and then construct a suitable *reduced* LTS of the system. The reduced LTS is a kind of a projection of the behaviour of the system onto the visible actions.

Before going into the details, let us have a look at what reduced LTSs corresponding to the formulae $\Box\neg(g_1 \wedge g_2)$ and $\Box(r_1 \Rightarrow \Diamond g_1)$ might look like when $n = 3$. Figure 8 shows such LTSs as produced by the ARA tool. As a matter of fact, the LTS in Figure 8(b) shows more actions than is necessary for checking eventual access, but we will soon see that also the extra actions are interesting. The numbering of states has been added when re-drawing the LTSs into this article. We will later see that precisely the same figures are obtained also with any $n > 3$.

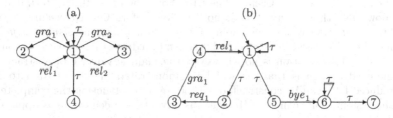

Fig. 8. (a) A mutual exclusion and (b) an eventual access view to the three-server system.

The LTS on the left hand side is obtained after hiding all other visible actions than gra_1, gra_2, rel_1 and rel_2. That is, it is a reduced version of

$$\textbf{hide } \Sigma_3^{\textsf{Sys}} - \{gra_1, gra_2, rel_1, rel_2\} \textbf{ in System}_3$$

We have that g_1 holds in state 2 and only in it, while g_2 holds precisely in state 3. There is thus no state where g_1 and g_2 hold simultaneously, so $\Box\neg(g_1 \wedge g_2)$ holds.

The LTS on the right hand side is a reduced version of

$$\textbf{hide } \Sigma_3^{\textsf{Sys}} - \{req_1, gra_1, rel_1, bye_1\} \textbf{ in System}_3$$

That there are no output transitions from state 7 means that the system can halt or deadlock. However, this state can be reached only after Client$_1$ has executed

bye_1, so the system cannot halt unless Client_1 chooses to never or never again request the permission. The possibility of halting is shown also by state 4 of the mutual exclusion LTS, but that LTS does not show that bye_1 is executed before halting, because bye_1 is not visible in that LTS.

The τ-loops adjacent to states 1 and 6 indicate that the system can execute forever without Client_1 being involved. It is easy to think of such executions: it suffices that the other clients request the permission again and again. What is important in the figure is that there are neither τ-loops nor deadlocks adjacent to state 3. This means that if Client_1 has executed req_1, then the system cannot halt or execute forever before Client_1 executes gra_1. In other words, if Client_1 has requested the permission, it will get the permission within a finite number of steps by the system. Therefore, $\Box(r_1 \Rightarrow \Diamond g_1)$ holds.

If the visible actions are req_2, gra_2, rel_2 and bye_2 or req_3, gra_3, rel_3 and bye_3, then the resulting LTS is like the LTS in Figure 8(b) with, of course, the subscripts in question. If the visible actions are gra_1, rel_1, gra_2, rel_2, gra_3 and rel_3, then the result is otherwise like the LTS in Figure 8(a), but the τ-loop has been replaced by a gra_3-rel_3-loop. Therefore, the correctness formulae hold for every value of i and j when $n = 3$.

We see that if a formula is simple enough, the corresponding reduced LTS is so small that the validity of the formula can be checked directly from the LTS without any tool. Furthermore, the reduced LTS may also contain other useful information. For instance, the LTS in Figure 8(b) shows the whole behaviour of the system as seen by Client_1. The LTS shows the possibility of termination, but shows also that termination is not possible before Client_1 executes bye_1. This kind of analysis of the behaviour of a system is known as *visual verification*. It has been discussed in more detail and compared to ordinary verification in [39].

Visual verification is not, however, the main advantage of abstraction. The main advantage is that, as will be demonstrated in Sections 3.5 to 3.7, the reduced LTS can be constructed without ever constructing the complete LTS of the system. This can be a tremendous advantage, because, as is apparent from Table 1, the size of the complete LTS may be huge.

3.3   CFFD-Equivalence

Table 1 shows that System_3 has 1320 states, and Definitions 7 and 8 imply that **hide** $\Sigma_3^{\mathsf{Sys}} - \{gra_1, gra_2, rel_1, rel_2\}$ **in** System_3 has as many states as System_3. The LTS in Figure 8(a) cannot thus be the complete LTS of **hide** $\Sigma_3^{\mathsf{Sys}} - \{gra_1, gra_2, rel_1, rel_2\}$ **in** System_3. It was mentioned in Section 3.2 that it is some kind of a projection of the complete LTS onto the chosen visible actions. The goal of this section is to make precise the sense in which the LTS in the figure represents the complete LTS.

The main idea is to throw away information about the execution of invisible actions. For that purpose, a new notation is defined that resembles the "$-a_1 \cdots a_n \rightarrow$"-notation, but where τs are omitted from within $a_1 \cdots a_n$.

Definition 10. *Let* $(S, \Sigma, \Delta, \hat{s})$ *be an LTS,* $s, s' \in S$, $n \geq 0$, *and* $a, a_1, a_2, \ldots \in \Sigma$.

- $s = \varepsilon \Rightarrow s'$ if and only if there is an $i \geq 0$ such that $s - \tau^i \to s'$, where τ^i denotes the sequence of i copies of τ.
- $s = a \Rightarrow s'$ if and only if $\exists s_1, s_2 \in S : s = \varepsilon \Rightarrow s_1 \wedge s_1 - a \to s_2 \wedge s_2 = \varepsilon \Rightarrow s'$.
- $s = a_1 a_2 \cdots a_n \Rightarrow s'$ if and only if
  $\exists s_0, s_1, \ldots, s_n \in S : s_0 = s \wedge s_n = s' \wedge \forall i \in \{1, 2, \ldots, n\} : s_{i-1} = a_i \Rightarrow s_i$.
- $s = a_1 a_2 \cdots a_n \Rightarrow$ if and only if $\exists s' : s = a_1 a_2 \cdots a_n \Rightarrow s'$.
- $s = a_1 a_2 a_3 \cdots \Rightarrow$ if and only if
  $\exists s_0, s_1, s_2, \ldots \in S : s_0 = s \wedge \forall i \in \{1, 2, 3, \ldots\} : s_{i-1} = a_i \Rightarrow s_i$.

An execution of a system is *complete*, if and only if it is as long as possible, that is, it is either infinite or ends up in a state that has no output transitions. The number of visible actions in an infinite execution may be finite or infinite. In the former case, the sequence of visible actions that arises from the infinite execution is called a *divergence trace*, and in the latter case it is an *infinite trace* of the system. An execution that corresponds to a divergence trace has an infinite end part that consists of only invisible transitions. Such a situation is called a *livelock*, because then the system is busy executing, but does not make any visible progress.

If an execution ends up in a halted state, then the corresponding sequence of visible actions is finite, and is called a *deadlock trace*.

Sometimes it is useful to talk about the sequence of visible actions that arises from a finite and not necessarily complete execution of a system. The notion of *trace* is introduced for that purpose.

It has turned out that in order to derive the deadlock traces of a parallel composition, the deadlock traces of the components do not always suffice, but their generalisation called *stable failures* is needed. A state is *stable* if and only if it has no output transitions that are labelled with τ. The *initial stability* predicate records whether the initial state is stable. A stable state *refuses* some set of visible actions, if and only if none of its output transitions is labelled with an element from the set. A stable failure is a pair that consists of a trace and a set of visible actions, such that at least one of the states where the LTS may be in after executing the trace is stable and refuses the set. If the other component of a parallel composition is simultaneously in a stable state where it can execute only actions from the set, then the parallel composition is in a deadlock, although both processes may be willing to execute more actions.

Definition 11. *Let $P = (S, \Sigma, \Delta, \hat{s})$ be an LTS.*

- *The set of the* traces *of P is*
  $Tr(P) = \{ a_1 a_2 \cdots a_n \in \Sigma^* \mid \hat{s} = a_1 a_2 \cdots a_n \Rightarrow \}$.
- *The set of the* infinite traces *of P is*
  $Inftr(P) = \{ a_1 a_2 a_3 \cdots \in \Sigma^\omega \mid \hat{s} = a_1 a_2 a_3 \cdots \Rightarrow \}$.
- *The set of the* divergence traces *of P is*
  $Divtr(P) = \{ a_1 a_2 \cdots a_n \in \Sigma^* \mid \exists s \in S : \hat{s} = a_1 a_2 \cdots a_n \Rightarrow s \wedge s - \tau^\omega \to \}$,
  where τ^ω denotes the sequence of an infinite number of copies of τ.
- *The set of the* deadlock traces *of P is $Dltr(P) =$*
  $\{ \sigma \in \Sigma^* \mid \exists s \in S : \hat{s} = \sigma \Rightarrow s \wedge \neg(s - \tau \to) \wedge \forall a \in \Sigma : \neg(s - a \to) \}$.
- *The set of the* stable failures *of P is $Sfail(P) =$*
  $\{ (\sigma, A) \in \Sigma^* \times 2^\Sigma \mid \exists s \in S : \hat{s} = \sigma \Rightarrow s \wedge \neg(s - \tau \to) \wedge \forall a \in A : \neg(s - a \to) \}$.

- *The* initial stability *predicate of P is*
  $Stable(P) = \neg(\hat{s} - \tau \rightarrow)$.

Some useful laws that these sets obey are listed below.

Theorem 5. *Let $P = (S, \Sigma, \Delta, \hat{s})$ be an LTS.*

- $\varepsilon \in Tr(P)$.
- *If $a_1 a_2 \cdots a_n \in Tr(P)$ and $0 \leq i \leq n$, then $a_1 a_2 \cdots a_i \in Tr(P)$.*
- $Tr(P) = Divtr(P) \cup \{ \sigma \mid (\sigma, \emptyset) \in Sfail(P) \}$.
- $Dltr(P) = \{ \sigma \mid (\sigma, \Sigma) \in Sfail(P) \}$.
- *If $(\sigma, A) \in Sfail(P)$ and $B \subseteq A$, then $(\sigma, B) \in Sfail(P)$.*
- *If $a_1 a_2 a_3 \cdots \in Inftr(P)$ and $0 \leq i$, then $a_1 a_2 \cdots a_i \in Tr(P)$.*
- *If S is finite, then*
  $Inftr(P) = \{ a_1 a_2 a_3 \cdots \in \Sigma^\omega \mid \forall i \in \{0, 1, 2, \dots\} : a_1 a_2 \cdots a_i \in Tr(P) \}$.

The validity of the mutual exclusion property in the demand-driven token-ring system depends only on how gra_i, rel_i, gra_j and rel_j are interleaved in the executions of the system. An important feature of the mutual exclusion property is that if it is violated, then it is violated after a finite execution of the system. This execution need not be complete. Therefore, to check whether the mutual exclusion property holds, it suffices to know the traces of **hide** $\Sigma_n^{\text{Sys}} - \{gra_i, gra_j, rel_i, rel_j\}$ **in** System$_n$ for every $1 \leq i < j \leq n$. Properties that can be checked from the set of traces are called *safety properties*.

The eventual access property is not a safety property, and thus cannot be checked from the set of traces. It is a (proper) *liveness* property. Namely, that a request by a client is never granted cannot be reasoned from an incomplete execution, because it is possible that it is granted in the unknown continuation of the execution. However, if a request is not granted in a complete execution, then it is certain that the property does not hold. Therefore, the validity of the eventual access property can be reasoned from the infinite traces, divergence traces and deadlock traces of **hide** $\Sigma_n^{\text{Sys}} - \{req_i, gra_i\}$ **in** System$_n$.

We are now ready to define formally the sense in which the LTSs in Figure 8 are equivalent to the LTSs **hide** $\Sigma_3^{\text{Sys}} - \{gra_1, gra_2, rel_1, rel_2\}$ **in** System$_3$ and **hide** $\Sigma_3^{\text{Sys}} - \{req_1, gra_1, rel_1, bye_1\}$ **in** System$_3$.

Definition 12. *Let $P = (S, \Sigma, \Delta, \hat{s})$ and $Q = (S', \Sigma', \Delta', \hat{s}')$ be LTSs.*

- *The CFFD semantics of P is $(\Sigma, Sfail(P), Divtr(P), Inftr(P), Stable(P))$.*
- *CFFD-equivalence is defined by $P \simeq_{\text{CFFD}} Q$ if and only if $\Sigma = \Sigma'$, $Sfail(P) = Sfail(Q)$, $Divtr(P) = Divtr(Q)$, $Inftr(P) = Inftr(Q)$, and $Stable(P) = Stable(Q)$.*
- *CFFD-preorder is defined by $P \leq_{\text{CFFD}} Q$ if and only if $\Sigma = \Sigma'$, $Sfail(P) \subseteq Sfail(Q)$, $Divtr(P) \subseteq Divtr(Q)$, $Inftr(P) \subseteq Inftr(Q)$, and $Stable(P) \vee \neg Stable(Q)$.*

"Preorder" means a reflexive and transitive relation. Obviously, $P \simeq_{\text{CFFD}} Q$ if and only if $P \leq_{\text{CFFD}} Q$ and $Q \leq_{\text{CFFD}} P$. It follows from Theorem 5 that if $P \leq_{\text{CFFD}} Q$, then $Tr(P) \subseteq Tr(Q)$. It is also true that if $P =_{\text{sb}} Q$, then $P \simeq_{\text{CFFD}} Q$. (We write $P \simeq_{\text{CFFD}} Q$ instead of $P =_{\text{CFFD}} Q$ to emphasise that unlike "=", "$=_{iso}$" and "$=_{sb}$", CFFD-equivalence preserves less information on τ-transitions than on visible transitions.)

The CFFD semantics preserves the validity of stuttering-insensitive linear temporal logic formulae in the following sense: if the validity of each state proposition of a formula can be reasoned from the visible actions executed so far, if Q satisfies the formula, and if $P \leq_{CFFD} Q$, then also P satisfies the formula. A process P that is smaller in CFFD-preorder than Q is thus "better" than Q in the sense that P satisfies at least the same formulae as Q, and may satisfy more. It is also said that P is *more deterministic* than Q, because LTSs that are deterministic in the sense mentioned towards the end of Section 2.7 are locally minimal with respect to CFFD-preorder.

The LTSs in Figure 8 are CFFD-equivalent to **hide** $\Sigma_3^{Sys} - \{gra_1, gra_2, rel_1,$ $rel_2\}$ **in** System$_3$ and **hide** $\Sigma_3^{Sys} - \{req_1, gra_1, rel_1, bye_1\}$ **in** System$_3$. Therefore, it is correct to check the validity of $\Box\neg(\mathbf{g}_1 \wedge \mathbf{g}_2)$ and $\Box(\mathbf{r}_1 \Rightarrow \Diamond \mathbf{g}_1)$ from them.

It may seem peculiar that there is no τ-loop adjacent to state 5 of the LTS in Figure 8(b), although there are τ-loops adjacent to states 1 and 6. It looks as if the rest of the system decides not to livelock (state 5), but then cancels this decision when the client executes bye_1. However, the rest of the system does not synchronise to bye_1, and cannot thus know when it is executed.

The explanation of this phenomenon is that the only thing that the CFFD semantics preserves about the history of a state is the sequence of visible actions that have been executed. When looking at state 6, one should not reason that the possibility of livelocking was temporarily lost at state 5, because the CFFD semantics does not preserve this kind of information. What one may read is that both livelocking (state 1) and not livelocking (state 5) are possible without or before executing bye_1. One may also read that both livelocking (state 6) and not livelocking (state 7) are possible after executing bye_1. However, all these possibilities need not be available in the same execution, although Figure 8(b) seems to indicate so. In its attempt to produce as small an LTS as possible, the algorithm that reduced the LTS twisted the information that the CFFD semantics does not preserve. This might feel irritating at first, but it is the key to obtaining small LTSs.

CFFD-equivalence is a congruence with respect to action transformation, parallel composition, and many other operators found in the literature. Furthermore, CFFD-preorder is a *precongruence*, meaning that if $P \leq_{CFFD} P'$ and $Q \leq_{CFFD} Q'$, then $P \parallel Q \leq_{CFFD} P' \parallel Q'$, and similarly with the action transformer and many other operators. The reason for the presence of the initial stability predicate in the definition of the CFFD semantics is to ensure the (pre)congruence property with respect to the CCS and Lotos operators known as "choice". If only action transformation and parallel composition are used, then the initial stability predicate can be omitted without violating the (pre)congruence property.

The precongruence and linear temporal logic preservation properties imply that if the system has been verified with the clients Client$_i$ shown in Figure 6, then it works correctly also with any clients Client$'_i$ such that Client$'_i \leq_{CFFD}$ Client$_i$. Consider any client whose visible actions are req_i, gra_i, rel_i and bye_i, and that has the following properties:

1. It never livelocks. However, before the first visible action, between any two visible actions, and after the last visible action it may do any finite number of invisible actions.
2. After executing bye_i it halts, and this is the only situation where it can stop trying to execute visible actions. It need not ever try to execute bye_i.
3. After executing req_i it tries to execute gra_i and then rel_i. These are the only situations where it may try to execute gra_i and rel_i. When trying to execute gra_i, it does not try alternative visible actions, and similarly when trying to execute rel_i. It need not ever try to execute req_i.

These requirements are quite reasonable. For instance, they state that bye_i is used to indicate termination and only for that; req_i, gra_i and rel_i are executed in the correct order; and the client commits to gra_i and rel_i in the sense discussed in Section 2.5. It can be shown that if Client'_i has these properties, then $\mathsf{Client}'_i \leq_{\mathsf{CFFD}} \mathsf{Client}_i$. Therefore, if the system is proven correct with Client_i, then it is correct with any clients that satisfy the properties in the above list. The clients in Figure 6 are thus very adequate.

In addition to extending the validity of affirmative verification results to clients that are CFFD-smaller than the original clients, the precongruence property of the CFFD semantics is very helpful in constructing reduced LTSs, as will become obvious in Sections 3.5 to 3.7. What is more, it was shown in [16] that if "$\simeq$" is a congruence that preserves (1) stuttering-insensitive linear temporal logic formulae in the above-mentioned sense and (2) deadlocks, then $P \simeq Q$ implies $P \simeq_{\mathsf{CFFD}} Q$.[3] This implies that CFFD-equivalence can produce smaller reduced LTSs than any other congruence that can be used for the verification of the properties (1) and (2). CFFD-equivalence is thus optimal in a certain precise sense.

The reasons why the details of the definition of the CFFD semantics are as they are were analysed in more detail in [36].

3.4   The Meaning of "CFFD"

The name "CFFD" is an abbreviation of "Chaos-Free Failures Divergences". The semantics was given this name, because it resembles the "Failures Divergences" semantics of the CSP theory, but lacks the phenomenon of the latter that divergence implies "Chaos". Namely, the CSP failures divergences semantics of an LTS P whose alphabet is Σ_P can be defined as follows (essentially from [28, Sect. 7.4.1] or [24]):

---

[3] It is indeed the case that the presence or absence of deadlocks cannot be specified with linear temporal logic in this setting. The reason is that the logic cannot tell a deadlock apart from a livelock. Deadlock-freedom is sometimes specified as $\Box(\mathsf{en}_1 \lor \cdots \lor \mathsf{en}_n)$ where the en_i are the enabling conditions of the atomic statements of the system, but this specification assumes extensive knowledge of the inner structure of the system, and thus cannot be used simultaneously with abstraction. Abstraction does not prevent us from specifying and verifying $\Box(\mathsf{en}_1 \lor \cdots \lor \mathsf{en}_n)$, but it prevents us from knowing that it is equivalent to deadlock-freedom.

- $CSPdivtr(P) =$
  $\{\, a_1 a_2 \cdots a_n \in \Sigma_P^* \mid \exists i \in \{0, 1, \ldots, n\} : a_1 a_2 \cdots a_i \in Divtr(P)\,\}$
- $CSPfail(P) = Sfail(P) \cup (CSPdivtr(P) \times 2^{\Sigma_P})$
- The *CSP failures divergences semantics* of P is
  $(\Sigma_P, CSPfail(P), CSPdivtr(P))$.
- $P \simeq_{\mathsf{FD}} Q$ if and only if
  $\Sigma_P = \Sigma_Q$, $CSPfail(P) = CSPfail(Q)$ and $CSPdivtr(P) = CSPdivtr(Q)$.
- $P \leq_{\mathsf{FD}} Q$ if and only if
  $\Sigma_P = \Sigma_Q$, $CSPfail(P) \subseteq CSPfail(Q)$ and $CSPdivtr(P) \subseteq CSPdivtr(Q)$.[4]

The definition implies that if σ is a divergence trace of P, then all continuations of σ are CSP-divergence traces of P, and all pairs (ρ, A) where ρ is a continuation of σ and A is just any subset of Σ_P are CSP-failures of P, independently of what P can do after σ. In particular, if ε is a divergence trace of a system, then the system has every $\sigma \in \Sigma_P^*$ as its CSP-divergence trace and every $(\sigma, A) \in \Sigma_P^* \times 2^{\Sigma_P}$ as its CSP-failure. Such a system is known as *Chaos*. According to the CSP failures divergences semantics, any system that has executed a divergence trace becomes equivalent to Chaos. Therefore, the semantics preserves no information about the behaviour of a system that has executed a divergence trace. For instance, the CSP failures divergences semantics treats both LTSs in Figure 8 as equivalent to Chaos, and thus gives no other information about their behaviour than the possibility of livelocking initially.

The reason for this rather brutal treatment of divergence is that it gives the semantics some very nice mathematical properties. Perhaps the most important of them is that any process equation has a unique maximum solution in the semantics. As a consequence, equations such as $P = a; P \ [] \ b; \mathbf{stop}$ — or as in Figure 2, or even $P = P$ — can be immediately used to define processes. The CFFD semantics lacks this property.

Fortunately, most process equations have a unique solution with respect to strong bisimilarity. This makes it possible to define the CFFD semantics of a recursively defined process by converting the definition to an LTS with the aid of strong bisimilarity, and then extracting the semantics according to Definition 12. How to proceed from a recursive process definition to an LTS modulo strong bisimilarity is well known, and explained in [23], for instance.

3.5 Compositional LTS Construction

Theorems 3 and 4 together with the congruence property of CFFD-equivalence make it possible to construct a reduced LTS for the system in the *compositional* way, without ever constructing the big complete LTS of the system. Consider

---

[4] In the CSP literature this relation is usually written as $P \sqsupseteq Q$ or $P \sqsupseteq_{\mathsf{FD}} Q$. However, the present author likes to write the preorder symbol in the same direction as the subset symbols are in the definition, so that a smaller system has less behaviour than a bigger system.

hide $\Sigma_n^{\mathsf{Sys}} - \{req_1, gra_1, rel_1, bye_1\}$ **in** System_n as an example. It is isomorphic to

$$\begin{aligned}
&\textbf{hide } tkn_1, \ldots, tkn_n, dem_1, \ldots, dem_n \textbf{ in} \\
&\qquad (\mathsf{Server\_tkn}_1 \parallel \mathsf{Client}_1) \\
&\quad\parallel\quad \textbf{hide } req_2, gra_2, rel_2, bye_2 \textbf{ in } (\mathsf{Server}_2 \parallel \mathsf{Client}_2) \\
&\quad\parallel\quad \textbf{hide } req_3, gra_3, rel_3, bye_3 \textbf{ in } (\mathsf{Server}_3 \parallel \mathsf{Client}_3) \\
&\qquad\qquad\qquad\vdots \\
&\quad\parallel\quad \textbf{hide } req_n, gra_n, rel_n, bye_n \textbf{ in } (\mathsf{Server}_n \parallel \mathsf{Client}_n)
\end{aligned}$$

When $2 \leq i \leq n$, let

- $\mathsf{S}_1 =$ **hide** req, gra, rel, bye **in** $(\mathsf{Server} \parallel \mathsf{Client})$,
- $\mathsf{S}_i =$ **hide** tm, dm **in** $(\mathsf{S}_{i-1}[tm/tr, dm/dr] \parallel \mathsf{S}_1[tm/tl, dm/dl])$,
- $\mathsf{Station}_i = \mathsf{S}_1[tkn_i/tl, tkn_{i\oplus1}/tr, dem_i/dl, dem_{i\oplus1}/dr]$, and
- $\mathsf{Station}_{2\ldots i} =$
  hide $tkn_3, \ldots, tkn_i, dem_3, \ldots, dem_i$ **in** $(\mathsf{Station}_2 \parallel \cdots \parallel \mathsf{Station}_i)$.

Then **hide** $req_i, gra_i, rel_i, bye_i$ **in** $(\mathsf{Server}_i \parallel \mathsf{Client}_i) = \mathsf{Station}_i$, and the whole system is isomorphic to

$$\textbf{hide } tkn_1, tkn_2, dem_1, dem_2 \textbf{ in } (\mathsf{Server\_tkn}_1 \parallel \mathsf{Client}_1 \parallel \mathsf{Station}_{2\ldots n})$$

Induction yields that

$$\mathsf{Station}_{2\ldots i} =_{\mathsf{iso}} \mathsf{S}_{i-1}[tkn_2/tl, tkn_{i\oplus1}/tr, dem_2/dl, dem_{i\oplus1}/dr]$$

So the whole system is isomorphic to

$$\begin{aligned}
&\textbf{hide } tkn_1, tkn_2, dem_1, dem_2 \textbf{ in} \\
&\quad (\mathsf{Server\_tkn}_1 \parallel \mathsf{Client}_1 \parallel \mathsf{S}_{n-1}[tkn_2/tl, tkn_1/tr, dem_2/dl, dem_1/dr])
\end{aligned} \qquad (1)$$

Although this reasoning may seem complicated, it was just restructuring of the system, comparable to reorganisation of the terms of a finite series in mathematics. The correctness of the final isomorphism is intuitively obvious. The reasoning above was presented to make it possible to check that the correctness indeed formally follows from the definitions.

Let **red** be an algorithm that, given an LTS, produces a CFFD-equivalent and (hopefully) smaller LTS. That is, **red** is a *CFFD-preserving reduction algorithm*. Let $\mathsf{S}'_1 = \mathsf{red}(\mathsf{S}_1)$ and $\mathsf{S}'_i = \mathsf{red}(\mathsf{S}''_i)$ when $2 \leq i < n$, where S''_i is obtained from S'_{i-1} and S'_1 in the same way as S_i is obtained from S_{i-1} and S_1. Because CFFD-equivalence is a congruence, $\mathsf{S}'_i \simeq_{\mathsf{CFFD}} \mathsf{S}_i$. Table 2 shows the sizes of S''_i and S'_i for various values of i, when **red** is the reduction algorithm in ARA. (That algorithm has been described in [40].)

Because CFFD-equivalence is a congruence, the use of S'_{n-1} instead of S_{n-1} in (1) yields an LTS that is CFFD-equivalent to **hide** $\Sigma_n^{\mathsf{Sys}} - \{req_1, gra_1, rel_1, bye_1\}$ **in** System_n. This last computation step cannot multiply the number of states by more than 38, because the number of states in $\mathsf{Server\_tkn}_1 \parallel \mathsf{Client}_1$ is 38. A comparison to Table 1 shows that compositional LTS construction gives huge savings with this system, and makes it possible to verify the system with much bigger values of n than the naïve approach. Because the resulting LTS is valid for only one client, the procedure has to be repeated for each value of i in the case of $\Box(r_i \Rightarrow \Diamond g_i)$, and for each i-j-pair for $\Box\neg(g_i \wedge g_j)$. Even then the total amount of work grows very much slower than the figures in Table 1, and the S'_i need be computed only once.

Table 2. Sizes of reduced chains of client-server pairs.

i	S_i'' states	transitions	S_i' states	transitions
1	38	106	7	14
2	39	97	20	43
3	85	230	31	70
4	126	353	42	97
5	167	476	53	124
6	208	599	64	151
7	249	722	75	178

3.6 Interface Specifications

Although compositional LTS construction works spectacularly well in the demand-driven token-ring system, it does not always succeed. It sometimes happens that a subsystem that has been isolated from its environment has many more states than the full system. Consider a fifo queue of capacity n and two different messages. It has $2^{n+1} - 1$ states. If the fifo is within the well-known alternating bit protocol [1] and the two different messages correspond to the two values of the alternating bit, then the fifo may have at most one location in which the message is different from the message in the next location. This restricts the number of the possible contents of the fifo to $n^2 + n + 1$.

To solve this problem, *interface specifications* were presented in [9]. An interface specification is a means with which the user of a verification tool can present a guess about the behaviour of the system to the tool. The tool takes advantage of the guess to reduce the number of states, sometimes dramatically. If the guess is correct, the resulting LTS is what would have been obtained without the interface specification. Otherwise, the fact that the guess is incorrect can be seen from the LTS, in which case the LTS cannot be used for verification.

To present the interface specification method, [9] relied on the theory of partially defined processes and the so-called observation equivalence semantics [23]. Because CFFD-equivalence is rather different from observation equivalence, the theory used in [9] does not apply as such in the present framework. A theory of partially defined processes for the CFFD semantics was presented in [18, Section 5.3]. That theory could have been used as a basis for the development of the interface specification method for the CFFD semantics. We shall, however, adopt a different strategy. We modify the method a bit, and develop it in a way that is rather independent of the chosen semantics. This is advantageous, because extending a semantics to partially defined processes is often nontrivial. To our knowledge, our semantics-independent approach is new.

The use of interface specifications relies on extending LTSs with a fifth component, namely *cut states*. They are a subset of the states. Cut states have no output transitions, and are treated in a special way when computing parallel compositions. A state of the parallel composition is marked as a cut state if and only if any component process is in a cut state. No successors for cut states are

constructed, even if component processes that are not in a cut state are ready
to execute actions that the component processes that are in a cut state are not
interested in. An LTS with cut states can thus be thought of as an incomplete
LTS, where cut states mark points at which the LTS has been pruned.

If P is an LTS and Φ is an action transformer for it, then the cut states of
P are also cut states of $P\Phi$, and $P\Phi$ has no other cut states.

Definition 13. *An LTS with cut states is a five-tuple* $(S, \Sigma, \Delta, \hat{s}, Cut)$, *where*
$(S, \Sigma, \Delta, \hat{s})$ *is an LTS,* $Cut \subseteq S$, *and* $\forall s \in Cut : \forall a \in \Sigma \cup \{\tau\} : \neg(s -a\rightarrow)$. *Cut*
is a set of cut states.

Let $P = (S, \Sigma, \Delta, \hat{s}, Cut)$ and $P_i = (S_i, \Sigma_i, \Delta_i, \hat{s}_i, Cut_i)$ be LTSs with cut
states when $1 \leq i \leq n$, and let Φ be an action transformer for P.

- $\mathsf{repa}(S, \Sigma, \Delta, \hat{s}, Cut) = (S', \Sigma, \Delta', \hat{s}, Cut')$, where
  - $S' = \{ s \in S \mid \exists s_0, \dots, s_k : s_0 = \hat{s} \wedge s_k = s \wedge$
    $\qquad \forall i \in \{0, \dots, k-1\} : s_i \notin Cut \wedge \exists a_i : s_i -a_i\rightarrow s_{i+1} \}$,
  - $\Delta' = \{ (s, a, s') \mid s \in S' - Cut \wedge (s, a, s') \in \Delta \}$, and
  - $Cut' = Cut \cap S'$.
- $P_1 \| \cdots \| P_n = \mathsf{repa}(S', \Sigma', \Delta', \hat{s}', Cut')$, where
  - $(S', \Sigma', \Delta', \hat{s}') = (S_1, \Sigma_1, \Delta_1, \hat{s}_1) \times \cdots \times (S_n, \Sigma_n, \Delta_n, \hat{s}_n)$, and
  - $Cut' = \{ \langle s_1, \dots, s_n \rangle \in S' \mid s_1 \in Cut_1 \vee \cdots \vee s_n \in Cut_n \}$.
- $P\Phi = (S, \Sigma', \Delta', \hat{s}, Cut)$, where $(S, \Sigma', \Delta', \hat{s}) = (S, \Sigma, \Delta, \hat{s})\Phi$.

Ordinary LTSs can be thought of as LTSs with cut states by choosing $Cut = \emptyset$.
Strong bisimilarity of LTSs with cut states is defined like strong bisimilarity
of ordinary LTSs, with the additional requirement that if $s_P \sim s_Q$, then $s_P \in$
$Cut_P \Leftrightarrow s_Q \in Cut_Q$.

An interface specification $I = (S_I, \Sigma_I, \Delta_I, \hat{s}_I, Cut_I)$ is a particular kind of an
LTS with cut states. It is used to reduce the size of some parallel composition
$P_1 \| \cdots \| P_n$ that is a subsystem of a bigger system $f(P_1 \| \cdots \| P_n)$. It represents
the guess that if σ is what $P_1 \| \cdots \| P_n$ sees of an execution of the system as a
whole, and if ρ is obtained from σ by removing those actions that are not in Σ_I,
then ρ does not lead I to a cut state. In other words, the states and transitions
of I are chosen such that if the guess that the user has about the behaviour
of the system is correct, then no cut state of I is reached in the full system
$f(P_1 \| \cdots \| P_n \| I)$, although it may be reached in $P_1 \| \cdots \| P_n \| I$. (If it is not
reached in $P_1 \| \cdots \| P_n \| I$, then the interface specification fails to reduce the
number of states and gives thus no benefit, but the results remain correct.)

For example, a natural guess about the behaviour of the demand-driven
token-ring system is that there is at most one token in any part of the ring
at any time. Figure 9 shows an interface specification that represents this guess
for any S_i. The black state is a cut state. It is reached if a token enters (tl) the
ring segment before the previous token leaves (tr) it.

An interface specification $I = (S_I, \Sigma_I, \Delta_I, \hat{s}_I, Cut_I)$ for the parallel compo-
sition $P_1 \| \cdots \| P_n$ must have the following properties:

- $\Sigma_I \subseteq \Sigma_1 \cup \cdots \cup \Sigma_n$, where each Σ_i is the alphabet of P_i.
- I has no τ-transitions. (Some τ-transitions might be allowed, but stating the
  condition like this is simpler and does not restrict generality.)

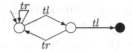

Fig. 9. An interface specification that represents the guess that a ring segment contains at most one token. The alphabet is $\{tl, tr\}$.

- $\forall s \in S_I - Cut_I : \forall a \in \Sigma_I : s -a\rightarrow_I$. That is, if a state is not a cut state, then it has an output transition for every visible action.
- $\hat{s}_I \notin Cut_I$. That is, the initial state is not a cut state. This is a meaningful requirement, because an interface specification whose initial state is a cut state would represent the certainly incorrect guess that the system cannot reach even its initial state.

These conditions imply that if each s_i, s_i', s_I and s_I' is a state of the corresponding LTS P_i or I, then

- if $\langle s_1, \ldots, s_n, s_I \rangle -a\rightarrow \langle s_1', \ldots, s_n', s_I' \rangle$, then $\langle s_1, \ldots, s_n \rangle -a\rightarrow \langle s_1', \ldots, s_n' \rangle$, and
- if $\langle s_1, \ldots, s_n \rangle -a\rightarrow \langle s_1', \ldots, s_n' \rangle$ and $s_I \in S_I - Cut_I$, then there is s_I' such that $\langle s_1, \ldots, s_n, s_I \rangle -a\rightarrow \langle s_1', \ldots, s_n', s_I' \rangle$.

Let I' be I with the cut states and their adjacent transitions removed. The result is an LTS because $\hat{s}_I \notin Cut_I$. Our modified interface specification method is as follows:

- Compute a reduced version of $Sys_I = f(P_1 || \cdots || P_n || I)$ using any semantics that preserves the presence of cut states. If the cut states are marked by, for instance, introducing a new action cut and adding a cut-transition from each cut state to a deadlock state, then the CFFD semantics can be used. Also many other semantic models can be used here, including the *trace semantics* which is defined by $P \simeq_{tr} Q$ if and only if $\Sigma_P = \Sigma_Q$ and $Tr(P) = Tr(Q)$, where Σ_P and Σ_Q are the alphabets of P and Q. The trace semantics is beneficial, because it gives very good LTS reduction results. Furthermore, it is correct to cut the LTSs at cut states during the computation of parallel compositions as was shown in Definition 13 (assuming that the cut-transitions are not removed), because the behaviour after a cut state does not affect the reachability of cut states.
- If Sys_I contains any cut states, then the guess that yielded I was incorrect. Then Sys_I is useless and one should try another I.
- If Sys_I contains no cut states, then the guess was correct. In this case, $f(P_1 || \cdots || P_n) =_{sb} f(P_1 || \cdots || P_n || I')$. Therefore, the original system can be analysed by computing a reduced version of $f(P_1 || \cdots || P_n || I')$ and analysing it. This is correct for any semantics x such that $P =_{sb} Q \Rightarrow P \simeq_x Q$. Almost every semantics presented in the literature has this property. Because I' contains no cut states, $f(P_1 || \cdots || P_n || I')$ can be computed using ordinary methods — no theory or algorithms for partially defined processes are needed.

To justify the correctness of the method we introduce two precongruence relations that are related to strong bisimilarity.

Definition 14. *Let* $P = (S_P, \Sigma_P, \Delta_P, \hat{s}_P, Cut_P)$ *and* $Q = (S_Q, \Sigma_Q, \Delta_Q, \hat{s}_Q, Cut_Q)$ *be LTSs with cut states.*

- $P \leq_{CB1} Q$ *if and only if* $\Sigma_P = \Sigma_Q$ *and there is "$\sim$"* $\subseteq S_P \times S_Q$ *such that* $\hat{s}_P \sim \hat{s}_Q$, *and for every* $s_P, s'_P \in S_P$ *and* $s_Q, s'_Q \in S_Q$ *such that* $s_P \sim s_Q$:
  - *If* $s_P \in Cut_P$, *then* $s_Q \in Cut_Q$.
  - *If* $s_P -a\rightarrow_P s'_P$, *then* $s_Q \in Cut_Q$ *or* S_Q *contains an* s *such that* $s_Q -a\rightarrow_Q s$ *and* $s'_P \sim s$.
  - *If* $s_Q -a\rightarrow_Q s'_Q$, *then* S_P *contains an* s *such that* $s_P -a\rightarrow_P s$ *and* $s \sim s'_Q$.
- $P \leq_{CB2} Q$ *if and only if* $\Sigma_P = \Sigma_Q$ *and there is "$\sim$"* $\subseteq S_P \times S_Q$ *such that* $\hat{s}_P \sim \hat{s}_Q$, *and for every* $s_P, s'_P \in S_P$ *and* $s_Q, s'_Q \in S_Q$ *such that* $s_P \sim s_Q$:
  - $s_P \in Cut_P \Leftrightarrow s_Q \in Cut_Q$.
  - *If* $s_P -a\rightarrow_P s'_P$, *then* S_Q *contains an* s *such that* $s_Q -a\rightarrow_Q s$ *and* $s'_P \sim s$.
  - *If* $s_Q -a\rightarrow_Q s'_Q$, *then* $s'_Q \in Cut_Q$ *(yes,* s'_Q*!) or* S_P *contains an* s *such that* $s_P -a\rightarrow_P s$ *and* $s \sim s'_Q$.

It follows from the definition that "$\leq_{CB1}$" and "$\leq_{CB2}$" are precongruences. Furthermore, if $P \leq_{CB1} Q$ and $Cut_Q = \emptyset$, then $P =_{sb} Q$; and if $P \leq_{CB2} Q$ and $Cut_Q = \emptyset$, then $P =_{sb} Q$. Also, $P \leq_{CB1} P \parallel I$ and $I' \leq_{CB2} I$. ¿From these it follows that $f(P) \leq_{CB1} f(P \parallel I)$ and $f(P \parallel I') \leq_{CB2} f(P \parallel I)$. Therefore, either $f(P \parallel I)$ has cut states, or $f(P) =_{sb} f(P \parallel I) =_{sb} f(P \parallel I')$.

Table 3 shows the sizes of the reduced versions of S_i obtained with repeated use of the interface specification I^9 in Figure 9. That is, it shows the sizes of S_i^I, where $S_1^I = S'_1$, and

$$S_i^I = \text{red}\big(\text{ hide } tm, dm \text{ in } (S_{i-1}^I[tm/tr, dm/dr] \parallel S'_1[tm/tl, dm/dl] \parallel I^9)\big)$$

when $i > 1$. The sizes include the above-mentioned *cut*-transitions and their end states. No other transitions have been constructed from the start states of the *cut*-transitions.

Table 3. Sizes of chains of client-server-pairs with interface specifications.

i	states	transitions
1	7	14
2	16	34
3	16	34
4	16	34

In the previous section we obtained the result that **hide** $\Sigma_n^{Sys} - \{req_1, gra_1, rel_1, bye_1\}$ **in** System_n is isomorphic to

hide $tkn_1, tkn_2, dem_1, dem_2$ **in**
    $(\text{Server\_tkn}_1 \parallel \text{Client}_1 \parallel S_{n-1}[tkn_2/tl, tkn_1/tr, dem_2/dl, dem_1/dr])$

In Section 3.2 we saw that its reduced behaviour when $n = 3$ is as in Figure 8(b). If S_{n-1}^I is used instead of S_{n-1} when $2 \leq n \leq 5$, then the resulting LTSs have no cut states. They are thus CFFD-equivalent to **hide** $\Sigma_n^{Sys} - \{req_1, gra_1, rel_1, bye_1\}$ in System$_n$, but they are obtained with less effort than with the ordinary compositional method, as comparison to Table 2 reveals. The savings are not significant. However, Table 3 drops a hint that interface specifications make a much better result possible. This result will be discussed in the next section.

3.7   Induction

An interesting aspect of the figures in Table 3 is that the LTS stops growing when $n = 2$. This makes it natural to ask: is S_3^I different from S_2^I?

This question can be answered with the ARA LTS comparison tool. The result is that $S_3^I \simeq_{\mathsf{CFFD}} S_2^I$.

This result has the consequence that $S_i^I \simeq_{\mathsf{CFFD}} S_2^I$ for any $i \geq 2$. Namely, if $S_i^I \simeq_{\mathsf{CFFD}} S_{i-1}^I$, then due to the facts that $\mathsf{red}(P) \simeq_{\mathsf{CFFD}} P$ and CFFD-equivalence is a congruence with respect to action transformation and parallel composition,

$$
\begin{aligned}
S_{i+1}^I &= \quad \mathsf{red}\big(\ \textbf{hide}\ tm, dm\ \textbf{in}\ (S_i^I[tm/tr, dm/dr] \parallel S_1[tm/tl, dm/dl] \parallel I^9)\ \big) \\
&\simeq_{\mathsf{CFFD}} \mathsf{red}\big(\ \textbf{hide}\ tm, dm\ \textbf{in}\ (S_{i-1}^I[tm/tr, dm/dr] \parallel S_1[tm/tl, dm/dl] \parallel I^9)\ \big) \\
&= \quad S_i^I
\end{aligned}
$$

from which the claim follows by induction. Furthermore, because of the congruence property of CFFD-equivalence,

$$
\begin{aligned}
&\quad\ \ \textbf{hide}\ \Sigma_n^{Sys} - \{req_1, gra_1, rel_1, bye_1\}\ \textbf{in}\ \mathsf{System}_n \\
&=_{\mathsf{Iso}}\ \textbf{hide}\ tkn_1, tkn_2, dem_1, dem_2\ \textbf{in} \\
&\qquad (\mathsf{Server\_tkn}_1 \parallel \mathsf{Client}_1 \parallel \mathsf{S}_{n-1}[tkn_2/tl, tkn_1/tr, dem_2/dl, dem_1/dr]) \\
&\simeq_{\mathsf{CFFD}}\ \textbf{hide}\ tkn_1, tkn_2, dem_1, dem_2\ \textbf{in} \\
&\qquad (\mathsf{Server\_tkn}_1 \parallel \mathsf{Client}_1 \parallel \mathsf{S}_{n-1}^I[tkn_2/tl, tkn_1/tr, dem_2/dl, dem_1/dr]) \\
&\simeq_{\mathsf{CFFD}}\ \textbf{hide}\ tkn_1, tkn_2, dem_1, dem_2\ \textbf{in} \\
&\qquad (\mathsf{Server\_tkn}_1 \parallel \mathsf{Client}_1 \parallel \mathsf{S}_2^I[tkn_2/tl, tkn_1/tr, dem_2/dl, dem_1/dr]) \\
&\simeq_{\mathsf{CFFD}}\ \text{the LTS in Figure 8(b)}
\end{aligned}
$$

whenever $n \geq 3$. This reasoning relies on the assumption that the final LTSs obtained with the interface specifications do not contain cut states. This is true because they did not when $n = 3$, and bigger systems are constructed in the same way except that S_2^I is replaced by the CFFD-equivalent LTS S_{n-1}^I.

Figure 8(b) is thus valid for any $n \geq 3$. A separate analysis shows that it is valid also when $n = 2$. Whatever useful information Figure 8(b) provides is thus valid for any $n \geq 2$. In particular, that the eventual access property holds for Client$_1$ has now been shown for all ring sizes of at least two.

A lot of work remains still to be done. The eventual access property must be proven for Client$_i$ when $2 \leq i \leq n$, and the mutual exclusion property must be proven for every $1 \leq i < j \leq n$. Because $S_i^I \simeq_{\mathsf{CFFD}} S_2^I$ whenever $i \geq 2$, more than two clients between Client$_1$ and Client$_i$ is equivalent to precisely two clients in the same interval. Thus the nine cases where i ranges from 2 to 4 and n ranges from i to $i + 2$ cover all the missing eventual access proofs, assuming, of course, that the final LTSs never contain cut states. But we can reason that this will hold: If the final LTS P contains cut states, then also **hide** Σ_n^{Sys} **in** P contains cut states. However, **hide** Σ_n^{Sys} **in** P is equivalent to **hide** $req_1, gra_1, rel_1, bye_1$ **in** (the LTS in Figure 8(b)), which does not contain cut states.

The mutual exclusion property can be fully verified by considering 36 cases: i ranges from 1 to 4, j ranges from $i + 1$ to $i + 3$, and n ranges from j to $j + 2$. In these cases, nothing, S_1, or S_2^I is used in the intervals between Client_1, Client_i, Client_j, and Client_1 again, depending on the width of the interval.

Thus 47 analyses suffice for verifying the correctness of the demand-driven token-ring system of any size $n \geq 2$. Although 47 is not too much for an automatic tool, there is still one trick left with which the number can be made smaller. Namely, now that it is known that cut states are never reached in a full system, the cut state and its incoming transition can be removed from the interface specification in Figure 9. Let S'^I_i be obtained like S_i^I, but with the modified interface specification. One can verify with ARA that $S'^I_1 \leq_{\mathsf{CFFD}} S'^I_2$. As was discussed in Section 3.3, together with the precongruence and logic-preservation properties of "$\leq_{\mathsf{CFFD}}$" this implies that although the final LTSs obtained with S'^I_1 are not necessarily the same nor even CFFD-equivalent to the LTSs obtained with S'^I_2, if any of the former violates the mutual exclusion or eventual access property, then also the corresponding latter LTS does.

As a consequence, the cases where $i = 3$, $j = i + 2$ or $n = j + 1$ for mutual exclusion and $i = 3$ or $n = i + 1$ for eventual access can be skipped. This leaves 17 cases.

In conclusion, 17 finite computer runs suffice for verifying the mutual exclusion property for every pair of clients and the eventual access property for every client of the demand-driven token-ring systems of all sizes ≥ 2.

As was mentioned in the introduction, induction-type of arguments have been utilised in automatic verification of concurrent systems at least in [44,20, 5]. Induction has been applied before this article also in the context of the CFFD semantics. The applications presented in [15,38] are particularly interesting.

In [15], the sliding window protocol [30] was verified independently of the capacities of the channels through which the protocol sender and receiver communicate. A data source or sending client was added to the system, the protocol sender was approximated from above using the variant of CFFD-preorder presented in [16], induction was used to show that the behaviour is independent of the number of channel positions, and so-called *data independency* [43] was appealed to in order to prove that the protocol is correct for arbitrary data. Data-independency means that the protocol does not look at the data it delivers, it only moves it around. It can be used to justify that if the protocol makes errors, then the errors can be found with certain fixed data sources that send only a small number of different messages, and send them in a specific order.

In [38], an integer counter that counts from some fixed value k towards 0 was represented as a chain of k processes. The counter was used as the retransmission counter of a modified version of the alternating bit protocol, where the transmission of any message is tried at most $k + 1$ times, while in the ordinary alternating bit protocol there is no upper limit. Induction was used to prove that the behaviour of the system is independent of the value of k. The same technique was used to show that if there is a finite upper limit to the number of messages that channels can lose in a row, then the ordinary alternating bit protocol behaves correctly independently of the value of the limit.

4   Discussion

We modelled the n-server demand-driven token-ring system as a parallel composition of labelled transition systems. Then we stated two requirements for the system: mutual exclusion and eventual access.

We used first the full system for verifying that the requirements hold, but this was possible only for small values of n because of the state explosion problem. Fortunately, we had divided mutual exclusion and eventual access to a number of "small" properties that refer to at most two component processes at a time. This made it possible to verify the small properties one by one by hiding most actions of the system, and then constructing a reduced LTS for the system with the compositional method. Already the basic compositional method reduced dramatically the number of states that had to be constructed, and made it possible to verify the system with much larger values of n. When it was used together with interface specifications and induction, it became possible to verify the system for *all* values of n ($n \geq 2$) by conducting 17 verification runs. The constructed reduced LTSs were either CFFD-equivalent to or CFFD-larger than the corresponding full LTSs.

The CFFD semantics is definitely not the only semantics that can be used or has been used in compositional LTS construction. Perhaps the three most commonly used semantics are *observation equivalence* [23] (also known as *weak bisimilarity*), the failures divergences model of the CSP theory [28,4,11], and the trace semantics.

The trace semantics was already mentioned in Section 3.6. It consists of the alphabet and the set of the traces of the LTS. It is thus essentially the same thing as a "language" in the classical theory of automata and formal languages. Because it throws almost all information on deadlocks and livelocks away, it cannot be used in the verification of the eventual access property. However, it can be used for mutual exclusion and other stuttering-insensitive safety properties. As a matter of fact, it is optimal for them in the sense that it gives at least as good reduction results as any other congruence that can be used for all stuttering-insensitive safety properties. The CFFD semantics was seen optimal in the same sense for a much larger set of properties towards the end of Section 3.3. Different sets of properties have different optimal equivalences, because the larger the set is, the more information the equivalence must preserve in order to not change the truth value of any property in the set.

The CFFD semantics was compared to the failures divergences semantics of CSP in Section 3.4. It was pointed out that they resemble each other a lot, but the CSP semantics could not have been used in this case study because of the way it treats divergence. A more detailed discussion on the relationship between the

CFFD semantics, the CSP semantics and some other semantics that are based on stable failures or related notions can be found in [36]. Some of these semantics are optimal for the verification of linear temporal logic [16], deadlocks [32] or livelocks [26] in the above-mentioned sense.

Like the definition of strong bisimilarity, the definition of observation equivalence states the existence of a certain kind of a simulation relation between the sets of the states of the LTSs that are compared. In the relation, instead of individual transitions $(s_1, a, s_2) \in \Delta$, abstracted transitions $s_1 = a \Rightarrow s_2$ for $a \in \Sigma \cup \{\varepsilon\}$ are simulated by $s'_1 = a \Rightarrow s'_2$, and similarly in the opposite direction. Because $s = \varepsilon \Rightarrow s$ is always true, observation equivalence allows the simulation of a local τ-loop $s - \tau \rightarrow s$ by nothing. Therefore, it does not preserve divergence information, and cannot be used for the verification of the eventual access property.

Observation equivalence can, however, be used for the verification of the property "in every reachable state, if a request from a client is pending, then there is at least one possible future in which the client is eventually served". This is a strictly weaker property than eventual access (which, in essence, promises service in *every* possible future instead of at least one), but is definitely better than nothing, and may well be sufficient in practice. This property talks about alternative futures in the middle of an execution, and is thus a *branching time* property. It is possible to demonstrate with an example that the CFFD semantics does not preserve this property. The CFFD semantics preserves only *linear time* properties. We have already seen an example of the CFFD semantics failing to preserve a branching time property, when we discussed in Section 3.3 the absence of a τ-loop adjacent to state 5 in Figure 8(b).

Observation equivalence can be made divergence-preserving by adding the extra requirement that a diverging and non-diverging state cannot simulate each other, where s is diverging if and only if $s - \tau^\omega \rightarrow$. Excluding the initial stability predicate, which is often not needed and is easy to take into account separately when needed, this variant of observation equivalence implies CFFD-equivalence. It can, therefore, be used in the verification of whatever can be verified with CFFD-equivalence, including eventual access. However, because it is strictly stronger than CFFD-equivalence, it does not allow reduction algorithms to throw as much information away as CFFD-equivalence allows, and therefore it does not give as good reduction results as CFFD-equivalence gives.[5]

In addition to other process-algebraic semantic models, there are many approaches to verification that are not based on process algebras. In addition to compositional LTS construction, interface specifications and induction, there are numerous other methods for alleviating the state explosion problem. We already mentioned the use of symmetries in Section 3.1 (and pointed out why it does not work in this case study), and data-independency in Section 3.7.

---

[5] It has been claimed that observation equivalence and its variants are more efficient in verification because they have faster algorithms than equivalences in the same family as CFFD. This claim is based on a misconception, confusing reduction with minimisation, as was pointed out in [33].

Two other methods that suit particularly well the framework in this article are *stubborn sets* [34,35] and *on-the-fly verification* [42,14,12,6,27,8,10, and others], which can be used also simultaneously [31].

Stubborn sets are a group of methods for reducing the number of states during the computation of a parallel composition or a more complicated expression such that certain properties of the system are preserved. They can be fully hidden in a tool, so that no special effort is required from the user. A natural application area for the CFFD-preserving and other process-algebraic stubborn set methods is expressions of the form **hide** A **in** $(P_1 \parallel \cdots \parallel P_n)$. The more actions are hidden, the better reduction results are obtained.

On-the-fly verification means the addition to the system of an observer that raises an alarm immediately when the system does something wrong. It can reduce states by

- stopping the construction of an LTS immediately when an error is found (this is more helpful than it might sound, because it prunes most of the usually very numerous extra states that an erroneous system has because of the error),
- preventing the system from entering parts of its LTS that are irrelevant for the property (one way to implement this is to remove from the observers of [10] the states and transitions from which no alarm states can be reached), and
- directing other methods, such as stubborn sets, to first investigate those parts of an LTS where an error is most likely found [31,29].

Perhaps surprisingly, with some support from the parallel composition tool, on-the-fly verification can be used for both safety and liveness properties.

The basic ideas of the above-mentioned and many other verification algorithms and methods are presented in the survey [35].

Acknowledgements. Mikko Tiusanen has given valuable comments on a draft of this article.

References

1. Bartlett, K. A., Scantlebury, R. A. & Wilkinson, P. T.: "A Note on Reliable Full-Duplex Transmission over Half-Duplex Links". *Communications of the ACM* 12(5) 1969, pp. 260–261.
2. Bolognesi, T. & Brinksma, E.: "Introduction to the ISO Specification Language LOTOS". *Computer Networks and ISDN Systems* 14 (1987), pp. 25–59.
3. Brookes, S. D., Hoare, C. A. R. & Roscoe, A. W.: "A Theory of Communicating Sequential Processes". *Journal of the ACM*, 31 (3) 1984, pp. 560–599.
4. Brookes, S. D. & Roscoe, A. W.: "An Improved Failures Model for Communicating Sequential Processes". *Proc. NSF-SERC Seminar on Concurrency*, Lecture Notes in Computer Science 197, Springer-Verlag 1985, pp. 281–305.
5. Clarke, E. M., Grumberg, O. & Jha, S.: "Verifying Parameterized Networks using Abstraction and Regular Languages". *Proc. CONCUR '95, 6th International Conference on Concurrency Theory*, Lecture Notes in Computer Science 962, Springer-Verlag 1995, pp. 395–407.

6. Courcoubetis, C., Vardi, M., Wolper, P. & Yannakakis, M.: "Memory-Efficient Algorithms for the Verification of Temporal Properties". *Formal Methods in System Design* 1 (1992), pp. 275–288.
7. Fernandez, J.-C.: "An Implementation of an Efficient Algorithm for Bisimulation Equivalence". *Science of Computer Programming* 13 (1989/90) pp. 219–236.
8. Gerth, R., Peled, D., Vardi, M. & Wolper, P.: "Simple On-the-fly Automatic Verification of Linear Temporal Logic". *Proc. Protocol Specification, Testing and Verification 1995*, Chapman & Hall 1995, pp. 3–18.
9. Graf, S. & Steffen, B.: "Compositional Minimization of Finite State Processes". *Proc. Computer-Aided Verification '90*, AMS-ACM DIMACS Series in Discrete Mathematics and Theoretical Computer Science, Vol. 3, 1991, pp. 57–73.
10. Helovuo, J. & Valmari, A.: "Checking for CFFD-Preorder with Tester Processes". *Proc. TACAS 2000, Tools and Algorithms for the Construction and Analysis of Systems, 6th International Conference*, Lecture Notes in Computer Science 1785, Springer-Verlag 2000, pp. 283–298.
11. Hoare, C. A. R.: *Communicating Sequential Processes*. Prentice-Hall 1985, 256 p.
12. Holzmann, G. J.: *Design and Validation of Computer Protocols*. Prentice-Hall 1991, 500 p.
13. *ISO 8807 International Standard: Information processing systems — Open Systems Interconnection — LOTOS — A formal description technique based on the temporal ordering of observational behaviour.* International Organization for Standardization 1989, 142 p.
14. Jard, C. & Jeron, T.: "On-Line Model Checking for Finite Linear Temporal Logic Specifications". *Proc. International Workshop on Automatic Verification Methods for Finite State Systems*, Lecture Notes in Computer Science 407, Springer-Verlag 1990, pp. 189–196.
15. Kaivola, R.: "Using Compositional Preorders in the Verification of Sliding Window Protocol". *Proc. Computer Aided Verification 1997*, Lecture Notes in Computer Science 1254, Springer-Verlag 1997, pp. 48–59.
16. Kaivola, R. & Valmari, A.: "The Weakest Compositional Semantic Equivalence Preserving Nexttime-less Linear Temporal Logic". *Proc. CONCUR '92, Third International Conference on Concurrency Theory*, Lecture Notes in Computer Science 630, Springer-Verlag 1992, pp. 207–221.
17. Kanellakis, P. C. & Smolka, S. A.: "CCS Expressions, Finite State Processes, and Three Problems of Equivalence". *Information and Computation* 86 (1) 1990 pp. 43–68.
18. Karvi, T.: *Partially Defined Lotos Specifications and their Refinement Relations.* Ph.D. Thesis, Report A-2000-5, Department of Computer Science, University of Helsinki, Finland, Helsinki University Printing House 2000, 157 p.
19. Kokkarinen, I.: *Reduction of Parallel Labelled Transition Systems with Stubborn Sets.* M. Sc. (Eng.) Thesis (in Finnish), Tampere University of Technology, Finland, 1995, 49 p.
20. Kurshan, R. P., Merritt, M., Orda, A. & Sachs, S. R.: "A Structural Linearization Principle for Processes". *Formal Methods in System Design* 5, 1994, pp. 227–244.
21. Madelaine, E. & Vergamini, D.: "AUTO: A Verification Tool for Distributed Systems Using Reduction of Finite Automata Networks". *Proc. Formal Description Techniques II (FORTE '89)*, North-Holland 1990, pp. 61–66.
22. Manna, Z. & Pnueli, A.: *The Temporal Logic of Reactive and Concurrent Systems, Volume I: Specification.* Springer-Verlag 1992, 427 p.
23. Milner, R.: *Communication and Concurrency*. Prentice-Hall 1989, 260 p.

24. Olderog, E.-R. & Hoare, C. A. R.: "Specification-Oriented Semantics for Communicating Processes". *Acta Informatica* 23 (1986) 9–66.
25. Park, D.: "Concurrency and Automata on Infinite Sequences". *Theoretical Computer Science: 5th GI-Conference*, Lecture Notes in Computer Science 104, Springer-Verlag 1981, pp. 167–183.
26. Puhakka, A. & Valmari, A.: "Weakest-Congruence Results for Livelock-Preserving Equivalences". *Proc. CONCUR '99 (Concurrency Theory)*, Lecture Notes in Computer Science 1664, Springer-Verlag 1999, pp. 510–524.
27. Roscoe, A. W.: "Model-Checking CSP". *A Classical Mind: Essays in Honour of C. A. R. Hoare*, Prentice-Hall 1994, pp. 353–378.
28. Roscoe, A. W.: *The Theory and Practice of Concurrency*. Prentice-Hall 1998, 565 p.
29. Schmidt, K.: "Stubborn Sets for Standard Properties". *Proc. Application and Theory of Petri Nets 1999*, Lecture Notes in Computer Science 1639, Springer-Verlag 1999, pp. 46–65.
30. Stenning, N. V.: "A Data Transfer Protocol". *Computer Networks*, vol. 11, 1976, pp. 99–110.
31. Valmari, A.: "On-the-fly Verification with Stubborn Sets". *Proc. Computer-Aided Verification (CAV) '93*, Lecture Notes in Computer Science 697, Springer-Verlag 1993, pp. 397–408.
32. Valmari, A.: "The Weakest Deadlock-Preserving Congruence". *Information Processing Letters* 53 (1995) 341–346.
33. Valmari, A.: "Failure-based Equivalences Are Faster Than Many Believe". *Proc. Structures in Concurrency Theory 1995*, Springer-Verlag "Workshops in Computing" series, 1995, pp. 326–340.
34. Valmari, A.: "Stubborn Set Methods for Process Algebras". *Proc. POMIV'96, Workshop on Partial Order Methods in Verification*, DIMACS Series in Discrete Mathematics and Theoretical Computer Science Vol. 29, American Mathematical Society 1997, pp. 213–231.
35. Valmari, A.: "The State Explosion Problem". *Lectures on Petri Nets I: Basic Models*, Lecture Notes in Computer Science 1491, Springer-Verlag 1998, pp. 429–528.
36. Valmari, A.: "A Chaos-Free Failures Divergences Semantics with Applications to Verification". *Millennial Perspectives in Computer Science, Proceedings of the 1999 Oxford–Microsoft Symposium in Honour of sir Tony Hoare*, Palgrave 2000, pp. 365–382.
37. Valmari, A., Kemppainen, J., Clegg, M. & Levanto, M.: "Putting Advanced Reachability Analysis Techniques Together: the 'ARA' Tool". *Proc. Formal Methods Europe '93: Industrial-Strength Formal Methods*, Lecture Notes in Computer Science 670, Springer-Verlag 1993, pp. 597–616.
38. Valmari, A. & Kokkarinen, I.: "Unbounded Verification Results by Finite-State Compositional Techniques: 10^{any} States and Beyond". *Proc. 1998 International Conference on Application of Concurrency to System Design*, IEEE Computer Society 1998, pp. 75–85.
39. Valmari, A. & Setälä, M.: "Visual Verification of Safety and Liveness". *Proc. Formal Methods Europe '96: Industrial Benefit and Advances in Formal Methods*, Lecture Notes in Computer Science 1051, Springer-Verlag 1996, pp. 228–247.
40. Valmari, A. & Tienari, M.: "An Improved Failures Equivalence for Finite-State Systems with a Reduction Algorithm". *Proc. Protocol Specification, Testing and Verification XI*, North-Holland 1991, pp. 3–18.
41. Valmari, A. & Tienari, M.: "Compositional Failure-Based Semantic Models for Basic LOTOS". *Formal Aspects of Computing* (1995) 7: 440–468.

42. Vardi, M. Y. & Wolper, P.: "An Automata-Theoretic Approach to Automatic Program Verification". *Proc. 1st Annual IEEE Symposium on Logic in Computer Science*, IEEE Computer Society Press 1986, pp. 332–344.
43. Wolper, P.: "Expressing Interesting Properties of Programs in Propositional Temporal Logic". *Proc. 13th ACM Symposium on Principles of Programming Languages*, 1986, pp. 184–193.
44. Wolper, P. & Lovinfosse, V.: "Verifying Properties of Large Sets of Processes with Network Invariants". *Proc. Workshop on Automatic Verification Methods for Finite State Systems*, Lecture Notes in Computer Science 407, Springer-Verlag 1989, pp. 68–80.

UPPAAL - Now, Next, and Future

Tobias Amnell[1], Gerd Behrmann[2], Johan Bengtsson[1], Pedro R. D'Argenio[3],
Alexandre David[1], Ansgar Fehnker[4], Thomas Hune[5], Bertrand Jeannet[2],
Kim G. Larsen[2], M. Oliver Möller[5], Paul Pettersson[1], Carsten Weise[6], and
Wang Yi[1]

[1] Department of Information Technology, Uppsala University, Sweden,
[tobiasa,johanb,adavid,paupet,yi]@docs.uu.se.
[2] Basic Research in Computer Science, Aalborg University, Denmark,
[behrmann,bjeannet,kgl]@cs.auc.dk.
[3] Faculty of Computer Science, University of Twente, The Netherlands,
dargenio@cs.utwente.nl.
[4] Computing Science Institute, University of Nijmegen, The Netherlands,
ansgar@cs.kun.nl.
[5] Basic Research in Computer Science, Aarhus University, Denmark,
[baris,omoeller]@brics.dk.
[6] Ericsson Eurolab Deutschland GmbH, Germany,
Carsten.Weise@eed.ericsson.se.

Abstract. UPPAAL is a tool for modeling, simulation and verification
of real-time systems, developed jointly by BRICS at Aalborg University
and the Department of Computer Systems at Uppsala University. The
tool is appropriate for systems that can be modeled as a collection of
non-deterministic processes with finite control structure and real-valued
clocks, communicating through channels or shared variables. Typical application areas include real-time controllers and communication protocols, in particular those where timing aspects are critical.

This paper reports on the currently available version and summarizes developments during the last two years. We report on new directions that
extends UPPAAL with cost-optimal exploration, parametric modeling,
stop-watches, probablistic modeling, hierachical modeling, executable
timed automata, and a hybrid automata animator. We also report on
recent work to improve the efficiency of the tool. In particular, we outline Clock Difference Diagrams (CDDs), new compact representations
of states, a distributed version of the tool, and application of dynamic
partitioning.

UPPAAL has been applied in a number of academic and industrial case
studies. We describe a selection of the recent case studies.

1 Current Version of UPPAAL

In the following, we give a brief overview on UPPAAL's maturing over the years
and explain the core functionalities of the current release version.

F. Cassez et al. (Eds.): MOVEP 2000, LNCS 2067, pp. 99–124, 2001.
© Springer-Verlag Berlin Heidelberg 2001

1.1 Background

UPPAAL [LPY97] is a tool for modeling, simulation and verification of real-time systems, developed jointly by BRICS at Aalborg University and the Department of Computer Systems at Uppsala University. The tool is appropriate for systems that can be modeled as a collection of non-deterministic processes with finite control structure and real-valued clocks, communicating through channels or shared variables. Typical application areas include real-time controllers and communication protocols.

UPPAAL consists of three main parts: a description language, a simulator and a model checker. The description language is a non-deterministic guarded command language with real-valued clock variables and simple data types. It serves as a modeling or design language to describe system behavior as networks of automata extended with clock and data variables. The simulator is a validation tool which enables examination of possible dynamic executions of a system during early design (or modeling) stages. It provides an inexpensive mean of fault detection prior to verification by the model checker which covers the exhaustive dynamic behavior of the system. The simulator also allows visualization of error traces found as result of verification efforts. The model checker is to check invariant and bounded-liveness properties by exploring the symbolic state-space of a system, i.e., reachability analysis in terms of symbolic states represented by constraints.

Since the first release of UPPAAL in 1995, the tool has been further developed by the teams in Aalborg and Uppsala. The run-time and space improvements in the period December 1996 to September 1998 are reported in [Pet99]. Figures 1 and 2 show the variations of time and space consumption in the period from November 1998 until January 2001 in terms of four examples: Fischer's mutual exclusion protocol with seven processes [Lam87], a TDMA start-up algorithm with three nodes [LP97], a CSMA/CD protocol with eight nodes [BDM+98], and the FDDI token-passing protocol with twelve nodes [Yov97]. We notice that the time performance has improved significantly whereas the space improvement is only marginal.

In July 1999 a new version of UPPAAL, called UPPAAL2k, was released. This new version, which required almost two years of development, is designed to improve the graphical interface of the tool, to allow for easier maintenance, and to be portable to the most common operating systems while still preserving UPPAAL's ease-of-use and efficiency. To meet these requirements, it is designed as a client/server application with a verification server providing efficient C++ services to a Java client over a socket based protocol. This design also makes it possible to execute the server and the GUI on two different machines.

The new GUI, shown in Figure 3, integrates the three main tool components of UPPAAL, i.e., the system editor, the simulator, and the verifier. Several new functionalities have been implemented in the tool. For example, the new system editor has been tailored and extended for the new system description language of UPPAAL2k (see below), the simulator can be used to display error traces generated by the verifier, and the verification interface has been enriched with a

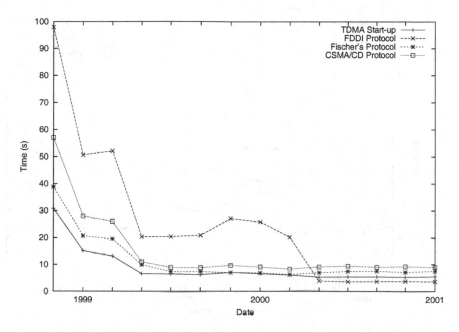

Fig. 1. Time (in seconds) benchmarks for the UPPAAL version 3.x, from internal version November 1998 to January 2001. Up to the second version in year 2000 the settings '-WA' (i.e. no warnings and convex-hull approximation) were used. For the later versions the settings '-WAa' (where '-a' activates the (in-)active clock reduction) were used. All tool versions were compiled with gcc 2.95.2 and executed on the same Sun UltraSPARC-II, 400 MHz machine.

requirement specification editor which stores the previous verification results of a logical property until the property or the system description is modified.

1.2   The Latest UPPAAL Release Version

The current UPPAAL version has a rich modeling language, that supports process templates and (bounded) data structures, such as data variables, constants, arrays, etc. A process template is a timed automaton extended with a list of formal parameters and a set of locally declared clocks, variables, and constants. Typically, a system description will consist of a set of instances of timed automata declared from the process templates, and of some global data, such as global clocks, variables, synchronization channels, etc. In addition, automata instances may be defined from templates re-used from existing system descriptions. Thus, the adopted notion of process templates (particularly when used in combination with the possibility to declare local process data) allows for convenient re-use of existing models.

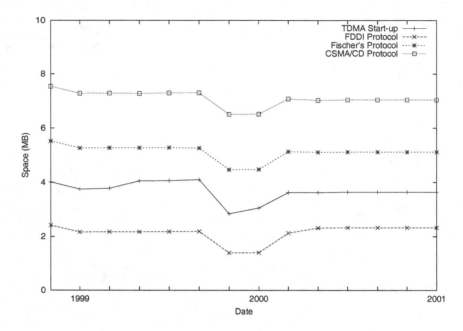

Fig. 2. Space (in MB) benchmarks for UPPAAL version 3.x, from internal version November 1998 to January 2001. Up to the second version in year 2000 the settings '-WAS' (where '-S' activates control-structure reduction [LLPY97]) were used. For the later versions the settings '-WAaS 2' (where '-S 2' is similar to '-S') were used.

The simulator allows both random and guided tracing through the model. One symbolic state is displayed at a time, where the control locations are visualized with red bullets in the timed automata graphs and data is shown by means of equations and clock constraints. Sub-windows can be scaled or dragged out, and the level of detail can be adjusted for user convenience. In the simulator, the user can steer to any point of an elapsed trace and save/load traces of the model. If the model checking engine detects an error trace, it can be handed over to the simulator for inspection.

The UPPAAL model-checking engine is the working horse of the tool. Therefore it is implemented in C++, whereas the GUI of the tool is implemented in Java. To interface the model-checking server, the GUI uses a socket-based protocol. This means that the GUI and verification server can be executed on two different machines. The verification server can also handle several simultaneous connections to serve several GUI clients running on different machines. By default the GUI automatically spawns a verification server process on the local machine [1].

---

[1] The command line options `-serverHost` *host* `-serverPort` *port* can be used to instruct the GUI to connect to a server at machine *host* on port *port*.

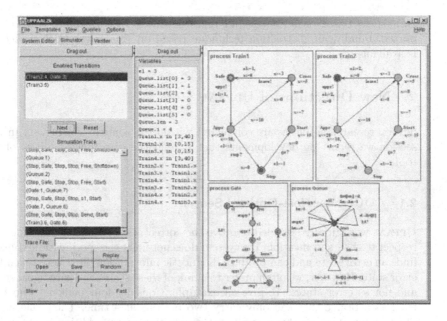

Fig. 3. UPPAAL2k's simulation tool on screen.

At the core of UPPAAL verification engine we find a forward-style state-space exploration algorithm. In principal, we might think of this as a variation of searching the states (nodes) of a directed graph. For this, two data structures are responsible for the potentially huge memory consumption. The first – the WAITING list – contains the states that have been encountered by the algorithm, but have not yet been explored, i.e., the successors have not been determined. The second – the PASSED list – contains all states that have been explored. The algorithm takes a state from the WAITING list, compares it with the PASSED list, and in case it has not been explored, the state itself is added to the PASSED list while the successors are added to the WAITING list.

The properties, that the model checking engine can check, describe a subset of timed computation tree logic (TCTL). In short, the four (un-nested) temporal quantifiers E<>, A[], E[], and A<> are supported, which stand for *possibly, always, inevitably,* and *potentially always*. In addition the operator ϕ --> φ is supported, which stands for the leadsto property A[] ($\phi \rightarrow$ A<> φ). An option for deadlock checking is also implemented but it is currently only available in the stand-alone verifier **verifyta**.

This UPPAAL2k verification server has been extended with various optimization options, described in our publications and elsewhere in the literature. The current version supports the *bit-state hashing* under-approximation technique which has been successfully used in the model-checking tool SPIN for several years. A technique for generating an over-approximation of a system's reachable state-space based on a *convex-hull* representations of constraints is also supported. Finally, an abstraction technique based on *(in-)active clock reductions* is available.

2   New Directions of UPPAAL

Several research activities are conducted within the context of UPPAAL. In this section we report on developments that extend the core functionalities of the tool.

2.1   COUPPAAL: Cost-Optimal Search

UPPAAL was initially intended to prove the correctness of real time systems with respect to their specification. If a system does not meet the specification UPPAAL finds an error state and can produce diagnostic information on how to reach this error state. However, we often prefer to think of these states as desired goal states and not as error states. To give an example. Consider four persons, who have to cross a bridge that can only carry two persons at a time. Then, one would like to know whether they can reach the safe side, given additional constraints and deadlines. This can be expressed with a timed reachability question, and if the goal state is reachable, the trace gives also a feasible schedule. We can use this approach to generally solve timed scheduling problems. In process industry for example, it is often valuable to know whether it is possible to schedule the production steps such that all constraints are met. In [Feh99,HLP00], we derive feasible schedules for a part of a steel plant in Ghent, Belgium, and a LEGO model of this plant.

Even though it is often hard to find a solution, as soon as a feasible solution is found, the question arises, whether this solution is optimal with respect to time or the number of actions. To address this, we included concepts that are well known from branch and bound algorithms to UPPAAL. It is then possible to derive optimal traces for *Uniformly Priced Timed Automata* (UPTA) [BFH+]. In this model the cost increases with a fixed rate as time elapses, or with a certain amount if a transition is taken. The cost is treated as a special clock with extra operations, but such that we can still use the efficient data structures currently used in UPPAAL. First results for the steel plant and several benchmark problems were obtained in [BFH+], and we hope to include an option that allows to find optimal traces to goal states in the next release of UPPAAL.

To be able to find time-optimal traces is very useful, but in many situations we would like to have a more general notion of cost. We proposed the model of *Linearly Priced Timed Automata* (LPTA) to be able to model for example machines that use a different amount of energy per time unit. This model extends timed automata with *prices* on all transitions and locations. In these models, the cost of taking an action transition is the price associated with the transition, and the cost of delaying d time units in a location is $d \cdot p$, where p is the price associated with the location. The cost of a trace is simply the accumulated sum of costs of its delay and action transitions.

To treat LPTA algorithmically, we introduce *priced zones*, which assign to a zone a linear function that defines the minimal cost of reaching a state in that zone. In [BFH+00] it was shown that given a set of goal states the cost-optimal trace is computable. This result is quite remarkable since several similar extensions of timed automata have been proven to be undecidable. A prototype implementation allows us to perform first experiments [LBB+01].

2.2 PARAMETRIC-UPPAAL: **Solving Parameterized Reachability Problems**

Timed model checking if frequently applied with the intention to find out, whether the timing constants of the model are correct. A common problem is to adjust timing parameters in a way, that yield a desired behavior. This can be achieved if we given a timed automaton with *parameters* in the guards and if some or all values for the parameters are synthesized to make the model behave correctly, i.e., satisfy a certain TCTL formula. We call this *parametric model checking*. This problem is addressed in [AHV93], where it is shown to be undecidable for systems with three clocks or more. A semi-decision procedures is suggested in [AHV93] which finds the correct values for the parameters when it terminates.

We extend the model of timed automata to *parametric timed automata* by adding a set of parameters. Guards in parametric timed automata can be on the form $x \bowtie e$ or $x - y \bowtie e$ where e is a linear expression over the parameters. Having guards of this type gives a natural way of defining a symbolic state-space including parameters. Instead of having integers in the entries of a DBM we use *parametric DBMs* (PDBMs) where the entries are linear expressions over the parameters.

All the operations on DBMs are based on adding or comparing entries of DBMs. Without knowing anything about the values of the parameters we can in general not compare linear expressions over the parameters to each other or to integers. Comparing a parameter p to the constant 3 has two possible outcomes depending on the value of p. When such comparisons arises we will have to distinguish both possibilities. We will do this by adding a *constraint set* to a PDBM, consisting of constraints of the form $e \bowtie e'$ where e and e' are linear expressions and $\bowtie \in \{<, \leq, >, \geq\}$. In the example from before we will then split into two cases, one where the constraint $p < 3$ is added to the constraint set and one where $p \geq 3$ is added to the constraint set. We can now compare entries of PDMs based on their constraint sets.

Changing DBMs to PDBMs and letting symbolic states consist of the location vector, a PDBM, and a constraint set, the standard algorithm for state-space exploration can be used. When a state satisfying the property is found the constraints in the constraint set of the state gives the constraints on the parameters needed for the state to be reachable. If we want to find all the possible values for the parameters we need to search the complete state-space to find all the different constraint sets making a goal state reachable.

We have implemented a parametric version of UPPAAL allowing parameters in clock guards and invariants. For deciding minimum between linear expressions we have borrowed a LP solver from the PMC tool [BSdRT01]. Parametric versions of the root-contention protocol and the bounded retransmission protocol have been analyzed using the implementation and minor errors in two published papers on these protocols have been discovered.

Since the problem is undecidable, UPPAAL is not guaranteed to terminate. As a pragmatic remedy, our algorithm outputs an explored state and the corresponding constraint set, as soon as it if found to satisfy the property. This allows the user to get partial results which can be very useful and in many cases are the full results though the search has not terminated. It is also possible to give initial constraints as input which in many case will make the search terminate much faster, or check whether partial results obtained are actually the full results.

2.3   STOPWATCH-UPPAAL: From Timed Automata to Hybrid Systems

For purposes of efficiency, the modeling language of UPPAAL was initially designed to be rather limited in expressive power. In particular, when modeling hybrid systems composed of discrete controller programs and continuous plants the timed automata model underlying UPPAAL is rather restrictive.

One useful extension of timed automata is that of linear hybrid automata [HHWT97]. In this model guards may be general linear constraints and the evolution rate of continuous variables may be given by arbitrary intervals. Consequently, model-checking and reachability checking is known to be undecidable for this model and more importantly the state-space exploration requires manipulation and representation of general polyhedra, which is computationally rather expensive.

In [CL00] an extension of UPPAAL with stopwatches (clocks that may be stopped occasionally) has been given allowing an approximate analysis of the full class of linear hybrid automata to be carried out using the efficient data structures and algorithms of UPPAAL.

In particular, this work investigates the expressive power of stopwatch automata, and shows as a main result that any finite or infinite *timed language* accepted by a *linear hybrid automaton* is also acceptable by a stopwatch automaton. The consequences of this result are two-fold: firstly, it shows that the seemingly minor upgrade from timed automata to stopwatch automata immediately yields the full expressive power of linear hybrid automata. Secondly, reachability analysis of linear hybrid automata may effectively be reduced to reachability analysis of stopwatch automata. This, in turn, may be carried out using an easy (over-approximating) extension of the efficient reachability analysis for timed automata to stopwatch automata. In [CL00] we also report on preliminary experiments on analyzing translations of linear hybrid automata using a stopwatch-extension of UPPAAL.

2.4   PrUppaal: Probabilistic Timed Automata

UPPAAL can check whether a network of timed automata satisfies a safety or a liveness (timed) property. Many times, this type of properties are not expressive enough to assert adequately the correctness of a system. Take for instance the well known Alternating Bit Protocol (ABP). Using UPPAAL, we can check whether the ABP satisfies properties like "*every message that is sent will eventually be received*" or "*every message that is sent will be received within Δ μsec.*" In fact we will see that the former is satisfied but not the latter, regardless of the value of Δ. If our interest is to provide quality of service, the latest property becomes as important as the former one. However, the fact that the ABP does not satisfy the second property does not necessarily make it an incorrect protocol. Knowing the probability with which a message is lost or damaged during transmission, we can determine the probability that a message is received within Δ μsec. The correctness of the ABP is now depend on whether we consider that such a probability measure is satisfactory.

Verification of probabilistic timed systems is one of the future directions pursued by UPPAAL. Probabilistic timed automata are a natural extension of timed automata with probabilities. The probabilistic information is attachted to edges. Now, an edge has the form $s \xrightarrow{g,a} p$ where s is a control node, g is a guard, a is an action name, and p is a probability function on pairs of set of clocks to be reset and control nodes. Figure 4 depicts a probabilistic timed automaton, that models a lossy channel. A message that is sent can be lost with probability $\frac{1}{100}$, otherwise it is transmitted within 10 to 20 nanoseconds. You can think of this automaton as model of the medium in the ABP.

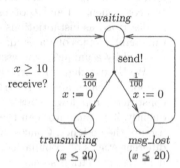

Fig. 4. A lossy channel.

On the setting of probabilistic timed systems we formally describe properties using PTCTL [HJ94]. PTCTL extends TCTL with modalities to express probabilities. For instance, $P_{\geq 0.95}(\forall \Box_{\leq 1000} received)$ expresses that with probability at least 0.95, every message is received within 1000 nanoseconds in any possible execution.

Solutions to model check probabilistic timed automata have been proposed in [Jen96] and [KNSS99]. Unfortunately these approaches are based on the construction of a region graph [ACD93] and therefore they heavily suffer from the state explosion problem. Another solution proposed in [KNSS99] is to use a modification of the forward reachability technique implemented in UPPAAL [YPD94]. Unfortunately, such a modification cannot decide the validity of simple reachability properties in general.

Our proposal is to use minimization techniques [ACH+92] in order to obtain (probabilistic) zone graphs that are stable and which behave in a similar manner to region graphs. However, this technique is still significantly more expensive when compared to the usual forward reachability analysis. In order to reduce the state space we plan to explore the use of CDD's [LWYP99] to represent non-convex zones as well as dynamic partition techniques [JHR99].

2.5   HUPPAAL: Hierarchical Structures for Modeling

Hierarchical structures are a popular theme in specification formalisms, such as statecharts [Har87] and UML [BRJ98]. The main idea is that locations not necessarily encode atomic points of control, but can serve as an abbreviation for more complex behavior. If a non-atomic location is entered, this may trigger a cascade of events irrelevant to a higher level of the system. If a more detailed view is required, the explicit description of the sub-component can be found isolated, since dependencies between the different levels of hierarchy are restricted.

The immediate benefit is a concise description, which allows to view a complex system on different levels of abstraction and nevertheless contains all information in detail. Moreover, symmetries can be expressed explicitly: If two sub-components A and B of a super-state S are structurally identical, they may be described as instantiations of the same template (with possibly different parameters). Copies of states may exist for notational convenience, ambiguities are resolved by a unique-name assumption.

We believe that UPPAAL can benefit greatly from these concepts, since they support a cleaner and more structured design of large systems. The model can be constructed top down, starting with a very abstract notion that is refined subsequently. The simulator can then be used to validate the model against the intuition of the designer. Conceptually, it is possible to reason about the model with different stages of granularity. Compositional verification can make use of this, if local information suffices to establish safety- and deadlock-properties. With respect to property-preserving abstractions, the structural information gives a natural refinement relation.

A second—however ambitious—goal is to exploit the structure in shaping more efficient model-checking algorithms. Related work [AW99] indicates, that locality of information can be exploited straightforward in reachability analysis. Also, the work in [LNAB+98] indicate that—at least for un-timed systems—one may exploit the hierarchical structure of a system during analysis. In UPPAAL this is more difficult, since all parallel processes implicitly synchronize on the passage of time. Approaches for local-time semantics [BJLY98] have yet to be shown to improve verification time in reasonable scenarios, i.e., where the dependency between parallel sub-components is low, thus that not all interleavings have to be taken into account.

As a first step towards this, we work on a careful definition of hierarchical timed automata, that support encapsulation and local definitions. In particular, the synchronization of joins raises semantic problems that can be resolved in various ways.

Case-studies are planned to test the naturalness of these definitions in complex examples. We experiment with a prototype translation of hierarchical timed automata into a parallel composition of (flat) timed automata. This flattened

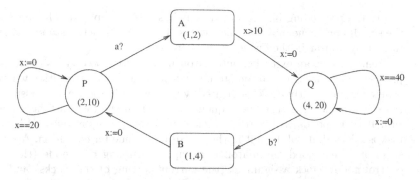

Fig. 5. Timed Automaton with Periodic and Sporadic Tasks.

system necessarily contains auxiliary constructs to imitate the behavior of the hierarchical ones. We expect the case-studies to give an intuition, whether this translation slack is tolerable.

The design of the hierarchical timed automata is meant to be close to UML statechart diagrams. As for the real-time aspect, one output of this considerations will be a real-time profile, that defines an extension of UML formalisms with clocks and timed invariants in a standard way. This work is carried out in the context of AIT-WOODDES project No IST-1999-10069.

2.6   ExUppaal: Executable Timed Automata

In this work we develop an executable version of timed automata. We view a timed automaton as an abstract model of a running software. The model describes the possible external events (alphabets accepted by the automaton) that may occur during the execution and the occurrence of the events must follow the timing constraints (given by the clock constraints). But the model gives no information on how these events should be handled. We use an extended version of timed automata ([EWY99]) with real time tasks that may be periodic and/or sporadic.

The main idea is to associate each node of an automaton with a task (or several tasks in the general case). A task is assumed to be an executable program with two given parameters: its worst case execution time and deadline. An example is shown in Figure 5. The system shown consists of 4 tasks as annotation on nodes, where P, Q are periodic with periods 20 and 40 respectively (specified by the constraints: x==20 and x==40), and A, B are sporadic or event driven (by event a and b respectively). The pairs in the nodes give the computation times and deadlines for tasks e.g. for P they are 2 and 10 respectively.

Intuitively, a discrete transition in an extended timed automaton denotes an event releasing a task and the guard (clock constraints) on the transition specifies all the possible arrival times of the associated task. Note that in the simple automaton shown in Figure 5, an instance of task A could be released before the preceeding instance of task P has been computed. This means that the scheduling queue may contains at least P and A. In fact, instances of all four tasks may appear in the queue at the same time.

Semantically, an extended automaton may perform two types of transitions just as an ordinary timed automaton. In addition, an action transition will release a new instance of the task associated with the destination node. Assume that there is a queue (the scheduling queue) holding all the task instances ready to run. It corresponds to the ready queue in an operating systems. Whenever a task is released, it will be put in the scheduling queue for execution. A semantic state of an extended automaton is a triple consisting of a node (the current control node), clock assignment (the current setting of the clocks) and a task queue (the current status of the ready queue). Then a delay transition of the timed automaton corresponds to the execution of the task with earliest deadline and idling for the other waiting tasks, and a sequences of discrete transitions corresponds to a sequence of arrivals of tasks. Naturally a sequence of tasks is *schedulable* if all the tasks can be executed within their deadlines and an automaton is schedulable if all task sequences are schedulable.

In [EWY99], it is shown that the schedulability problem for extended automata can be solved by reachability analysis for non-preemptive tasks. It is equivalent to prove that all schedulable states are schedulable. For preemptive tasks, unfortunately the problem is undecidable. In fact the model will be as expressive as timed automata with stop watches.

Currently we are working on automatic code synthesis for the extended model. Inspired by the design philosophy of synchronous languages e.g. Esterel, we assume that the underlying RT operating system guarantees the *Synchrony Hypothesis*, that is the OS system functions takes little time compared to the worst case execution times and deadlines of tasks. The idea is to use system functions (primitives) provided by the underlying operating system or run-time system, to code the discrete transitions (the control structure) of an automaton, and to compute the tasks on nodes by procedure calls or light weight threads.

If an automaton is schedulable (checked by schedulability analysis that all tasks instances can be computed within their deadlines), and the synchrony hypothesis is guaranteed by the underlying operating system, the generated code in execution will meet the constraints imposed on the tasks.

2.7   Hybrid Automata Animation

In several case-studies with UPPAAL we have identified a need to visualize the execution of the automata. Currently the simulator in UPPAAL's GUI allows an interactive "execution" of the modeled system. The user can manually select one of the enabled transitions and go to the next state of the system. This can be very helpful in understanding the model, but it is still on the difficulty level of the actual automaton. To make good use of the simulator the user needs to understand all the details of the modelling language and all details of the specific system.

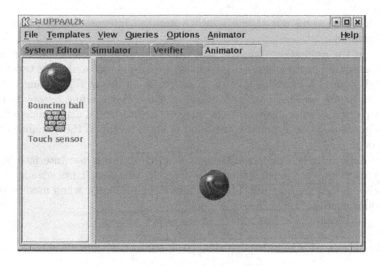

Fig. 6. A protoype of the hybrid automata animation tool in UPPAAL.

To describe a typical situation, consider one person performing the modeling and verification of a system, whereas another person wants to validate that the model is "correct" in the sense that it is an accurate description of the actual system. Exploring all possible simulation traces is often a very tedious work. With a visualization tool, where the user can interact with the underlying model on a higher level via buttons, sliders, and other objects in a graphical environment this validation task becomes much simpler.

Several other tools have responded to this demand, for example MATLAB/-Simulink and Statemate, where graphical animation of the models are possible. By considering simulation and animation of hybrid automata, we adopt these techniques and aim at taking them one step further. The plan is to generalize the model of timed automata in UPPAAL to the more expressive model of hybrid automata, where changes of a state is defined by ordinary differential equations (ODE). To each location we associate a set of ODE's that describe how real-valued variables change over time. This more expressive model will be used only in the animator to model and visualize the behavior a system's environment. The system itself will still normally be modeled with timed automata.

The animation is based on the values of the variables, the current location, and the signals. The values of the variables are calculated at discrete time points using numerical solution methods. To solve the ODE's we use a free package named CVODE [2]. Around this we have implemented a *Hybrid Automata Interpreter* that handles the automata transitions, synchronizations, etc., and allows the user to define the ODE's using a library of mathematical functions. The

---

[2] More information about the CVODE package can be found at the web site http://www.netlib.org.

values that come out of the Hybrid Automata Interpreter are used to drive the animation.

In the animation tool, the user defines a *view* of the whole system by setting certain parameters. For instance, in a 2-dimensional view two variables x and y could be used to give the position of an image illustrating the modeled component, and the current location of the corresponding automaton could be visualized as color-changes in the image. The user could also decide what actions (e.g. mouse-clicks) should correspond to signals sent to the visualized automata model.

Following the example of UPPAAL's multi-platform user interface (see Section 1), the animator is implemented in Java. In this way it fits seamlessly into the existing tool architecture. Figure 6 shows the animator when used to simulate a bouncing ball.

3   Recent Developments in UPPAAL

In this section we describe the recent developments in UPPAAL, which are primarily aimed at improving the efficiency of the model-checker of the tool. In particular, the development of new internal data-structures, and approximation and partial-order reduction techniques are considered relevant.

3.1   CDD's: Clock Difference Diagrams

Difference Bound Matrices (DBM's) as the standard representation for time zones in analysis of Timed Automata have a well-known shortcoming: they are not closed under set-union. This comes from the fact that a set represented by a DBM is convex, while the union of two convex sets is not necessarily convex.

Within the symbolic computation for the reachability analysis of UPPAAL, set-union however is a crucial operation which occurs in every symbolic step. The shortcoming of DBM's leads to a situation, where symbolic states which could be treated as one in theory have to be handled as a collection of several different symbolic states in practice. This leads to trade-offs in memory and time consumption, as more symbolic states have to be stored and visited during in the algorithm.

DBM's represent a zone as a conjunction of constraints on the differences between each pair of clocks of the timed automata (including a fictitious clock representing the value 0). The major idea of CDD's (Clock Difference Diagrams) is to store a zone as a decision tree of clock differences, generalizing the ideas of BDD's (Binary Decision Diagrams, see [Bry86]) and IDD's (Integer Decision Diagrams, see [ST98])

The nodes of the decision tree represent clock differences. Nodes on the same level of the tree represent the same clock difference. The order of the clock differences is fixed a-priori, all CDD's have to agree on the same ordering. The leaves of the decision tree are two nodes representing true and false, as in the case of BDD's.

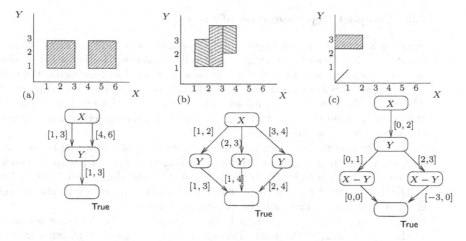

Fig. 7. Three example CDD's. Intervals not shown lead implicitly to **False**.

Each node can have several outgoing edges. Edges are labeled with integral intervals: open, half-closed and closed intervals with integer values as the borders. A node representing the clock difference $X - Y$ together with an outgoing edge with interval I represents the constraint "$X - Y$ within I". The leafs represent the global constraints true and false respectively.

A path in a CDD from a node down to a leaf represents the set of clock values with fulfill the conjunction of constraints found along the path. Remember that a constraint is found from the pair node and outgoing edge. Paths going to false thus always represent the empty set, and thus only paths leading to the true node need to be stored in the CDD. A CDD itself represents the set given by the union of all sets represented by the paths going from the root to the true node. From this clearly CDD's are closed under set-union. Figure 7 gives three examples of two-dimensional zones and their representation as CDDs. Note that the same zone can have different CDD representations.

All operations on DBM's can be lifted straightforward to CDD's. Care has to be taken when the canonical form of the DBM is involved in the operation, as there is no direct equivalent to the (unique) canonical form of DBM's for CDD's.

CDD's generalize IDD's, where the nodes represent clock values instead of clock differences. As clock differences, in contrast to clock values, are not independent of each other, operations on CDD's are much more elaborated than the same operations on IDD's. CDD's can be implemented space-efficient by using the standard BDD's technique of sharing common substructure. This sharing can also take place between different CDD's.

Experimental results have shown that using CDD's instead of DBM's can lead to space savings of up to 99%. However, in some cases a moderate increase in run time (up to 20%) has to be paid. This comes from the fact that operations involving the canonical form are much more complicated in the case of CDD's compared to DBM's. More on CDD's can be found in [LWYP99] and [BLP$^+$99].

3.2   Compact Representation of States

Symbolic states are the core objects of state space search and their representation is one of the key issues in implementing an efficient verifier. In the earlier versions of UPPAAL each entity in a state (i.e., an element in the location vector, the value of an integer variable or a bound in the DBM) is mapped on a machine word. The reason for this is simplicity and speed. However, the number of possible values for each entity is usually small, and using a whole machine word for each of them is often a waste of space.

To solve this problem two additional, more compact, state representations have been implemented. In both of them the discrete part of each state is encoded as a number, using a multiply and add scheme. This encoding is much like looking at the discrete part as a number, where each digit is an entity in the discrete state and the base varies with the number of different digits.

In the first packing scheme, a DBM is encoded using the same technique as the discrete part of the state. This gives a very space efficient but computationally expensive representation, where each state takes a minimum amount of memory but where a number of bignum division operations have to be performed to check inclusion between two DBMs.

In the second packing scheme, some of the space performance is sacrificed to allow a more efficient inclusion check. Here each bound in the DBM is encoded as a bit string long enough to represent all the possible values of this bound plus one *test bit*, i.e., if a bound can have 10 possible values then five bits are used to represent the bound. This allows cheap inclusion checking based on ideas of Paul and Simon [PS80] on comparing vectors using subtraction of bit strings.

In Figure 8 we see that the space performance of these representations are both substantially better than the traditional representation, with space savings of between 25% and 70%. As we expect, the performance of the first packing scheme, with an expensive inclusion check, is somewhat better, space-wise, than the packing scheme with the cheap inclusion check.

Considering the time performance for the packed state representations (see Figure 9), we note that the price for using the encoding with expensive inclusion check is a slowdown of 2 – 12 times, while using the other encoding sometimes is even faster than the traditional representation.

3.3   Partial Order Reduction for Timed Systems

Partial-order reduction is a well developed technique, whose purpose is to reduce the usage of time and memory in state-space exploration by avoiding to explore unnecessary interleavings of independent transitions. It has been successfully applied to finite-state systems. However, for timed systems there has been less progress. The major obstacle to the application of partial order reduction to timed systems is the assumption that all clocks advance at the same speed, meaning that all clocks are implicitly synchronized. If each process contains (at least) one local clock, this means that advancement of the local clock of a process is not independent of time advancements in other processes. Therefore, different interleavings of a set of independent transitions will produce different

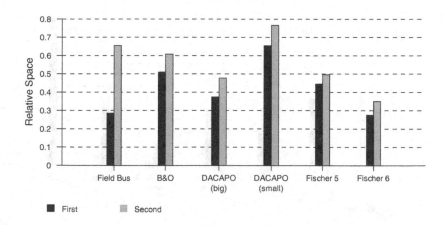

Fig. 8. Space performance for the two packing schemes (denoted First and Second).

combinations of clock values, even if there is no explicit synchronization between the processes or their clocks.

In [BJLY98], we have presented a partial-order reduction method for timed systems based on a *local-time* semantics for networks of timed automata. The main idea is to remove the implicit clock synchronization between processes in a network by letting local clocks in each process advance independently of clocks in other processes, and by requiring that two processes *resynchronize* their local time scales whenever they communicate. The idea of introducing local time is related to the treatment of local time in the field of parallel simulation. Here, a simulation step involves some local computation of a process together with a corresponding update of its local time. A snapshot of the system state during a simulation will be composed of many local time scales. In our work, we are concerned with verification rather than simulation, and we must therefore represent sets of such system states symbolically.

A symbolic version of the local-time semantics is developed in terms of predicate transformers, which enjoys the desired property that two predicate transformers are independent if they correspond to disjoint transitions in different processes. Thus we can apply standard partial order reduction techniques to the problem of checking reachability for timed systems, which avoid exploration of unnecessary interleavings of independent transitions. The price is that we must introduce extra machinery to perform the resynchronization operations on local clocks. A variant of DBM representation has been developed for symbolic states in the local time semantics for efficient implementation of our method.

We have developed a prototype implementation based on the technique. Unfortunately, our experimental results are not so satisfactory, which is not so surprising due to the large number of local clocks introduced. We are still struggling for an efficient implementation.

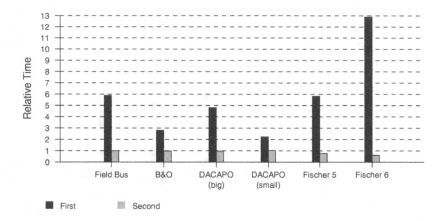

Fig. 9. Time performance for the two packing schemes (denoted **First** and **Second**).

3.4   DUᴘᴘᴀᴀʟ: **Distributed State Space Exploration**

Real time model checking is a time and memory consuming task, quite often reaching the limits of both computers and the patience of users. An increasingly common solution to this situation is to use the combined power of computers connected in a cluster. Good results have recently been achieved for Uᴘᴘᴀᴀʟ by distributing both the model checking algorithm and the main data structures [BHV00].

Recall the basic state-space exploration described briefly in Section 1.2. The distributed version of this algorithm is similar. Each node (processing unit) in the cluster will hold fragments of both the Wᴀɪᴛɪɴɢ list and the Pᴀssᴇᴅ list according to a distribution function mapping states to nodes. In the beginning, the distributed Wᴀɪᴛɪɴɢ list will only hold the initial state. What ever node hosts this state will compare it to its still empty Pᴀssᴇᴅ list fragment and consequently explore it. Now, the successors are distributed according to the distribution function and put into the Wᴀɪᴛɪɴɢ list fragment on the respective nodes. This process will be repeated, but now several nodes contain states in their fragment of the Wᴀɪᴛɪɴɢ list and quickly all nodes become busy exploring their part of the state space. The algorithm terminates when all Wᴀɪᴛɪɴɢ list fragments are empty and no states are in the process of being transfered between nodes.

The distribution function is in fact a hash function. It distributes states uniformly over its range and hence implements what is called *random load balancing*. Since states are equally likely to be mapped to any node, all nodes will receive approximately the same number of states and hence the load will be equally distributed.

This approach is very similar to the one taken by [SD97]. The difference is that UPPAAL uses symbolic states, each covering (infinitely) many concrete states. In order to achieve optimal performance, the lookup performed on the PASSED list is an inclusion check. An unexplored symbolic state taken from the WAITING list is compared with all the explored symbolic states on the PASSED list, and only if non of those states cover (include) the unexplored symbolic state it is explored. For this to work in the distributed case, the distribution function needs to guarantee that potentially overlapping symbolic states are mapped to the same node in the cluster. A symbolic state can be divided into a discrete part and a continuous part. By only basing the distribution on the discrete part, the above is ensured.

Peculiarly, the number of explored states is heavily dependent on the search order. For instance, let s and t be two symbolic states such that s includes t. Thus, if s is encountered before t, t will not be explored because s is already on the PASSED list and hence covers t. On the other hand, if we encounter t first, both states will be explored. Experiments have shown that breadth first order is close to optimal when building the complete reachable state-space. Unfortunately, ensuring strict breadth first order in a distributed setting requires synchronizing the nodes, which is undesirable. Instead, we order the states in each WAITING list fragment according to their distance from the initial state, exploring those with the smallest distance first. This results in an approximation of the breadth first order. Experiments have shown that this order drastically reduces the number of explored states compared to simply using a FIFO order.

This version of UPPAAL has been used on a Sun Enterprise 10000 with 24 CPUs and on a Linux Beowulf cluster with 10 nodes. Good speedups have been observed on both platforms when verifying large systems (around 80% of optimal at 23 CPUs on the Enterprise 10000).

3.5   Dynamic Partitioning: Tackling the State Explosion Problem

This line of work addresses the *state-space explosion* problem that has to be overcomed in the verification of systems described by a parallel composition of several automata.

Recall that basic algorithm implemented in UPPAAL is an *exact* reachability algorithm that computes for each reachable location of the global system a finite union of zones. One promising idea here is to make use of *approximations* in order to reduce the complexity of this algorithm, and nevertheless stay conservative with respect to safety properties. In many cases, this greatly improves performance without sacrificing relevant information.

The current release of UPPAAL already contains options for convex-hull approximation of zones, basically associating one unique zone to each reachable control location. Such a zone represents then an upper-approximation of the exact reachable clock values in the considered location. Another possible approximation would consist in associating the same zone to *several* locations. We will use a combination of these two techniques.

Now, a major difficulty is to adjust the level of approximation used. A tradeoff has to be found between precision and efficiency. Rough approximations make analysis cheaper but may fail in showing non-trivial properties; more precise analyses may be too expensive to be able to deal with big systems.

The solution we propose [JHR99,Jea00,Jea] is defined within the framework of abstract interpretation theory [CC77]. It relies on the use of an abstract lattice combining Boolean and numerical properties (e.g. zones), and exploits the partitioning of the state space of the system in order to adjust the precision of the analysis. Now, given a safety property, it is hardly possible to guess the good partition to check it, i.e., the coarsest partition that is still detailed enough to enable the proof of this property. We propose to start the analysis with a very coarse partition, and to automatically refine it according to the needs of verification, until the obtained precision enables a proof of the property, or until the partition cannot be refined in a reasonable way any more.

This technique has been implemented in the tool NBAC, using convex polyhedra to represent numerical properties, and has been successfully applied to the verification of synchronous programs [Jea00,Jea]. Work is currently done to extend the tool with continuous time semantic, and to connect it to the UPPAAL language for timed automata. We are also considering to replace the convex polyhedra lattice used in the tool by the cheaper lattice of zones, used in UPPAAL, or possibly the new lattice of octagons [Min00], that generalizes zones by allowing constraints of the form $m \leq x_i + x_j \leq M$.

4   Recent Case Studies

UPPAAL2k has been applied in a number of case studies. In this section we briefly describe a selection of the more recent ones. A more complete overview is given on the UPPAAL home page http://www.uppaal.com/ (see the section "Documentation").

In [DY00], David and Wang report on an industrial application of UPPAAL to model and debug a commercial field bus communication protocol, AF100 (Advant Field-bus 100) developed and implemented by process control industry for safety-critical applications. The protocol has been running in various industrial environments over the world for the past ten years. Due to the complexity of the protocol and various changes made over the years, it shows occasionally unexpected behaviors. During the case study, a number of imperfections in the protocol logic and its implementation are found and the error sources are debugged based on abstract models of the protocol; respective improvements have been suggested.

In [HLP00], Hune et al. address the problem of synthesizing production schedules and control programs for the batch production plant model built in LEGO® MINDSTORMS™ RCX™ shown in Figures 10. A timed automata model of the plant which faithfully reflects the level of abstraction needed to synthesize control programs is described. This makes the model very detailed and complicated for automatic analysis. To solve this problem a general way of adding guidance to a model by augmenting it with additional guidance variables and transition guards is presented. Applying the technique makes synthesis of control problems feasible for a plant producing as many as 60 batches. In comparison, only two

Fig. 10. An overview of the LEGO® plant.

batches could be scheduled without guides. The synthesized control programs have been executed in the plant. Doing this revealed some model errors.

The papers [Hun99,IKL+00] also consider systems controlled by LEGO® RCX™ bricks. Here the studied problem is that of checking properties of the actual programs, rather than abstract models of programs. It is shown how UPPAAL models can be automatically synthesized from RCX™ programs, written in the programming language *Not Quite C*, NQC. Moreover, a protocol to facilitate the distribution of NQC programs over several RCX™ bricks is developed and proved to be correct. The developed translation and protocol are applied to a distributed LEGO® system with two RCX™ bricks pushing boxes between two conveyer belts moving in opposite directions. The system is modeled and some verification results with UPPAAL2k are reported.

In [KLPW99], Kristoffersen et. al. present an analysis of an experimental batch plant using UPPAAL2k. The plant is modeled as a network of timed automata where automata are used for modeling the physical components of the plant, such as the valves, pumps, tanks etc. To model the actual levels of liquid in the tanks, integer variables are used in combination with real-valued clocks which control the change between the (discrete) levels at instances of time which may be predicted from a more accurate hybrid automata model. An crucial assumption of this discretization is that the interaction between the tanks and the rest of the plant must be such that any plant event affecting the tanks only occurs at these time instances. If this assumption can be guaranteed (which is one of the verification efforts in this framework), the verification results are exact and not only conservative with respect to a more accurate model, where the continuous change of the levels may have been given by some suitable differential equation.

The paper [LAM99] reports on the first time, that a part of the Ada run-time complex has been formally verified. To eliminate most implementation dependencies and constructs with not clearly specified behavior in Ada, the Ravenscar Tasking Profile is used to implement the concurrency part. This significantly advances the possibility to formally verify properties of concurrent programs. The case study uses UPPAAL to prove fourteen properties, where one depends directly on an upper bound on a real-time clock value.

In an ongoing case study [AJ01], UPPAAL is applied to model and analyze a generalized version of a car looking system developed by Saab Automobile. The looking system is distributed over several nodes in the internal communication network that exists in all modern vehicles. The system consists of a central node gathering information and based on this instructing sub nodes attached to the physical hardware to lock or unlock doors, trunk lid, etc. The input sources are different kinds of remote controllers, speed sensors, automatic re-locking time-outs etc. which based on predefined rules may activate the locking mechanism. The model of the system is derived from the actual functional requirements of the looking system used at Saab Automobile. During the currently ongoing work with verifying the functional requirements of the model, some inconsistencies and other problems between requirement have been found and pointed out to the engineers.

5   Online Available Distributions

UPPAAL2k is currently available for Linux, SunOS and MS Windows platforms. It can be downloaded from the UPPAAL home page http://www.uppaal.com/. Since July 1999, the tool has been downloaded by more than 800 different users in 60 countries. On the home page, you also find answers to frequently asked questions, online documentation, tutorials, and related research articles.

An open mailing list at http://groups.yahoo.com/group/uppaal serves as a lively discussion forum for both UPPAAL users and developers.

References

[ACD93]   Rajeev Alur, Costas Courcoubetis, and David Dill. Model Checking in Dense Real Time. *Information and Computation*, 104:2–34, 1993.

[ACH+92]   Rajeev Alur, Costas Courcoubetis, Nicolas Halbwachs, David Dill, and Howard Wong-Toi. Minimization of Timed Transition Systems. In *Proc. of CONCUR '92, Theories of Concurrency: Unification an d Extension*, pages 340–354, 1992.

[AHV93]   Rajeev Alur, Thomas A. Henzinger, and Moshe Y. Vardi. Parametric
             Real-time Reasoning. In *Proceedings of the Twenty-Fifth Annual ACM
             Symposium on the Theory of Computing*, pages 592–601, 1993.

[AJ01]   Tobias Amnell and Pontus Jansson. Report from astec-rt auto project
             — central locking system case study. In preparation, 2001.

[AW99]   Rajeev Alur and Bow-Yaw Wang. "Next" Heuristic for On-the-fly Model
             Checking. In *Proc. of CONCUR '99: Concurrency Theory*, number 1664
             in Lecture Notes in Computer Science, pages 98–113. Springer–Verlag,
             1999.

[BDM+98]   Marius Bozga, Conrado Daws, Oded Maler, Alfredo Olivero, Stavros Tri-
             pakis, and Sergio Yovine. Kronos: A model-Checking Tool for Real-Time
             Systems. In *Proc. of the 10th Int. Conf. on Computer Aided Verifica-
             tion*, number 1427 in Lecture Notes in Computer Science, pages 546–550.
             Springer–Verlag, 1998.

[BFH+]   Gerd Behrmann, Ansgar Fehnker, Thomas Hune, Kim G. Larsen, Paul
             Pettersson, and Judi Romijn. Efficient Guiding Towards Cost-Optimality
             in UPPAAL. Accepted for publication in TACAS'2001.

[BFH+00]   Gerd Behrmann, Ansgar Fehnker, Thomas Hune, Kim G. Larsen,
             Paul Pettersson, Judi Romijn, and Frits Vaandrager. Minimum-
             Cost Reachability for Priced Timed Automata. Submitted for
             publication. Available at http://www.docs.uu.se/docs/rtmv/papers/-
             bfhlprv-sub00-1.ps.gz, 2000.

[BHV00]   Gerd Behrmann, Thomas Hune, and Frits Vaandrager. Distributing
             Timed Model Checking – How the Search Order Matters. In *Proc. of the
             12th Int. Conf. on Computer Aided Verification*, number 1855 in Lecture
             Notes in Computer Science, pages 216–231. Springer–Verlag, 2000.

[BJLY98]   Johan Bengtsson, Bengt Jonsson, Johan Lilius, and Wang Yi. Partial
             Order Reductions for Timed Systems. In *Proc. of CONCUR '98: Con-
             currency Theory*, number 1466 in Lecture Notes in Computer Science.
             Springer–Verlag, 1998.

[BLP+99]   Gerd Behrmann, Kim G. Larsen, Justin Pearson, Carsten Weise, and
             Wang Yi. Efficient Timed Reachability Analysis Using Clock Difference
             Diagrams. In *Proc. of the 11th Int. Conf. on Computer Aided Verifi-
             cation*, number 1633 in Lecture Notes in Computer Science. Springer–
             Verlag, 1999.

[BRJ98]   Grady Booch, James Rumbaugh, and Ivar Jacobson. *The Unified Mod-
             eling Language User Guide*. Addison-Wesley, 1998.

[Bry86]   Randal E. Bryant. Graph-Based Algorithms for Boolean-Function Ma-
             nipulation. *IEEE Trans. on Computers*, C-35(8):677–691, August 1986.

[BSdRT01]   Giosuè Bandini, R. F. Lutje Spelberg, R. C. M. de Rooij, and W. J.
             Toetenel. Application of Parametric Model Checking - The Root Con-
             tention Protocol. In *Proc. of the 34th Annual Hawaii International Con-
             ference on System Sciences (HICSS-34)*, 2001.

[CC77]   Patrick Cousot and Radhia Cousot. Abstract Interpretation: a Unified
             Lattice Model for Static Analysis of Programs by Construction or Ap-
             proximation of Fixpoints. *Proc. of the 4th ACM Symposium on Princi-
             ples of Programming Languages*, January 1977.

[CL00]   Franck Cassez and Kim G. Larsen. The Impressive Power of Stopwatches.
             In *Proc. of CONCUR '2000: Concurrency Theory*, number 1877 in Lec-
             ture Notes in Computer Science, pages 138–152. Springer–Verlag, 2000.

[DY00]   Alexandre David and Wang Yi. Modelling and Analysis of a Commercial
            Field Bus Protocol. In *Proc. of 12th Euromicro Conference on Real-Time
            Systems*, pages 165–172. IEEE Computer Society Press, June 2000.
[EWY99]   Christer Ericsson, Anders Wall, and Wang Yi. Timed Automata as Task
            Models for Eventdriven Systems. In *Proceedings of RTSCA 99*. IEEE
            Computer Society Press, 1999.
[Feh99]   Ansgar Fehnker. Scheduling a Steel Plant with Timed Automata. In
            *Proc. of the 6th International Conference on Real-Time Computing Sys-
            tems and Applications (RTCSA99)*, pages 280–286. IEEE Computer So-
            ciety Press, 1999.
[Har87]   David Harel. Statecharts: A Visual Formalism for Complex Systems.
            Science of Computer Programming, 8:231–274, 1987.
[HHWT97]   Thomas A. Henzinger, Pei-Hsin Ho, and Howard Wong-Toi. HyTech: A
            Model Checker for Hybrid Systems. In Orna Grumberg, editor, *Proc. of
            the 9th Int. Conf. on Computer Aided Verification*, number 1254 in Lec-
            ture Notes in Computer Science, pages 460–463. Springer–Verlag, 1997.
[HJ94]   Hans A. Hansson and Bengt Jonsson. A Logic for Reasoning about Time
            and Reliability. *Formal Aspects of Computing*, 6:512–535, 1994.
[HLP00]   Thomas Hune, Kim G. Larsen, and Paul Pettersson. Guided Synthesis of
            Control Programs Using UPPAAL. In Ten H. Lai, editor, *Proc. of the IEEE
            ICDCS International Workshop on Distributed Systems Verification and
            Validation*, pages E15–E22. IEEE Computer Society Press, April 2000.
[Hun99]   Thomas Hune. Modelling a Real-time Language. In *Proceedings of
            FMICS*, 1999.
[IKL+00]   Torsten K. Iversen, Kåre J. Kristoffersen, Kim G. Larsen, Morten
            Laursen, Rune G. Madsen, Steffen K. Mortensen, Paul Pettersson, and
            Chris B. Thomasen. Model-Checking Real-Time Control Programs —
            Verifying LEGO Mindstorms Systems Using UPPAAL. In *Proc. of 12th
            Euromicro Conference on Real-Time Systems*, pages 147–155. IEEE
            Computer Society Press, June 2000.
[Jea]   Bertrand Jeannet. Dynamic Partitioning in Linear Relation Analysis.
            Application to the Verification of Reactive Systems. to appear in *Formal
            Methods and System Design*, Kluwer Academic Press.
[Jea00]   Bertrand Jeannet. *Partitionnement dynamique dans l'analyse de rela-
            tions linéaires et application à la vérification de programmes synchrones*.
            PhD thesis, Institut National Polytechnique de Grenoble, September
            2000.
[Jen96]   Henrik E. Jensen. Model Checking Probabilistic Real Time Systems. In
            B. Bjerner, M. Larsson, and B. Nordström, editors, *Proceedings of the 7th
            Nordic Workshop on Programming Theory*, Göteborg Sweden, Report 86,
            pages 247–261. Chalmers University of Technolog, 1996.
[JHR99]   Bertrand Jeannet, Nicolas Halbwachs, and Pascal Raymond. Dynamic
            Partitioning in Analyses of Numerical Properties. In *Static Analysis
            Symposium, SAS'99*, Venezia (Italy), September 1999.
[KLPW99]   Kåre Kristoffersen, Kim G. Larsen, Paul Pettersson, and Carsten Weise.
            Vhs Case Study 1 - experimental Batch Plant using UPPAAL. BRICS,
            University of Aalborg, Denmark, http://www.cs.auc.dk/research/-
            FS/VHS/cs1uppaal.ps.gz, May 1999.

[KNSS99]   Marta Z. Kwiatkowska, Gethin Norman, Roberto Segala, and Jeremy
            Sproston. Automatic Verification of Real-Time Systems with Proba-
            bility Distributions. In J.-P. Katoen, editor, *Proceedings of the 5th
            AMAST Workshop on Real-Time and Probabilistic System,* Bamberg,
            Germany, number 1601 in Lecture Notes in Computer Science, pages 75–
            95. Springer–Verlag, 1999. An extended version will appear in Theoretical
            Computer Science.

[Lam87]   Leslie Lamport. A Fast Mutual Exclusion Algorithm. *ACM Trans. on
            Computer Systems,* 5(1):1–11, February 1987. Also appeared as SRC
            Research Report 7.

[LAM99]   Kristina Lundqvist, Lars Asplund, and Stephen Michell. A Formal Model
            of the Ada Ravenscar Tasking Profile; Protected Objects. In Springer-
            Verlag, editor, *Proc. of the Ada Europe Conference,* pages 12–25, 1999.

[LBB+01]   Kim G. Larsen, Gerd Behrmann, Ed Brinksma, Ansgar Fehnker, Thomas
            Hune, Paul Pettersson, and Judi Romijn. As Cheap as Possible: Efficient
            Cost-Optimal Reachability for Priced Timed Automata. Submitted for
            publication, 2001.

[LLPY97]   Fredrik Larsson, Kim G. Larsen, Paul Pettersson, and Wang Yi. Effi-
            cient Verification of Real-Time Systems: Compact Data Structures and
            State-Space Reduction. In *Proc. of the 18th IEEE Real-Time Systems
            Symposium,* pages 14–24. IEEE Computer Society Press, December 1997.

[LNAB+98]   Jørn Lind-Nielsen, Henrik Reif Andersen, Gerd Behrmann, Henrik Hul-
            gaard, Kåre J. Kristoffersen, and Kim G. Larsen. Verification of Large
            State/Event Systems Using Compositionality and Dependency Analy-
            sis. In Bernard Steffen, editor, *Proc. of the 4th Workshop on Tools and
            Algorithms for the Construction and Analysis of Systems,* number 1384
            in Lecture Notes in Computer Science, pages 201–216. Springer–Verlag,
            1998.

[LP97]   Henrik Lönn and Paul Pettersson. Formal Verification of a TDMA Pro-
            tocol Startup Mechanism. In *Proc. of the Pacific Rim Int. Symp. on
            Fault-Tolerant Systems,* pages 235–242, December 1997.

[LPY97]   Kim G. Larsen, Paul Pettersson, and Wang Yi. UPPAAL in a Nutshell.
            Int. Journal on Software Tools for Technology Transfer, 1(1–2):134–152,
            October 1997.

[LWYP99]   Kim G. Larsen, Carsten Weise, Wang Yi, and Justin Pearson. Clock
            Difference Diagrams. *Nordic Journal of Computing,* 6(3):271–298, 1999.

[Min00]   Antoine Miné. The Numerical Domain of Octagons and Application to
            the Automatic Analysis of Programs. Master's thesis, École Normale
            Supérieure de Paris, 2000.

[Pet99]   Paul Pettersson. *Modelling and Analysis of Real-Time Systems Using
            Timed Automata: Theory and Practice.* PhD thesis, Department of Com-
            puter Systems, Uppsala University, February 1999.

[PS80]   Wolfgang J. Paul and Janos Simon. Decision Trees and Random
            Access Machines. In *Logic and Algorithmic,* volume 30 of *Monogra-
            phie de L'Enseignement Mathématique,* pages 331–340. L'Enseignement
            Mathématique, Université de Genève, 1980.

[SD97]   Ulrich Stern and David L. Dill. Parallelizing the Murφ Verifier. In
            Orna Grumberg, editor, *Proc. of the 9th Int. Conf. on Computer Aided
            Verification,* volume 1254 of *Lecture Notes in Computer Science,* pages
            256–267. Springer–Verlag, June 1997. Haifa, Isreal, June 22-25.

[ST98]   Karsten Strehl and Lothar Thiele. Symbolic Model Checking of Process Networks Using Interval Diagram Techniques. In *Proceedings of the IEEE/ACM International Conference on Computer-Aided Design (ICCAD-98)*, pages 686–692, 1998.

[Yov97]   Sergio Yovine. Kronos: A verification Tool for Real-Time Systems. *Springer International Journal of Software Tools for Technology Transfer*, 1(1/2), October 1997.

[YPD94]   Wang Yi, Paul Pettersson, and Mats Daniels. Automatic Verification of Real-Time Communicating Systems By Constraint-Solving. In Dieter Hogrefe and Stefan Leue, editors, *Proc. of the 7th Int. Conf. on Formal Description Techniques*, pages 223–238. North–Holland, 1994.

HMSCs as Partial Specifications ... with PNs as Completions

Benoit Caillaud, Philippe Darondeau, Loïc Hélouët, and Gilles Lesventes

IRISA, campus de Beaulieu, F35042 Rennes Cedex
Name.Surname@irisa.fr

Abstract. The paper presents ongoing work aiming at understanding the nature of specifications given by High Level Message Sequence Charts and the ways in which they can be put into effective use. Contrarily to some authors, we do not set finite state restrictions on HMSCs as we feel such restrictions do not fit in with the type of distributed systems encountered today in the field of telecommunications. The talk presents first a series of undecidability results about general HMSCs following from corresponding undecidability results on rational sets in product monoids. These negative results which with one exception do not appear yet in the literature on HMSCs do indicate that the sole way in which general HMSCs may be usefully handed as behavioural specifications is to interpret their linear extensions as minimal languages, to be approximated from above in any realization. The problem is then to investigate frameworks in which these incomplete specifications may be given a meaning by a closure operation. The second part of the paper presents a closure operation relative to Petri net languages. This closure operation is an effective procedure that relies on semilinear properties of HMSCs languages. We finally present some decidability results for the distribution and verification of HMSCs transformed into Petri nets.

1 Introduction

Message Sequence Charts (MSC) are a modern form of the old timing diagrams, adapted so as to describe scenarios in which the agents of a distributed system communicate by end-to-end message passing. High Level MSCs (HMSC) are not MSCs but finite generators of MSCs used to describe in a compact way a whole family of scenarios in quite the same way as a finite automaton generates a set of words, but using a different concatenation since MSCs are partial words rather than words. Indeed a MSC is drawn in graphical form as the Hasse diagram of a partially ordered multiset (pomset, or partial word) whose linear extensions form a language (set of words). The concatenation of MSCs is therefore the concatenation of pomsets, and it induces a somewhat complex operation of composition on the associated languages. As a result, the language formed of all linear extensions of all MSCs produced from a finite generator (HMSC) is generally not finitely recognizable. Before discussing consequences, let us introduce first precise definitions. The following is not a literal reproduction of the

F. Cassez et al. (Eds.): MOVEP 2000, LNCS 2067, pp. 125–152, 2001.
© Springer-Verlag Berlin Heidelberg 2001

definitions for MSCs and HMSCs produced by the normalizing committee of the
ITU [16] but we choosed to keep compatibility of our simplified definitions with
this standard. The reader should be warned that we disregard the branching semantics of HMSCs (for more on this, see Mauw and Reniers's paper [18], where
HMSCs are given a process algebra semantics): we are concerned here exclu-
sively with the linear behaviours of HMSCs. Owing to this option, we feel free
to ignore co-regions as they may always be expanded by interleaving without
affecting linear behaviours.

1.1   Notations

A MSC describes the joint behaviour of a fixed family of agents each of which
executes a process defined by a fixed finite sequence of events. Events may be
autonomous (e.g., message emissions or private events) or non autonomous (e.g.,
message receptions). We assume a finite family of agents $[n] = \{1, \ldots, n\}$, a finite
set of private events P owned by agents, and a finite set M of messages each of
which determines its sender and its receiver. This yields an alphabet of events
E that decomposes into a partition $P \cup S \cup R$ as follows:

- P (for private) is the set of private events,
- S (for sending) is the set of message emissions ($S = \{!m | m \in M\}$),
- R (for receiving) is the set of message receptions ($R = \{?m | m \in M\}$).

Let $\phi : E \to [n]$ be the map such that:

- for $e \in P$, $\phi(e)$ is the owner of the private event e,
- for $e = !m$, $\phi(e)$ is the emitter of the message m,
- for $e = ?m$, $\phi(e)$ is the receiver of the message m.

The alphabet of events E may be partitioned accordingly into $E_1 \cup \cdots \cup E_n$,
where $E_i = \{e \in E \mid \phi(e) = i\}$. Now for any word $w \in E^*$, let $\pi_i(w)$ denote the
projection of w on E_i thus $\pi_i(w) \in E_i^*$, and let $\delta(w)$ denote the distribution of w
on $E_1^* \times \cdots \times E_n^*$ thus $\delta(w) = (\pi_1(w), \ldots, \pi_n(w))$. The operation of distribution
will play an important role in the sequel. To end up with generalities, let us
recall that a word u is a prefix of w ($u \in pref(w)$) if $w = uv$ for some v, and
that $|w|_e$ is the number of occurrences of the symbol e in w. We come now to
the main definitions.

1.2   Basic Message Sequence Charts

Definition 1. *A word $w \in E^*$ is said to be* admissible *if $|u|_{!m} \geq |u|_{?m}$ for every
$u \in pref(w)$ and for every message $m \in M$. A vector $W = (w_1, \ldots, w_n) \in
E_1^* \times \cdots \times E_n^*$ is said to be* admissible *if $W = \delta(w)$ for some admissible word
$w \in E^*$. A* scenario *is an admissible vector $W \in E_1^* \times \cdots \times E_n^*$, and it is a*
closed *scenario if moreover $W = \delta(w)$ entails $|w|_{!m} = |w|_{?m}$ for every $m \in M$.
A* basic Message Sequence Chart *(or bMSC) is a closed scenario.*

Remark 1. When M is the empty set of messages, every word $w \in E^*$ and every
vector of words $(w_1, \ldots, w_n) \in E_1^* \times \cdots \times E_n^*$ are admissible.

Definition 1 calls for a few comments. In a scenario $W = (w_1, \dots, w_n)$, each word $w_i \in E_i^*$ defines the process of the corresponding agent $i \in [n]$. The admissibility condition guarantees there is at least one way to interleave these processes in a joint process such that all receptions of messages are preceded by matching emissions. The additional condition on bMSCs guarantees that all messages sent are received later on in this joint process. However, this prevents us from representing communication via gates (e.g., environmental communications) in bMSCs and HMSCs. Before defining the latter, let us introduce a concatenation operation on scenarios.

Definition 2. *Given scenarios* $U = (u_1, \dots, u_n)$ *and* $V = (v_1, \dots, v_n)$ *let their* concatenation *be defined as* $U \cdot V = (u_1.v_1, \dots, u_n.v_n)$.

It is easily seen that $U \cdot V = \delta(uv)$ if $U = \delta(u)$ and $V = \delta(v)$; it follows from this observation that the concatenation of two scenarios (resp. bMSCs) is a scenario (resp. a bMSC). Basic Message Sequence Charts form therefore a monoid, with the distribution of the empty word as the neutral element. This allows to define families of bMSCs using finite automata interpreted in this monoid.

1.3   High Level Message Sequence Charts

Definition 3. *A High-Level Message Sequence Chart (or HMSC) is a pair* $(H, \mathcal{I})$ *where* H *is a finite automaton on a set of symbols* B, *with one initial state and all states final, and* $\mathcal{I}$ *is a map from* B *to the set of Basic Message Sequence Charts. This map extends to a unique morphism of monoids from* B^* *to the monoid of bMSCs, such that* $\mathcal{I}(\epsilon) = (\epsilon, \dots, \epsilon)$ *and* $\mathcal{I}(uv) = \mathcal{I}(u) \cdot \mathcal{I}(v)$ *for* $u, v \in B^*$. *The language* $L(H)$ *of the automaton* H *in the free monoid* B^* *is called the* meta-language *of the HMSC. The image of* $L(H)$ *under* $\mathcal{I}$, *let* $\overrightarrow{\mathcal{L}}(H) = \{\mathcal{I}(w) \mid w \in L(H)\}$, *is called the* vector language *of the HMSC (it is a subset of* $E_1^* \times \cdots \times E_n^*$). *The admissible words* $w \in E^*$ *such that* $\delta(w) \in \overrightarrow{\mathcal{L}}(H)$ *are called* terminated *sequences of the HMSC. The set of prefixes of the terminated sequences is called the* language *of the HMSC and it is denoted* $\mathcal{L}(H)$ *(it is a subset of* E^*).

This definition calls for several comments. By considering all states of H as final states and all prefixes of terminated sequences as elements of $\mathcal{L}(H)$, we adopt an operational view on HMSCs as on line computing devices. One could alternatively specify an explicit subset of final states for H and restrict the definition of $\mathcal{L}(H)$ to terminated sequences. Results given in this paper do carry unchanged to this more general setting. A second simplification which is achieved here is to present bMSCs as vectors of words $(w_1, \dots, w_n) \in E_1^* \times \cdots \times E_n^*$ rather than pomsets labelled on $E = E_1 \cup \cdots \cup E_n$. If one assumes that multiple copies of the *same* message are always received in the order they are sent, this makes no real difference since the partial order on the occurrences of events in the vector $(w_1, \dots, w_n)$ can actually be reconstructed as soon as this vector is admissible: as all occurrences of events are already ordered in each process, it suffices to make explicit for each message m with respective emitter i and receiver j the ordering

$(w_i, k) < (w_j, l)$ for all occurences (w_i, k) and (w_j, l) of the respective events $!m$ and $?m$ such that $|w_i|_{!m} = |w_j|_{?m}$. Now it is easily seen that a word $w \in E^*$ represents a linear extension of the partial order thus obtained if and only if w is admissible and $(w_1, \ldots, w_n) \in \delta(w)$. Our presentation is therefore consistent with other presentations of HMSCs that may be found in the literature.

1.4   Using HMSCs as Behavioural Specifications?

The topic of this paper is to try understanding how HMSCs can be used as behavioural specifications of distributed systems to be realized. Let us briefly review a few studies where this question is addressed directly or indirectly. The *matching problem* for MSCs and HMSCs was solved in [21] by Muscholl, Peled and Su. This membership problem is as follows: given a bMSC and a HMSC, does the former belong to the set of bMSCs defined by the latter? It was shown by these authors that the matching problem is NP-complete, while the intersection problem for HMSCs (given two HMSCs, does there exist some bMSC generated by both?) is undecidable. Incidentally, there are significant differences between our HMSCs and those dealt with in [21], where no specific order can be imposed on the reception of two messages unless the emission of one depends on the reception of the other. The negative answer to the intersection problem may be reworded as follows: given a system modelled by a HMSC, one cannot decide whether this system is compatible with the specifications given by another HMSC. One may take this negative result as an indication that most problems for HMSCs are undecidable. We shall see that this intuition is right. A different approach was proposed by Damm and Harel in [5]. One of the ideas developed in that work is to interpret concatenation of bMSCs as an operation that may synchronize agents and that explicitly prevents multiple instances of a bMSC to be entered concurrently. With this interpretation, languages of HMSCs stay within rational languages; this enables the model checking of HMSCs, which is EXP-SPACE complete according to Alur and Yannakakis [1]. HMSCs with this strong form of concatenation may be realized by communicating automata with synchronous control [13]. Although we have chosen here a purely asynchronous framework, we could have set weaker constraints of *boundedness* on HMSCs so that HMSC languages would stay rational, following [1] and [14]. We did not take this option for we feel it does not suit well the field of telecommunications in which HMSCs are used for partial specifications at early design stages. We nevertheless adopt the objective of synthesizing distributed realizations of HMSCs by communicating automata, like was done for bounded HMSCs in [13] and in [14] [15]. Our approach to distribution shares little with the language-theoretical approach proposed in the last two references: we regard communicating automata as systems whose runs or partial runs take place in the real world, and hence cannot be accepted or rejected by a posteriori acceptance conditions.

To end this introduction we give a flavour of the contents of the remaining sections. Section 2 establishes a series of undecidability results for HMSC languages, following from similar results on rational sets in product monoids. We show the undecidability of inclusion and rationality of HMSC languages. More precisely, we show that both inclusion and reverse inclusion between HMSC languages and rational languages are undecidable. This leaves no hope to deal with HMSCs as complete specifications of distributed systems amenable to automated verification, without cutting down HMSCs by strong restrictions. The alternative is to consider general HMSCs as *incomplete* specifications of behaviours. The language of an HMSC should thus be seen as the minimal behaviour required from systems realizing these specifications. The meaning of specifications is now relative to a fixed class of potential realizations, and a main question is to identify classes of realizations in which each HMSC has an optimal realization, determined in a unique way. We give a selective answer to this question in section 3, where we prove that Petri Nets form such a class. We show for this purpose that HMSC languages are semilinear, and it follows from the theory of regions that they have closures in Petri net languages. Hints are given at the issues of distribution and verification, and case studies are finally dealt with before a short conclusion.

2   Undecidability Results

It is shown in this section that inclusion and rationality are undecidable for HMSC languages, and similarly for the inclusion and for the reverse inclusion between HMSC languages on the one hand and rational languages on the other hand. In order to obtain these negative results, we shall focus on HMSCs with an empty set of messages, depriving them of communication between processes. We could alternatively eliminate private events and then concentrate on HMSCs with an even number of processes $n = 2k$ where every message is sent from process i ($\leq k$) to process $i + k$, such that process $i + k$ is a replica of process i up to substituting $?m$ for $!m$ for each $m \in M$. The results given in this section apply also to this case (as we shall see). Now, if we assume that M is the empty set of messages, scenarios and bMSCs are *arbitrary* elements of the product monoid $E_1^* \times \cdots \times E_n^*$. As the concatenation of scenarios (resp. bMSCs) agrees by definition with the concatenation in this monoid, vector languages of HMSCs are certainly rational subsets of $E_1^* \times \cdots \times E_n^*$, but they cannot coincide with the latter since we did not equip HMSCs with specific final states. Neither does the distribution map $\delta : E^* \to E_1^* \times \cdots \times E_n^*$ yield a bijective correspondence between languages and vector languages of HMSCs since we imposed on languages of HMSCs to be closed under prefix. Both disagreements derive from our operational view on HMSCs. Notwithstanding, it is possible to reduce undecidable problems on rational subsets of $E_1^* \times \cdots \times E_n^*$ to decision problems on languages of HMSCs, thus proving their undecidability, and this is what is achieved in this section. The organization is as follows. Basic definitions and results about recognizable and rational sets and relations are recalled in 2.1; auxiliary definitions and lemmas needed to compensate for the discrepancies between rational sets and HMSC languages (regarding final states and prefix closure) are stated in 2.2; a series of undecidable problems on rational subsets of $E_1^* \times \cdots \times E_n^*$ are reduced in 2.3 to decision problems on HMSC languages; the consequences of these reductions on the potential use of HMSCs as system specifications are examined in 2.4.

2.1   Recognizable and Rational Sets and Relations

Let us recall classical definitions and results that may be found in many good books on language theory, e.g. in [3].

Let $E_1, \ldots, E_n$ be finite disjoint alphabets and let $E = \bigcup_{i=1}^n E_i$. The free monoid (finitely) generated from E is denoted E^*. The cartesian product $E_1^* \times \cdots \times E_n^*$ of the E_i^* is a monoid with neutral element $(\varepsilon, \ldots, \varepsilon)$ and with composition as follows: $(w_1, \cdots, w_n)(w_1', \ldots, w_n') = (w_1 w_1', \ldots, w_n w_n')$. This monoid is finitely generated (its generators are vectors of words $(w_1, \cdots, w_n)$ such that $w_i \in E_i$ for some i and $w_j = \varepsilon$ for all $j \neq i$) but it is not a free monoid (the composition of generators is commutative). The subsets of $E_1^* \times \cdots \times E_n^*$ are also called *relations*.

Definition 4. *Let M be a monoid and A a subset of M. A is* recognizable *($A \in Rec(M)$) if there exists a finite monoid N, a morphism of monoids $\alpha : M \to N$, and a subset P of N such that $A = \alpha^{-1}(P)$.*

Definition 5. *Let M be a monoid with neutral element $1 \in M$. The family $Rat(M)$ of rational subsets of M is the least family of subsets X of M such that :*
  a) the empty set $\emptyset$ and every singleton set $\{m\}$ are rational,
  b) if A, B are rational then $A \cup B$ and AB are rational,
  c) if A is rational then A^* is rational,
where $AB = \{ \alpha\beta \mid \alpha \in A \wedge \beta \in B \}$ and A^* is the least subset of M such that $X = \{1\} \cup AX$ (hence $\emptyset^* = \{1\}$).

It follows from the definitions that monoid morphisms $\alpha : M \to N$ preserve rationality (if A is a rational subset of M then αA is a rational subset of N) while they reflect recognizability (if αA is a recognizable subset of N then A is a recognizable subset of M). Both notions are ideally linked as follows.

Theorem 1 (Kleene). *Let M be a free monoid. Then $Rec(M) = Rat(M)$.*

Kleene's theorem states that recognizable and rational subsets coincide in free monoids but it does not apply to $E_1^* \times \cdots \times E_n^*$ since this monoid is not free. However $E_1^* \times \cdots \times E_n^*$ is a finitely generated monoid and a weaker theorem still applies.

Theorem 2 (McKnight). *Let M be a finitely generated monoid.*
Then $Rec(M) \subset Rat(M)$.

Another crucial Kleene's theorem connects rational sets with finite automata.

Theorem 3 (Kleene). *The rational subsets of E^* coincide with the languages generated by finite automata with alphabet E.*

It follows that rational subsets of any monoid M must coincide with subsets of M generated by finite automata interpreted in M (the singleton sets $\{m\}$ used to express a rational subset of M form the alphabet of the associated automaton). In the specific case of the monoid $E_1^* \times \cdots \times E_n^*$, the set of generators is the bijective image of $E = \bigcup_{i=1}^n E_i$ by the distribution map δ, and this map is moreover a monoid morphism $\delta : E^* \to E_1^* \times \cdots \times E_n^*$. Seeing that any $m \in M$ may be finitely expressed in terms of generators, it follows clearly that the rational subsets of $E_1^* \times \cdots \times E_n^*$ coincide with the images under δ of the rational subsets of E^*. Let us add a few words about the inverse δ^{-1} of the distribution map.

Definition 6. *Given $A \subseteq E_1^* \times \cdots \times E_n^*$, the* mix *of A is the language $\delta^{-1}(A) = \{w \in E^* \mid \delta(w) \in A\}$.*

Given a HMSC $(H, \mathcal{I})$ with an empty set of messages, the words in $\mathcal{L}(H)$ are the prefixes of the words in the mix of $\overrightarrow{\mathcal{L}}(H)$; if moreover each bMSC $\mathcal{I}(b)$ contains at most one occurrence of event, then $\mathcal{L}(H)$ is equal to the mix of $\overrightarrow{\mathcal{L}}(H)$. Now the main source of problems with HMSC languages lays in that $\mathcal{L}(H)$ may not be rational even though $\overrightarrow{\mathcal{L}}(H)$ is rational. To get convinced of this fact, it suffices to consider e.g. the vector language $(e_1, e_2)^*$.

2.2   Marked Sets and Prefix Sets

In order to compensate for the mismatch between rational subsets of $E_1^* \times \cdots \times E_n^*$ and vector languages of HMSCs, one may envisage to represent a rational subset A of this monoid as $Pref(A_\top)$ using the following definitions.

Definition 7 (Marked subset). *Given $A \subseteq E_1^* \times \cdots \times E_n^*$ and a set of markers $\{\top_1, \ldots, \top_n\}$ disjoint from E, let $A_\top = \{W \cdot (\top_1, \ldots, \top_n) \mid W \in A\}$.*

Definition 8 (Prefix set). *Given a monoid M and a subset $A \subseteq M$ let $Pref(A) = \{m \in M \mid \exists m' \in M : mm' \in A\}$.*

Lemmas below state that the above suggested representation is faithful, that $Pref(A_\top)$ is rational if A is rational, and that $\delta^{-1}(Pref(A_\top)) = Pref(\delta^{-1}(A_\top))$. Hence, one obtains altogether a representation of rational subsets of $E_1^* \times \cdots \times E_n^*$ by HMSC languages.

Lemma 1. *Let $A, B \subseteq E_1^* \times \cdots \times E_n^*$ then the following inclusions are equivalent :*
a) $A \subseteq B$
b) $A_\top \subseteq B_\top$
c) $Pref(A_\top) \subseteq Pref(B_\top)$

Lemma 2. *$A \in Rat(E_1^* \times \cdots \times E_n^*) \Rightarrow Pref(A) \in Rat(E_1^* \times \cdots \times E_n^*)$.*

Proof. Let $E = \bigcup_{i=1}^n E_i$. As A is rational, $A = \delta R$ for $R \in Rat(E^*)$ accepted by some finite automaton $\mathcal{A} = (Q, E, T, q_0, Q_F)$. Let $\mathcal{A}' = (Q', E, T', q_0', Q_F')$ with $Q' = Q \times \mathcal{P}([n])$, $q_0' = (q_0, [n])$, $Q_F' = Q_F \times \mathcal{P}([n])$, and with T' ($\subseteq Q' \times E \times Q'$) defined as the least set of transitions such that, for all $i \in [n]$, $e_i \in E_i$, and

$J \subseteq [n]$:

if $q_1 \xrightarrow{e_i} q_2 \in T$, then:

$(q_1, J) \xrightarrow{e_i} (q_2, J) \in T'$ if $i \in J$, and

$(q_1, J) \xrightarrow{\varepsilon} (q_2, J \setminus \{i\}) \in T'$ in any case.

Clearly, $Pref(A) = \delta R'$ where R' is the rational subset accepted by $\mathcal{A}'$, hence $Pref(A)$ is rational.   □

Lemma 3. $Pref \circ \delta^{-1}(A) = \delta^{-1} \circ Pref(A)$ for any $A \subseteq E_1^* \times \cdots \times E_n^*$.

Proof. Let $W' \in Pref(A)$ then by definition of Prefix sets, $W = W' \cdot W''$ for some $W \in A$ and $W'' \in E_1^* \times \cdots \times E_n^*$. Since δ is a morphism of monoids, $\delta^{-1}\{W'\} \cdot \delta^{-1}\{W''\} \subseteq \delta^{-1}\{W\}$, showing that $\delta^{-1} \circ Pref(A) \subseteq Pref \circ \delta^{-1}(A)$. Let $w' \in Pref \circ \delta^{-1}(A)$ then by definition of Prefix sets, $w = w'w''$ for some $w \in \delta^{-1}(A)$ and $w'' \in E^*$. Let $W' = \delta(w')$ and $W'' = \delta(w'')$. Since δ is a morphism of monoids, $\delta(w'w'') = W' \cdot W'' \in A$, hence $Pref \circ \delta^{-1}(A) \subseteq \delta^{-1} \circ Pref(A)$.   □

The following fact is also used.

Lemma 4. Let M be a monoid. If $A \in Rec(M)$ then $Pref(A) \in Rec(M)$.

Proof. Let $A \in Rec(M)$, let $\alpha : M \to N$ be a morphism from M into a finite monoid N, and let P be a subset of N such that $A = \alpha^{-1}(P)$. Then $Pref(A) = \alpha^{-1}(P')$ where $P' = \{n \in N \mid \exists m \in M : n.\alpha(m) \in P\}$.   □

2.3   A Reduction Yielding Negative Decision Results for HMSCs

We recall first a classical theorem claiming the undecidability of several questions about rational relations (we refer the reader to [12] or to [3] p.90 for the proof of this theorem that relies on the undecidability of Post's Correspondence Problem). We establish next a reduction of these questions to similar questions on HMSC languages, showing that the latter are undecidable.

Theorem 4 (Fischer-Rosenberg). *Let* X, Y *be alphabets with at least two letters. Given rational subsets* $A, B \subseteq X^* \times Y^*$, *it is undecidable to determine whether:*

  i) $A \cap B = \emptyset$;

  ii) $A \subseteq B$;

  iii) $A = B$;

  iv) $A = X^* \times Y^*$;

  v) $(X^* \times Y^*) \setminus A$ *is finite;*

  vi) A *is recognizable.*

Theorem 5. *Let* $E = \bigcup_{i=1}^n E_i$ *be an alphabet of events partitioned into subalphabets* $E_1, \ldots, E_n$ *such that* $n \geq 2$ *and each alphabet* E_i *defines at least three private events for process* i. *Given two HMSCs* H_1 *and* H_2 *over the alphabet* E, *and given a rational subset* $R \subseteq E^*$, *it is undecidable to determine whether*

$i)$ $\mathcal{L}(H_1) = \mathcal{L}(H_2)$;
$ii)$ $\mathcal{L}(H_1) \subseteq \mathcal{L}(H_2)$;
$iii)$ $R \subseteq \mathcal{L}(H_2)$;
$iv)$ $\mathcal{L}(H_1) \subseteq R$;
$v)$ $\mathcal{L}(H_1) \subseteq \delta^{-1}\delta R$;
$vi)$ $\mathcal{L}(H_1) = R$;
$vii)$ $\mathcal{L}(H_1)$ *is rational* .

In order to establish Theo. 5, we will show that each problem in the above list amounts to a reduction of some undecidable problem among problems (ii,iii,iv,vi) from Theo. 4 (a different proof of the undecidability of (vii) was sketched in [14]). So, let $A, B \in Rat(X^* \times Y^*)$ where X and Y are disjoint alphabets with size at least 2. We prepare the way to the reductions by constructing first HMSCs H_1 and H_2 such that $\mathcal{L}(H_1) = \delta^{-1} \circ Pref(A_\top)$ and $\mathcal{L}(H_2) = \delta^{-1} \circ Pref(B_\top)$ (where $A_\top$ and $B_\top$ are marked sets). The alphabet of these HMSCs is $E = E_1 \cup E_2$ with $E_1 = X \cup \{\top_1\}$ and $E_2 = Y \cup \{\top_2\}$, letting $\top_1$ and $\top_2$ be distinct markers (such that $\{\top_1, \top_2\} \cap (X \cup Y) = \emptyset$). All events in E_i are private events of process i (for $i \in [2]$). The construction of H_1 is described hereafter.

As $A \in Rat(X^* \times Y^*)$, the marked set $A_\top$ is a rational subset of $E_1^* \times E_2^*$, hence $A_\top = \delta R$ for some $R \in Rat(E^*)$. Let $\mathcal{A}$ be a finite automaton on the alphabet E such that $R = L(\mathcal{A})$ (the language generated by automaton $\mathcal{A}$) and the reachability set of each state of $\mathcal{A}$ includes a nonempty subset of final states. Let H_1 be the automaton on E that derives from $\mathcal{A}$ by making all states final so that $L(H_1) = Pref(R)$. The HMSC associated with A is the pair $(H_1, \mathcal{I})$ where the interpretation map $\mathcal{I} : E \to E_1^* \times E_2^*$ is defined as the restriction on E ($\subseteq E^*$) of the distribution map $\delta : E^* \to E_1^* \times E_2^*$ (hence $\mathcal{I}(x) = (x, \varepsilon)$ for $x \in X \cup \{\top_1\}$ and $\mathcal{I}(y) = (\varepsilon, y)$ for $y \in Y \cup \{\top_2\}$). Lemmas below show that the construction works as expected.

Lemma 5. $Pref \circ \delta L(H_1) = Pref(A_\top)$

Proof. $A_\top = \delta R \Rightarrow R \subseteq \delta^{-1} A_\top \Rightarrow Pref(R) \subseteq Pref \circ \delta^{-1}(A_\top) \Rightarrow Pref(R) \subseteq \delta^{-1} \circ Pref(A_\top)$ (lemma 3) $\Rightarrow L(H_1) \subseteq \delta^{-1} \circ Pref(A_\top) \Rightarrow \delta L(H_1) \subseteq \delta\delta^{-1} \circ Pref(A_\top) \Rightarrow \delta L(H_1) \subseteq Pref(A_\top)$ ($\delta\delta^{-1}$ is the identity) $\Rightarrow Pref \circ \delta(L(H_1)) \subseteq Pref(A_\top)$. Conversely, $A_\top = \delta R \subseteq \delta L(H_1) \Rightarrow Pref(A_\top) \subseteq Pref \circ \delta(L(H_1))$.

Lemma 6. $\mathcal{L}(H_1) = Pref \circ \delta^{-1}\delta(L(H_1))$.

Proof. As the interpretation map of H_1 has been defined as the restriction of δ on E, and seeing that every word in $\delta^{-1}\delta(L(H_1))$ is admissible because H_1 has an empty set of messages, this follows directly form the definition of HMSCs. □

Lemma 7. $\mathcal{L}(H_1) = \delta^{-1} \circ Pref(A_\top)$

Proof. $\mathcal{L}(H_1) = Pref \circ \delta^{-1}\delta(L(H_1))$ (lemma 6)
$= \delta^{-1} \circ Pref \circ \delta(L(H_1))$ (lemma 3) $= \delta^{-1} \circ Pref(A_\top)$ (lemma 5). □

Lemma 8. $\delta^{-1}\delta(\mathcal{L}(H_1)) = \mathcal{L}(H_1)$.

Proof. $\delta^{-1}\delta(\mathcal{L}(H_1)) = \delta^{-1}\delta \circ Pref \circ \delta^{-1}\delta(L(H_1))$ (lemma 7)
$= \delta^{-1}\delta\delta^{-1} \circ Pref \circ \delta(L(H_1))$ (lemma 3) $= \delta^{-1} \circ Pref \circ \delta(L(H_1))$ ($\delta\delta^{-1}$ is the
identity) $= Pref \circ \delta^{-1}\delta(L(H_1))$ (lemma 3) $= \mathcal{L}(H_1)$ (lemma 6)   □

Proof of theorem 5.   Given $A, B \in Rat(X^* \times Y^*)$ let H_1, H_2 be HMSCs such
that $\mathcal{L}(H_1) = \delta^{-1} \circ Pref(A_\top)$ and $\mathcal{L}(H_2) = \delta^{-1} \circ Pref(B_\top)$. We show that (i)
to (vii) are reductions of undecidable problems on A or B or A and B.
* *ad (i)* $A = B$ iff $Pref(A_\top) = Pref(B_\top)$ (lemma 1) iff
$\mathcal{L}(H_1) = \mathcal{L}(H_2)$ (lemma 7, seeing that $\delta\delta^{-1}$ is the identity).
The undecidability of $\mathcal{L}(H_1) = \mathcal{L}(H_2)$ follows from (iii) in Theo. 4.
* *ad (ii)*   this is an obvious consequence of (i).
* *ad (iii)* $A \subseteq B$ iff $Pref(A_\top) \subseteq Pref(B_\top)$ (lemma 1) iff
$\mathcal{L}(H_1) \subseteq \mathcal{L}(H_2)$ (lemma 7, seeing that $\delta\delta^{-1}$ is the identity).
We claim that $\mathcal{L}(H_1) \subseteq \mathcal{L}(H_2)$ iff $L(H_1) \subseteq \mathcal{L}(H_2)$.
The direct implication follows from
$L(H_1) \subseteq \delta^{-1}\delta L(H_1) \subseteq Pref \circ \delta^{-1}\delta L(H_1) = \mathcal{L}(H_1)$ (lemma 6).
For the reverse implication, note that $\mathcal{L}(H_2) = Pref \circ \delta^{-1}\delta(\mathcal{L}(H_2))$
(as $\mathcal{L}(H_2) = Pref(\mathcal{L}(H_2))$ and by lemma 8 $\mathcal{L}(H_2) = \delta^{-1}\delta\mathcal{L}(H_2)$)
and $\mathcal{L}(H_1) = Pref \circ \delta^{-1}\delta(L(H_1))$ (lemma 6),
hence $L(H_1) \subseteq \mathcal{L}(H_2) \Rightarrow \mathcal{L}(H_1) \subseteq \mathcal{L}(H_2)$.
The undecidability of $R \subseteq \mathcal{L}(H_2)$ follows from (ii) in Theo. 4 with $R = L(H_1)$.
* *ad (iv)* $A \cap B \neq \emptyset$ iff $A_\top \cap B_\top \neq \emptyset$ iff $Pref(A_\top) \cap B_\top \neq \emptyset$ iff
$Pref \circ \delta(\mathcal{L}(H_1)) \cap B_\top \neq \emptyset$ (lemma 7, seeing that $\delta\delta^{-1}$ is the identity).
Let $S \in Rat(E^*)$ such that $B_\top = \delta S$.
We claim that $Pref \circ \delta(\mathcal{L}(H_1)) \cap B_\top \neq \emptyset$ iff $\mathcal{L}(H_1) \cap S \neq \emptyset$.
For the direct implication, we observe:
$Pref \circ \delta(\mathcal{L}(H_1)) \cap B_\top \neq \emptyset \Rightarrow S \cap \delta^{-1} \circ Pref \circ \delta(\mathcal{L}(H_1)) \neq \emptyset \Rightarrow$
$S \cap Pref \circ \delta^{-1}\delta(\mathcal{L}(H_1)) \neq \emptyset$ (lemma 3) $\Rightarrow S \cap Pref(\mathcal{L}(H_1)) \neq \emptyset$ (lemma 8)
$\Rightarrow S \cap \mathcal{L}(H_1) \neq \emptyset$ (since $\mathcal{L}(H_1) = Pref(\mathcal{L}(H_1))$.
For the reverse implication, we note that $\mathcal{L}(H_1) = Pref(\mathcal{L}(H_1))$
and that $\delta \circ Pref(\mathcal{L}(H_1)) \subseteq Pref \circ \delta(\mathcal{L}(H_1))$ because δ is a morphism of monoids,
hence $\mathcal{L}(H_1) \cap S \neq \emptyset \Rightarrow \delta(\mathcal{L}(H_1)) \cap B_\top \neq \emptyset \Rightarrow Pref \circ \delta(\mathcal{L}(H_1)) \cap B_\top \neq \emptyset$.
Altogether $A \cap B = \emptyset$ iff $\mathcal{L}(H_1) \cap S = \emptyset$ iff $\mathcal{L}(H_1) \subseteq R$ where $R = E^* \setminus S$.
The undecidability of $\mathcal{L}(H_1) \subseteq R$ follows from (i) in Theo. 4.
* *ad (v)* $A \subseteq B$ iff $Pref(A_\top) \subseteq Pref(B_\top)$ (lemma 1) iff
$\mathcal{L}(H_1) \subseteq \delta^{-1} \circ Pref(B_\top)$ (lemma 7).
As $Pref(B_\top) \in Rat(E_1^* \times E_2^*)$, $Pref(B_\top) = \delta R$ for some $R \in Rat(E^*)$.
Thus $A \subseteq B$ iff $\mathcal{L}(H_1) \subseteq \delta^{-1}\delta R$ and the undecidability of $\mathcal{L}(H_1) \subseteq \delta^{-1}\delta R$
follows from (ii) in Theo. 4.
* *ad (vi)* $A = X^* \times Y^*$ iff $Pref(A_\top) = Pref(X^*\top_1 \times Y^*\top_2)$
iff $\delta^{-1} \circ Pref(A_\top) = R = \mathcal{L}(H_1)$ (lemma 7) where we let
$R = Pref((X \cup Y)^* \top_1 (X \cup Y)^* \top_2 \cup (X \cup Y)^* \top_2 (X \cup Y)^* \top_1)$.
The undecidability of $\mathcal{L}(H_1) = R$ follows from (iv) in Theo. 4.
* *ad (vii)*   We show that $A \in Rec(X^* \times Y^*)$ if and only if $\mathcal{L}(H_1) \in Rat(E^*)$.
The direct implication may be established as follows:
$A \in Rec(X^* \times Y^*) \Rightarrow A \in Rec(E_1^* \times E_2^*) \Rightarrow A_\top \in Rec(E_1^* \times E_2^*)$

(as the recognizable sets are closed under composition ([3], p.61) and seeing that $(T_1, T_2) \in Rec(E_1^* \times E_2^*))$

$\Rightarrow Pref(A_T) \in Rec(E_1^* \times E_2^*)$ (lemma 4) $\Rightarrow \delta^{-1}(Pref(A_T) \in Rec(E^*)$

(as the recognizable sets are closed under inverse morphisms ([3], p.53) and $\delta : E^* \to E_1^* \times E_2^*$ is a monoid morphism)

$\Rightarrow \mathcal{L}(H_1) \in Rec(E^*)$ (lemma 7) $\Rightarrow \mathcal{L}(H_1) \in Rat(E^*)$ (Theo 2).

The reverse implication may be established as follows:

$\mathcal{L}(H_1) \in Rat(E^*) \Rightarrow \mathcal{L}(H_1) \in Rec(E^*)$ (Theo 1)

$\Rightarrow Pref(\mathcal{L}(H_1)) \in Rec(E^*)$ (lemma 4)

$\Rightarrow Pref \circ \delta^{-1} \circ Pref(A_T) \in Rec(E^*)$ (lemma 7)

$\Rightarrow \delta^{-1} \circ Pref(A_T) \in Rec(E^*)$ (lemma 3)

$\Rightarrow Pref(A_T) \in Rec(E_1^* \times E_2^*)$

(by direct application of a proposition stated in [8] (p.33) and [9] (p.172) for morphisms from a free monoid E^* onto an arbitrary monoid, applied here to the surjective morphism $\delta : E^* \to E_1^* \times E_2^*$)

$\Rightarrow Pref(A_T) \cap (E_1^* \times E_2^*) \cdot (T_1, T_2) \in Rec(E_1^* \times E_2^*)$

(the recognizable sets are closed under intersection)

$\Rightarrow A_T \in Rec(E_1^* \times E_2^*)$ (as $A_T = Pref(A_T) \cap (E_1^* \times E_2^*) \cdot (T_1, T_2)$) .

Thus there exists a finite monoid N, a morphism α from $(E_1^* \times E_2^*)$ into N, and a subset P of N such that $A_T = \alpha^{-1}(P)$. Let α' be the restriction of α on $(X^* \times Y^*)$ and let $P' = \{s \in N \mid s.\alpha(T_1, T_2) \in P\}$ then clearly $A = \alpha'^{-1}(P')$, and therefore $A \in Rec(X^* \times Y^*)$.

We have thus shown that $A \in Rec(X^* \times Y^*)$ iff $\mathcal{L}(H_1) \in Rat(E^*)$ and the undecidability of $\mathcal{L}(H_1) \in Rat(E^*)$ follows from (vi) in Theo. 4. □

We will now show that the undecidability of relations (i) to (v) in Theo. 5 extends to purely communicating HMSCs (i.e. such that all events are emissions or receptions). This may be done by reducing undecidable problems on non communicating HMSCs to decision problems on purely communicating HMSCs. Given (non communicating) HMSCs $H_1 = (H_1, \mathcal{I})$ and $H_2 = (H_2, \mathcal{I})$ on the set of events $E = E_1 \cup E_2$ with an interpretation map $\mathcal{I} : E \to E_1^* \times E_2^*$ such that $\mathcal{I}(e) = \delta(e)$ for all $e \in E$, define (communicating) HMSCs $H_1' = (H_1, \mathcal{I}')$ and $H_2' = (H_2, \mathcal{I}')$ on the same automata H_1 and H_2 by choosing a new interpretation map $\mathcal{I}'$ such that $\mathcal{I}'(e) = (!e, \varepsilon, ?e, \varepsilon)$ for $e \in E_1$ and $\mathcal{I}'(e) = (\varepsilon, !e, \varepsilon, ?e)$ for $e \in E_2$. Thus the $\mathcal{I}'(e)$ are bMSCs on the set of events $E' = R \cup S$ where $S = \{!e \mid e \in E\}$ and $R = \{?e \mid e \in E\}$. It is easily seen that for $i \in \{1, 2\}$, $\mathcal{L}(H_i') = \cup \{!(u) \sqcup\!\sqcup ?(v) \mid u \in \mathcal{L}(H_i) \ \& \ v \in pref(u)\}$ where $! : E^* \to S^*$ and $? : E^* \to R^*$ are the respective morphisms such that $!(e) = !e$ and $?(e) = ?e$, while $\sqcup\!\sqcup$ is the shuffle operator. As a consequence:

$\mathcal{L}(H_1) \subseteq \mathcal{L}(H_2)$ iff $\mathcal{L}(H_1') \subseteq \mathcal{L}(H_2')$,

$A \subseteq \mathcal{L}(H_2)$ iff $!(A) \subseteq \mathcal{L}(H_2')$ for $A \in Rat(E^*)$,

$\mathcal{L}(H_1) \subseteq A$ iff $\mathcal{L}(H_1') \subseteq !(A) \sqcup\!\sqcup R^*$ for $A \in Rat(E^*)$,

$\mathcal{L}(H_1) \subseteq \delta^{-1}\delta A$ iff $\mathcal{L}(H_1') \subseteq \delta^{-1}\delta(!(A) \sqcup\!\sqcup R^*)$ for $A \in Rat(E^*)$,

and the undecidability of relations (i) to (v) for purely communicating HMSCs follows from Theo. 5 (seeing that $A \sqcup\!\sqcup R^* \in Rat(E'^*)$ for $A \in Rat(S^*)$).

2.4   Should HMSCs Be Considered as Specifications?

There are several ways to consider HMSCs as specifications of distributed systems. By interpreting HMSCs as abstract generators for languages $\mathcal{L}(H)$, we admittedly restrict the scope of our investigations in this respect, but the generated languages may be given at least three different meanings: $\mathcal{L}(H)$ may be considered as a subset of the behaviour of the specified system (specifications of service), as an exact definition of the behaviour of the specified system (complete specifications), or as a superset of the behaviour of the specified system (specifications of safety). Needless to say, all interpretations may co-exist in a logical framework for distributed system specification based on HMSCs. Sharing the common opinion that any practical specification framework should enable some decision of conformity of systems with specifications, let us examine these various interpretations under the light shed by Theo. 5.

By (ii) in Theo. 5 one cannot check HMSCs considered as representations of systems against HMSCs expressing safety conditions or service requirements. By (iii) and (iv) in Theo. 5, one cannot check bounded systems against HMSCs expressing safety conditions or service requirements; and one cannot check HMSCs considered as representations of systems against regular safety conditions or regular service requirements. As Theo. 5 is not conclusive for star-free regular languages, this leaves open the problem of checking HMSCs against linear temporal logic formulas (but we bet the situation is not better). Finally, by (vii) in Theo. 5 one cannot decide whether a given HMSC generates a rational language (in which case most difficulties vanish since we are brought back to the realm of effective boolean algebras).

The above observations leave two ways out. One is to impose constraints on HMSCs strong enough to guarantee that languages of HMSCs are kept within rational languages [1] [5] [14]. The price to pay is to give up with unbounded systems, nicely modelled with HMSCs and largely present as partial specifications of telecommunication systems. The alternative way, yet unexplored, is to consider languages of HMSCs as specifications of minimal service for a given class of (potentially) unbounded systems. The price to pay is to accept that the realized behaviours may be strictly *larger* than the specified behaviours. The difference between realized behaviours and specified behaviours is an inverse measure for the quality of realizations.

An ideal class of unbounded systems for the realization of HMSC specifications should come equipped with an effective procedure able to synthesize optimal realizations of all HMSC specifications; it should also allow for model-checking systems against safety assertions in order to verify that the added part of the realized behaviours makes no problem. These criteria are demanding but they are reasonable. Next section shows that they are met by Petri nets and more importantly by *distributable* Petri nets, a variety of Petri nets that translate easily to clusters of automata communicating by asynchronous message passing. We do *not* claim that HMSC specifications are implemented at best via Petri net synthesis. Petri nets are used only as an illustration aiming to show that general HMSCs may really play a central role in the design of distributed systems. The search for other (more) adequate classes of realizations for HMSC specifications is an open direction for further work.

3   Petri Net Realization of HMSC Languages

It is shown in this section that HMSC languages $\mathcal{L}(H)$ may be mapped to closures $\overline{\mathcal{L}}(H)$ in the class $\mathbf{G_0}^{\mathbf{f}}$ of (free) Petri net languages [23], such that $\overline{\mathcal{L}}(H) = \mathcal{L}(N)$ for some net N effectively computed from H, thus providing an optimal realization of H. In order to get distributed realizations of HMSCs, we will specialize the construction of closures to *distributable* Petri nets, that may be compiled to distributed implementations on an asynchronous network. Petri nets may be model-checked against safety assertions, hence they are an adequate class of realizations for HMSC specifications, according to the criteria stated in section 2. Two results will complete the picture: on the negative side, the problem whether a HMSC language may be realized exactly by some Petri net is undecidable; on the positive side, Petri net realizations of HMSCs may be model-checked against (possibly non regular) safety assertions represented as Petri nets.

It is not the goal of the paper to give a presentation on the topic of Petri net synthesis, hence we shall only present here the necessary results (for more on the topic, the reader may consult [2] [4] [6] [7]). The corner-stone of the methods developed so far for deriving Petri nets from formal languages is the semilinearity of their commutative images. The main contribution of the section is to show that commutative images of HMSC languages are precisely semilinear.

The section is organized as follows. The semilinearity of commutative images of HMSC languages is established in 3.1; using this fact, Petri net closures of HMSC languages are constructed in 3.2; distributable Petri nets are considered in 3.3; the undecidability of the Petri net synthesis problem for HMSC languages is proved in 3.4; the issue of model-checking realizations of HMSCs is finally addressed in 3.5.

3.1   Commutative Images of HMSC Languages Are Semilinear

First, let us recall the definitions of linear subsets and semilinear subsets of a monoid.

Definition 9. *Let M be a monoid. A subset of M is* linear *if it may be expressed as $m \cdot P^*$ where $m \in M$ and P is a finite subset of M. A semilinear subset of M is a finite union of linear subsets of M.*

Let $k = |E|$ where E is the alphabet of events fixed for HMSCs. The monoid we shall consider here is $\mathbb{N}^k$ (with the all zero k-vector as the neutral element and the addition of k-vectors as the composition operation). Words $w \in E^*$ may be sent into $\mathbb{N}^k$ by counting the occurences of each letter $e_i \in E$, resulting in an k-vector $\psi(w) = (|w|_{e_1}, \ldots, |w|_{e_k})$ that represents the commutative image of w; the mapping $\psi : E^* \to \mathbb{N}^k$, known as Parikh mapping, is actually a monoid morphism. We aim at showing that for any HMSC H with set of events E, the Parikh image $\psi\mathcal{L}(H)$ of the language of H is a semilinear subset of $\mathbb{N}^k$. To that effect, we shall use the crucial fact that semilinear subsets and rational subsets coincide in any commutative monoid [10] (hence in particular in $\mathbb{N}^k$) and a series of technical lemmas about scenarios. In the sequel, notations are like those in section 1.1, except that $u \leq w$ and $U \leq W$ are used as abbreviations for $\exists v \; w = u \cdot v$ and $\exists V \; W = U \cdot V$ respectively in the (unit divisor free) monoids E^* and $E_1^* \times \cdots \times E_n^*$.

Lemma 9. *Let $U \leq W$ where U and W are scenarios. For any admissible word u such that $U = \delta(u)$ there exists an admissible word w such that $u \leq w$ and $W = \delta(w)$.*

Proof. Let $W = U \cdot V$ (V is not necessarily admissible). By induction on the size of V, with the trivial case $W = U$ as a basis, it suffices to establish: $W \neq U \Rightarrow \exists e \in E$ such that $\delta(e) \leq V$ and ue is admissible. We proceed with a proof by contradiction. Suppose $\forall e \in E \;\; \delta(e) \leq V \Rightarrow ue$ is not admissible. As u is admissible $\delta(e) \leq V$ entails $e = ?m$ for some m such that $?m$ and $!m$ occur an equal number of times in u. Let $W = (w_1, \ldots, w_n)$, $U = (u_1, \ldots, u_n)$ and $I = \{i \in [n] \mid w_i \neq u_i\}$. Thus $I \neq \emptyset$ and for each $i \in I$, $w_i = u_i \cdot ?m_i \cdot u'_i$ where $?m_i$ and $!m_i$ occur an equal number of times in u. Fix some admissible word w such that $W = \delta(w)$ (there must exist such words since W is admissible). Let $w' \leq w$ be the least prefix of w such that $|u|_{?m_i} < |w'|_{?m_i}$ for some $i \in I$. If we set $\delta(w') = (w'_1, \ldots, w'_n)$ then necessarily $w'_i = u_i \cdot ?m_i$ for some $i \in I$, and $w'_j \leq u_j$ for all $j \neq i$. Now let $m = m_i$ (hence $\phi(?m) = i$) and $\phi(!m) = k$. As w' is admissible, $|w'|_{?m} \leq |w'|_{!m}$. Seeing that $|w'|_{!m} = |w'_k|_{!m} \leq |u_k|_{!m} = |u|_{!m}$ and $|w'|_{?m} = |w'_i|_{?m} = 1 + |u_i|_{?m} = 1 + |u|_{?m}$ it follows that $|u|_{!m} \geq 1 + |u|_{?m}$, contradicting $m = m_i$ or the fact that $!m_i$ and $?m_i$ occur an equal number of times in u. $\square$

Lemma 10. *Let $H = (H, \mathcal{I})$ be a HMSC on E whose underlying automaton has set of symbols B (hence $\mathcal{I}$ maps symbols $b \in B$ to bMSCs on E). A word $u \in E^*$ belongs to the language of the HMSC ($u \in \mathcal{L}(H)$) if and only if it is admissible and there exists some word $\beta \in B^*$ accepted by the underlying automaton ($\beta \in L(H)$) such that $\delta(u) \leq \mathcal{I}(\beta)$.*

Proof. Suppose $u \in \mathcal{L}(H)$, then by definition, $u \leq w$ for some admissible word w such that $\delta(w) = \mathcal{I}(\beta)$ for some $\beta \in L(H)$, and prefixes of admissible words are admissible. Conversely, let u be an admissible word and suppose that $\delta(u) \leq \mathcal{I}(\beta)$ for some $\beta \in L(H)$. It then follows directly from lemma 9 that $u \in \mathcal{L}(H)$. $\square$

Lemma 11. *Let $W = W_1 \cdot \ldots \cdot W_m$, where for each $i \in [m]$, $W_i = (w_{i_1}, \ldots, w_{i_n})$ is a bMSC (thus W is a bMSC). A vector $U \in E_1^* \times \cdots \times E_n^*$ is an admissible prefix of W if and only if it may decomposed as $U = W'_1 \cdot \ldots \cdot W'_m$ such that: for all $i \in [m]$, $W'_i = (w'_{i_1}, \ldots, w'_{i_n})$ is an admissible prefix of W_i and for all $p \in [n]$, $w'_{i_p} \neq w_{i_p} \Rightarrow w'_{j_p} = \varepsilon$ for all $j > i$.*

Proof. The delicate part of the proof is the direct implication. The reverse relation may be established as follows. Let $U = W'_1 \cdot \ldots \cdot W'_m$ as above, hence $U \leq W$. For each $i \in [m]$ let w'_i be an admissible word such that $W'_i = \delta(w'_i)$ (such words must exist by definition) and let $u = w'_1 \cdot \ldots w'_m$. Then $U = \delta(u)$ and u is an admissible word, and U is therefore an admissible prefix of W. Let us show now the direct implication. Every prefix U of $W = W_1 \cdot \ldots \cdot W_m$ has a unique decomposition $U = W'_1 \cdot \ldots \cdot W'_m$ satisfying all requirements of the lemma but the admissibility of the W'_i. We shall prove by induction on the size of U, with the trivial case $U = \delta(\varepsilon)$ as a basis, that this requirement is met when U is an admissible prefix of W. Hence let $u = ve$ (with $e \in E$) be an admissible word such that $U = \delta(u)$, and assume by induction that $\delta(v) = W''_1 \cdot \ldots \cdot W''_m$ and the W''_i satisfy all conditions expressed in the lemma (for W'_i). Since $\delta(u) = \delta(v) \cdot \delta(e)$ and the considered decomposition of $\delta(v)$ is unique, there must exist $i \in [m]$ such that $W'_i = W''_i \cdot \delta(e)$ and $W'_j = W''_j$ for $j \neq i$ (hence W'_j is admissible for $j \neq i$). It remains to show that W'_i is admissible. For the sake of contradiction, suppose the opposite. Let $W''_i = (w''_{i_1}, \ldots, w''_{i_n})$, and let $w''_i \in E^*$ be an admissible word such that $W''_i = \delta(w''_i)$. From our supposition $w''_i e$ is not admissible. As w''_i is admissible, the only possibility is that $e = ?m$ for some m such that $!m$ and $?m$ occur an equal number of times in w''_i. Hence, assuming $\phi(?m) = p$ and $\phi(!m) = q$, we have: $|w'_{i_p}|_{?m} = 1 + |w''_{i_p}|_{?m} = 1 + |w''_{i_q}|_{!m} = 1 + |w'_{i_q}|_{!m}$. Now $W'_i \leq W_i \Rightarrow w'_{i_p} \leq w_{i_p} \Rightarrow |w'_{i_p}|_{?m} \leq |w_{i_p}|_{?m}$, and $|w_{i_p}|_{?m} = |w_{i_q}|_{!m}$ since W_i is a bMSC (closed scenario). Altogether we obtain the inequality $1 + |w'_{i_q}|_{!m} \leq |w_{i_q}|_{!m}$. Hence $w'_{i_q} \neq w_{i_q}$ and therefore $w'_{j_q} = \varepsilon$ for $j > i$. Moreover, $w'_{i_p} \neq \varepsilon \Rightarrow w'_{j_p} = w_{j_p}$ for $j < i$. Recalling that $|w_{j_p}|_{?m} = |w_{j_q}|_{!m}$ for all j and summing up one obtains the inequality $\sum_k |w'_{k_q}|_{!m} < \sum_{k \leq i} |w'_{k_p}|_{?m}$. It follows from this inequality that $|u|_{!m} < |u|_{?m}$ for any word u such that $U = \delta(u)$, hence U is not an admissible prefix of W, which contradicts the assumption. □

One can now easily derive from any HMSC H on E a finite automaton $\overline{H}$ on $E_1^* \times \cdots \times E_n^*$ whose generated language of vectors is the set of admissible prefixes of vectors in $\overrightarrow{\mathcal{L}}(H)$. The construction is sketched below.

Let $H = (A, \mathcal{I})$ where the automaton A has set of symbols B and $\mathcal{I}$ maps symbols $b \in B$ to bMSCs on E. Let $A = (S, B, T, s_0)$ where S is the set of states, $s_0 \in S$ is the initial state, and $T \subseteq S \times B \times S$ is the set of transitions. Then $\overline{H} = (\overline{S}, \overline{B}, \overline{T}, \overline{s_0})$ where $\overline{S} = S \times \mathcal{P}[n]$ (the second component represents a collection of dead agents), $\overline{B} \subseteq E_1^* \times \cdots \times E_n^*$ is the set of admissible prefixes of the bMSCs $\mathcal{I}(b)$ for b ranging over B, $\overline{s_0} = (s_0, \emptyset)$, all states are final, and $\overline{T}$

is the least set of transitions such that, for all $J, J' \subseteq [n]$ and $V \in \overline{B}$:
if $s \xrightarrow{b} s'$ in A then $(s', J) \xrightarrow{V} (s, J')$ in $\overline{H}$ whenever
V is an admissible prefix of $\mathcal{I}(b)$ and the following hold,
letting $V = (v_1, \ldots, v_n)$ and $\mathcal{I}(b) = (w_1, \ldots, w_n)$:
* $v_j = \varepsilon$ for all $j \in J$,
* $J \subseteq J'$,
* $v_j \neq w_j \Rightarrow j \in J'$.
The correctness of the construction follows directly from lemma 11.

The automaton $\overline{H}$ can easily be transformed into an automaton $\psi(\overline{H})$ on $\mathbb{N}^k$, whose set of accepted vectors is the set of Parikh images of the words in $\mathcal{L}(H)$. The transformation consists in replacing labels $V \in \overline{B}$ by corresponding vectors $\psi(V) \in \mathbb{N}^k$, where the Parikh mapping $\psi : E^* \to \mathbb{N}^k$ is extended to $E_1^* \times \cdots \times E_n^*$ by setting $\psi(v_1, \ldots, v_n) = \psi(v_1) + \ldots + \psi(v_n)$. The correctness of the construction follows directly from lemmas 9 and 10.

Recalling that rational subsets and semilinear subsets coincide in $\mathbb{N}^k$ (where this correspondence is effective in both directions), we have obtained a complete proof of the following theorem.

Theorem 6. *Let H be a HMSC, then $\psi\mathcal{L}(H)$ is effectively semilinear.*

A little more is needed if we want to compute closures of HMSC languages with respect to general Petri nets. We need for each $e \in E$ a semilinear expression of the Parikh image of the *e-terminating* sublanguage $\mathcal{L}(H) \cap E^*e$. A semilinear expression of $\psi(\mathcal{L}(H) \cap E^*e)$ may be obtained as shown for $\psi\mathcal{L}(H)$ by specializing the basic automaton $\overline{H}$ according to e. For $e \in E$, let $\overline{H}_e$ be the automaton that derives from H by carrying the following list of modifications:
* each state (s, J) is replaced with two states $(s, J, 0)$ and $(s, J, 1)$,
* $(s_0, \emptyset, 0)$ is the initial state,
* the states $(s, J, 1)$ are the final states,
* $(s, J) \xrightarrow{V} (s', J')$ splits to $(s, J, 0) \xrightarrow{V} (s', J', 0)$ and $(s, J, 1) \xrightarrow{V} (s', J', 1)$,
* $(s, J, 0) \xrightarrow{V} (s', J', 1)$ is added for each transition $(s, J) \xrightarrow{V} (s', J')$ such that $V = \delta(ue)$ for some admissible word ue with $\phi(e) \in J'$.

Verifying that the set of vectors accepted by $\psi(\overline{H}_e)$ is equal to the Parikh image of $\mathcal{L}(H) \cap E^*e$ is left to the reader (note: use the fact that bMSCs are closed scenarios).

3.2   Petri Net Closures of HMSC Languages

This part recalls the definition of Petri nets, brings in a general theorem that connects Parikh semilinear languages with Petri nets, and applies this theorem to HMSC languages in order to define and compute their Petri net closures.

Definition 10. *A Petri net (system) is a quadruple $N = (P, E, F, M_0)$ where: P and E are finite disjoint sets of places and events, $F : (P \times E) \cup (E \times P) \to \mathbb{N}$,* and $M_0 : P \to \mathbb{N}$. Maps $M : P \to \mathbb{N}$ are called markings. M_0 is the initial marking. The net is pure if for all e and p, $F(p, e) = 0 \vee F(e, p) = 0$. An event e may be fired at M if $(\forall p \in P)$ $F(p, e) \leq M(p)$. The firing of e results in a transition $M [e > M'$ such that $(\forall p \in P)$ $M'(P) = M(p) - F(p, e) + F(e, p)$. A firing sequence of N is a (nonempty) sequence $M_0 [e_1 > M_1 \ldots [e_n > M_n$. The $\mathbf{G_0}$ language of the net is the set of labels $e_1 \ldots e_n$ of the firing sequences, plus the empty word (ε). A marking M is reachable if $M = M_0$ or $M = M_n$ for some firing sequence. N is bounded if the set of reachable markings is finite.

In the sequel, $\mathcal{L}(N)$ denotes the $\mathbf{G_0}$ language of the net N. In the basic version of nets defined above, events do not bear extra labels; for this reason, languages $\mathcal{L}(N)$ are called free Petri net languages; thus $\mathcal{L}(N) \in \mathbf{G_0}^{\mathbf{f}}$ (where $\mathbf{G_0}$ means that all prefixes are included and $\mathbf{f}$ means that the labelling is free). In the sequel, we say that a language $\mathcal{L} \subseteq E^*$ is Parikh semilinear if its Parikh image $\psi\mathcal{L}$ is a semilinear set.

Theorem 7. If a language $\mathcal{L} \subseteq E^*$ is Parikh semilinear, one can effectively compute from $\psi\mathcal{L}$ a pure Petri net N such that $\mathcal{L} \subseteq \mathcal{L}(N)$ and $\mathcal{L} \subseteq \mathcal{L}(N') \Rightarrow \mathcal{L}(N) \subseteq \mathcal{L}(N')$ for every pure Petri net N'. This assertion remains true if one replaces pure Petri nets with pure and bounded Petri nets.
If all the e-terminating sublanguages of a language $\mathcal{L} \subseteq E^*$ are Parikh semilinear, one can effectively compute from the respective sets $\psi(\mathcal{L} \cap E^*e)$ a Petri net N such that $\mathcal{L} \subseteq \mathcal{L}(N)$ and $\mathcal{L} \subseteq \mathcal{L}(N') \Rightarrow \mathcal{L}(N) \subseteq \mathcal{L}(N')$ for every Petri net N'. This assertion remains true if one replaces Petri nets with bounded Petri nets.

The reader may find a brief presentation of the construction of N in [7], with enough indications for a complete proof of the above theorem (that extends Prop. 3.9 of [6]). If we now apply this theorem to HMSC languages, we get immediately the following.

Theorem 8. Let H be a HMSC on E. One can effectively compute from H a general (resp. pure resp. bounded resp. pure and bounded) Petri net N_H with set of events E such that $\mathcal{L}(N_H)$ is the least language of a general (resp. bounded resp. pure resp. pure and bounded) Petri net N satisfying $\mathcal{L}(H) \subseteq \mathcal{L}(N)$.

Proof. By lemma 6, the conditions of application of Theo. 7 are valid.   □

The net N_H is not totally determined by the theory (several nets may have an identical language even though they have no redundant places), but also by the algorithm chosen for the construction. On the contrary, the language of the net N_H does not depend on the chosen algorithm. In the sequel, the language $\mathcal{L}(N_H)$ is denoted $\overline{\mathcal{L}}(H)$ and is called the Petri net closure of the HMSC language $\mathcal{L}(H)$. Every net N such that $\mathcal{L}(N) = \overline{\mathcal{L}}(H)$ is called a Petri net realization of the HMSC H or more properly of the HMSC language $\mathcal{L}(H)$. It is important to observe that all the words in $\overline{\mathcal{L}}(H)$ are admissible (this property may be enforced on the behaviours of a net by supplying for each message m one place p_m such that $F(!m, p_m)$ and $F(p_m, ?m)$). On the contrary, semilinearity is generally not preserved by the closure operation.

3.3   An Undecidability Result

At this stage, a question naturally arises: if one sticks to the strict requirement of equality of the specified and realized languages, does the subset of HMSCs which may be realized in the strict sense using Petri nets form a recursive subset? The answer is negative, and we produce hereafter evidence for this. In the meantime, let us recall an important result of Petri net theory due to Elisabeth Pelz [22].

Definition 11. *A labeled Petri net is a Petri net N equipped with a labeling map $\ell : E \to (A \cup \{\varepsilon\})$, where ε is the empty word. The labeled net is deterministic if at each reachable marking at most one event can be fired for each label. The labeled net is ε-free if $\ell(e) \neq \varepsilon$ for all $e \in E$. The language of the labeled net (N, ℓ) is the set of all images under ℓ of firing sequences from the initial marking. A Petri net generator is a labeled Petri net equipped with a finite subset of final markings (or partial markings) $\mathcal{F}$. The language of the generator is the set of all images under ℓ of firing sequences from the initial marking to final markings (or partial markings).*

Theorem 9 (Pelz). *The complement of the language of a deterministic ε-free labeled net N is the language of a Petri net generator $\mathcal{C}N$ constructible from N.*

Corollary 1. *Let N and N' be Petri net generators. If N' is deterministic and ε-free, one can decide on the inclusion $\mathcal{L}(N) \subseteq \mathcal{L}(N')$.*

Proof. $\mathcal{L}(N) \subseteq \mathcal{L}(N')$ if and only if the language of N'' is empty, where N'' is the Petri net generator defined as the synchronized product of N and $\mathcal{C}N'$, with events defined as pairs of events with common label, and with final (partial) markings defined as inverse projections of the final (partial) markings of $\mathcal{C}N'$. Deciding on the emptyness of $\mathcal{L}(N')$ reduces to the (partial) reachability problem for Petri nets, which is decidable [19].   □

The basic Petri nets introduced in Def. 10 are a particular case of deterministic ε-free Petri net generators: their labelling map $\ell : E \to (E \cup \{\varepsilon\})$ acts as the identity on E, and their set of final partial markings $\mathcal{F}$ has the totally undefined marking as its unique element. We proceed with the proof of the announced result.

Theorem 10. *Relation $\overline{\mathcal{L}}(H) = \mathcal{L}(H)$ is undecidable (from H).*

Proof. By lemma 7, from any rational subset $A \in Rat(X^* \times Y^*)$, one can construct a HMSC H on $E = E_1 \cup E_2$ (with $E_1 = X \cup \{\top_1\}$, $E_2 = Y \cup \{\top_2\}$, $\top_1 \neq \top_2$, and $(X \cup Y) \cap \{\top_1, \top_2\} = \emptyset$) such that $\mathcal{L}(H) = \delta^{-1} \circ Pref(A_\top)$ (with $\phi(e) = i$ for $e \in E_i$). It should be clear from this relation that $\mathcal{L}(H) \subseteq Pref(X^*\top_1) \sqcup\!\sqcup Pref(Y^*\top_2)$, where $\sqcup\!\sqcup$ is the shuffle operator, and that equality is met if and only if $A = X^* \times Y^*$. Since $Pref(X^*\top_1)$ and $Pref(Y^*\top_2)$ are languages of (one-place) nets N_1 and N_2 with disjoint sets of events, their shuffle is the language of the net N obtained by putting N_1 and N_2 side by side. Hence $\mathcal{L}(H) \subseteq \mathcal{L}(N)$, and $\mathcal{L}(H) = \mathcal{L}(N)$ if and only if $A = X^* \times Y^*$.

By Theo. 8, one can construct from H another Petri net N_H such that $\mathcal{L}(N_H) = \overline{\mathcal{L}}(H)$. As $\mathcal{L}(H) \subseteq \mathcal{L}(N)$, $\mathcal{L}(N_H) = \overline{\mathcal{L}}(H) \subseteq \mathcal{L}(N)$ by definition of Petri net closures of HMSC languages.

Suppose for contradiction that one can decide on the relation $\mathcal{L}(H) = \overline{\mathcal{L}}(H)$. We derive a decision procedure for the relation $A = X^* \times Y^*$, thus contradicting (iv) in Theo. 4. The procedure is as follows. If $\mathcal{L}(H) = \overline{\mathcal{L}}(H)$ has a negative answer (thus $\mathcal{L}(H) \subset \overline{\mathcal{L}}(H)$) then $\mathcal{L}(H) \subset \mathcal{L}(N)$ (since $\overline{\mathcal{L}}(H) \subseteq \mathcal{L}(N)$) and therefore $A \neq X^* \times Y^*$ (as $\mathcal{L}(H) = \mathcal{L}(N)$ iff $A = X^* \times Y^*$). If $\mathcal{L}(H) = \overline{\mathcal{L}}(H)$ has a positive answer (thus $\mathcal{L}(H) = \mathcal{L}(N_H)$) then $A = X^* \times Y^*$ if and only if $\mathcal{L}(N) \subseteq \mathcal{L}(N_H)$ (as $A = X^* \times Y^*$ iff $\mathcal{L}(H) = \mathcal{L}(N)$ iff $\mathcal{L}(N_H) = \mathcal{L}(N)$, and $\mathcal{L}(N_H) = \overline{\mathcal{L}}(H) \subseteq \mathcal{L}(N)$). By Theo. 9 and corollary 1, the last relation can be decided. Hence we have obtained a decision of the relation $A = X^* \times Y^*$.   □

3.4   Distributed Net Realizations of HMSCs

Of special interest for the realization of HMSCs are the *distributable* Petri nets introduced in [4]. Let us recall the definition.

Definition 12. *A* distributable *Petri net system with set of locations* $[n]$ *is a quintuple* $\mathcal{N} = (P, E, F, M_0, \phi)$ *where* (P, E, F, M_0) *is a Petri net system and* $\phi : (P \cup E) \to [n]$ *is a placement map such that* $F(p, e) \neq 0 \Rightarrow \phi(p) = \phi(e)$ *for every place* $p \in P$ *and for every event* $e \in E$.

The range $[n]$ of the placement map represents the collection of sites on an asynchronous communication network where no message is ever lost or duplicated. Places and events located at different sites may be connected by the flow (multi) relation F. Hence an event $e \in E$ may produce tokens for a distant place $p \in P$. As the flow of tokens must be implemented on the network by asynchronous message passing, tokens produced will be available only after some delay, but this remains compatible with the asynchronous nature of Petri nets. On the contrary, if events $e \in E$ were allowed to consume tokens from distant places, one would immediately be faced with the problem of distributed conflict that cannot be solved without building first a synchronous layer on top of the asynchronous network. The condition $F(p, e) \neq 0 \Rightarrow \phi(p) = \phi(e)$ guarantees that conflicts cannot occur between events at different sites. A straightforward procedure for the implementation of distributable nets on asynchronous networks then follows. Let us postpone the description of this procedure and come back to HMSCs.

By definition, the set of events of a HMSC comes equipped with a placement map $\phi : E \to [n]$ (we recall that $\phi(e) = i$ if e is a private event owned by process i, or $e =!m$ and i is the emitter of m, or $e =?m$ and i is the receiver of m). Thus, it makes sense to try realizing HMSCs with distributable Petri nets such that processes $i \in [n]$ are mapped identically to sites. Next theorem shows that this special form of the realization problem may be solved with little effort.

Theorem 11. *Theorem 7 extends to distributable Petri nets with fixed placement map* $\phi : E \to [n]$. *Theorem 8 extends similarly to distributable Petri nets with the placement map* $\phi : E \to [n]$ *inherited from* H.

So, given a HMSC H on E with placement map $\phi : E \to [n]$, one can compute a distributable Petri net $\mathcal{N}_H = (P, E, F, M_0, \phi)$ whose generated language is the closure of $\mathcal{L}(H)$ with respect to distributable Petri nets. In order to obtain a distributed realization of H, it remains to implement the distributable net $\mathcal{N}_H$ on the asynchronous network. To this effect, we propose a two stage procedure.

In a first stage, we expand $\mathcal{N}_H = (P, E, F, M_0, \phi)$ into a distributable net $\mathcal{N}'_H = (P', E', F', M'_0, \phi')$ where both new places and new events are added in order to model the buffered mode of transmission of tokens on the asynchronous network. The idea is to let $F'(e, p) = 0$ for all $e \in E$ and $p \in P$ such that $\phi(e) \neq \phi(p)$ (as an instantaneous transmission of tokens between different sites is not possible) and to compensate for the distorsion by introducing auxiliary message emissions and receptions (new events) which implement the asynchronous transmission of the tokens produced by e and passed to p from $\phi(e)$ to $\phi(p)$. The set of auxiliary messages $\mathcal{M}$ is the set of nonempty multisets μ on P such that $\mu = \mu(i, e, j)$ for some $i, j \in [n]$ and $e \in E$, letting:

$$\mu(i, e, j)(p) = F(e, p) \quad \text{if} \quad i = \phi(e) \neq \phi(p) = j \quad \text{and} \quad 0 \quad \text{otherwise.}$$

The sets $E_!$ (resp. $E_?$) of auxiliary message emissions (resp. receptions) are:

$$E_! = \{ \mu^i_! \mid \exists e \, \exists j \, \mu = \mu(i, e, j) \neq \emptyset \} \quad \text{and} \quad E_? = \{ \mu_? \mid \exists i \, \exists e \, \exists j \, \mu = \mu(i, e, j) \neq \emptyset \}.$$

Auxiliary places are introduced in order to condition the emissions resp. receptions of auxiliary messages, giving the respective sets:

$$P_! = \{ p^i_\mu \mid \exists e \, \exists j \, \mu = \mu(i, e, j) \neq \emptyset \} \quad \text{and} \quad P_? = \{ p_\mu \mid \exists i \, \exists e \, \exists j \, \mu = \mu(i, e, j) \neq \emptyset \}.$$

The sets of places and events of $\mathcal{N}'_H$ are $P' = P \cup P_! \cup P_?$ and $E' = E \cup E_! \cup E_?$. The initial marking M_0 is extended to M'_0 by setting $M'_0(p') = 0$ for all $p' \notin P$. The localisation map ϕ is extended to ϕ' by setting $\phi'(p^i_\mu) = \phi'(\mu^i_!) = i$ and $\phi'(p_\mu) = \phi'(\mu_?) = j$ where j is the (unique) location such that $\mu = \mu(i, e, j)$ for some i and e. The definition of $\mathcal{N}'_H$ is completed by setting the flow relations as follows ($e \in E$ and $p \in P$):

$F'(p, e) = F(p, e)$,

$F'(e, p) = F(e, p)$ if $\phi(e) = \phi(p)$ and 0 otherwise,

$F'(e, p^i_\mu) = 1$ if $\mu = \mu(i, e, j)$ for some j and 0 otherwise,

$F'(p^i_\mu, \mu^i_!) = F'(\mu^i_!, p_\mu) = F'(p_\mu, \mu_?) = 1$,

$F'(\mu_?, p) = \mu(p)$,

$F' = 0$ in all cases left unspecified.

It is proved in [2] that when all auxiliary events in $P' \setminus P$ are considered unobservable, the reachable state graph of $\mathcal{N}'_H$ is *divergence free*, which means that no infinite sequence of unobservable transitions can occur, and *branching bisimilar* to the reachable state graph of $\mathcal{N}_H$ (see [24]), which entails that the observable behaviours of the two nets are identical.

In a second stage, we remove from $\mathcal{N}'_H$ the auxiliary places p_μ which were used to represent tokens in transit on the network. The effect of the removal is to disconnect $\mathcal{N}'_H$ and to produce n component nets $\mathcal{N}_i$. For each $i \in [n]$, the net $\mathcal{N}_i$ is the restriction of $\mathcal{N}'_H$ on the (remaining) places and events with location i. One is left with implementing each $\mathcal{N}_i$ on the corresponding site i such that auxiliary events are interpreted as follows:

* each auxiliary event $\mu^i_!$ is interpreted as sending message μ to the (unique) destination j on the network such that $\mu = \mu(i, e, j)$,
* each auxiliary event $\mu_?$ in $\mathcal{N}_i$ is interpreted as receiving message μ from the network.

We obtain in this way a distributed (and provably correct) realization of the (distributable) Petri net closure $\overline{\mathcal{L}}(H)$ of the language $\mathcal{L}(H)$ of the HMSC H.

In case when $\mathcal{N}_H$ is a bounded Petri net, one can go a step further by translating the component nets $\mathcal{N}_i$ to *finite* automata A_i. As the component nets are generally unbounded, even though $\mathcal{N}_H$ is bounded, the translation is not immediate. The trick is to introduce for each place p of $\mathcal{N}_i$ with bound $\overline{p}$ in $\mathcal{N}_H$ (thus $p \in P$) a new place representing $\overline{p} - p$. The effect of the complementary places is to transform each $\mathcal{N}_i$ to a bounded net by pruning away behaviours of the autonomous net $\mathcal{N}_i$ that could not occur anyway in the context of $\mathcal{N}'_H$. Indeed, $\mathcal{N}'_H$ is bounded if $\mathcal{N}_H$ is bounded, and bounds agree on common places. The finite automata A_i are finally obtained by computing the reachable state graphs of the bounded versions of the components nets $\mathcal{N}_i$. We obtain in this way distributed realizations of HMSCs by finite automata communicating with asynchronous message passing.

3.5   Model-Checking Petri Net Realizations of HMSCs

As $\overline{\mathcal{L}}(H)$ is by definition the closure of $\mathcal{L}(H)$, realized behaviours $\overline{\mathcal{L}}(H)$ may be larger than specified behaviours $\mathcal{L}(H)$. One may want to verify that extra behaviours cause no problems, which amounts to model-check Petri net realizations N_H of HMSCs against safety assertions. In view of the results recalled hereafter, this is certainly possible. Model-checking Petri nets w.r.t. the linear time μ-calculus is decidable [11]. More generally, one can decide on the inclusion $\mathcal{L}(N) \subseteq A$ for a net N labelled on E and $A \in Rat(E^*)$ [17]. Last but not least, by Theo. 9, one can decide on the inclusion $\mathcal{L}(N) \subseteq \mathcal{L}(N')$ for two nets N and N' labelled on E provided that N' is deterministic.

The decision techniques supplied in the above references apply to arbitrary Petri nets N. In the particular case where $N = N_H$ is the net realization of a HMSC, one may try to exploit this specific fact. For instance, let H and N have the same set of events, then $\mathcal{L}(N_H) \subseteq \mathcal{L}(N)$ if and only if every place p of N coincides with a *region* of $\mathcal{L}(H)$ (see [7]). This may be checked directly and efficiently from the automaton $\psi(\overline{H})$ which was constructed in section 3.1. One may decide in a similar way on the equivalent inclusions $\mathcal{L}(H_1) \subseteq \overline{\mathcal{L}}(H_2)$ or $\overline{\mathcal{L}}(H_1) \subseteq \overline{\mathcal{L}}(H_2)$ for two different HMSCs. It is not clear that the use of regions may help to decide more efficiently on the inclusion $\overline{\mathcal{L}}(H) \subseteq A$ for $A \in Rat(E^*)$.

4   Case Studies

Two case studies taken from telecommunication applications are now presented. They embrace typical behaviours of communication protocols. Both consist in synthesizing communicating finite state machines (CFSM) from a given HMSC (H). We apply for this purpose the method sketched in 3.4 and explained in [2]: i) synthesize a distributable (bounded) Petri net, where places and transitions have locations and transitions take tokens only from co-located places, and ii) transform the Petri net into a set of asynchronously communicating automata. However, we make here an advanced use of Petri net synthesis: we compute the Petri net closure of the language $\mathcal{L}(H)$ *projected* on the subset of private events P of E ($= P \cup S \cup R$). In view of Theo. 7, this makes sense since the projection of a language on a sub-alphabet preserves the semi-linearity of its commutative image. Messages in a bMSC are then considered only as a means to specify the partial order on events in P; therefore we don't attribute labels to message emissions (in S) and receptions (in E). The goal of reconstructing a dialogue between agents which enforces the specified partial order on P is achieved in step (ii), where auxiliary messages are used in any case for achieving distribution.

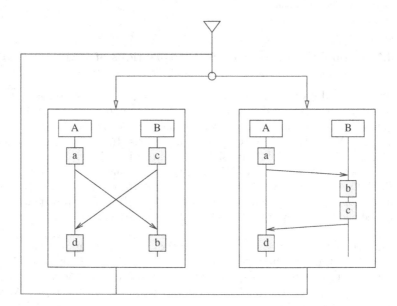

Fig. 1. A HMSC with non-local choice

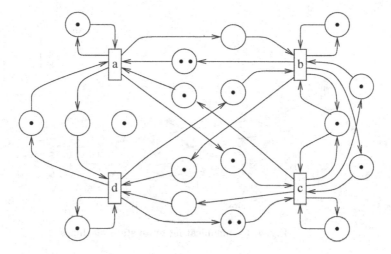

Fig. 2. Synthesized Petri net

4.1   A HMSC with Non-local Choice

The HMSC H in figure 1 defines two instances of agents (A and B) repeatedly performing four local actions a, b, c and d which are ordered thanks to a pair of messages. Two cases can occur: either (right-hand side case) all actions are performed in sequence, or (left-hand side case) some events can be performed concurrently. The commutative image of $\mathcal{L}(H)$ is given by the regular expression:

$$(abcd)^* \left(0 + a + c + ab + ac + abc + acd + abc^2 + a^2cd\right)$$

More precisely, for $x \in \{a, b, c, d\}$, the commutative images of the right residuals $\mathcal{L}(H)/x$ are given in this order by the respective regular expressions:

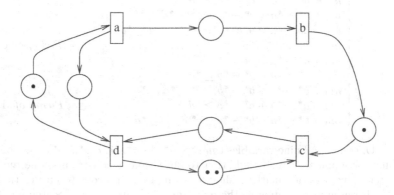

Fig. 3. Minimal Petri net

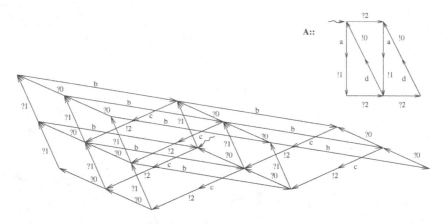

Fig. 4. Communicating finite state machines

$(abcd)^* (0 + c + acd)$
$(abcd)^* (a + ac + acd + a^2cd)$
$(abcd)^* (0 + a + ab + abc)$
$(abcd)^* (ac + abc)$

Hence each place $(m_0, {}^\bullet a, a^\bullet, {}^\bullet b, b^\bullet, {}^\bullet c, c^\bullet, {}^\bullet d, d^\bullet)$ marked with m_0 tokens in the net $N = \mathcal{N}_H$ which realizes the (bounded) Petri net closure $\overline{\mathcal{L}}(H)$ of $\mathcal{L}(H)$ should satisfy the following set of linear equations and inequations:

$$\left\{ \begin{array}{ll}
a^\bullet - {}^\bullet a + b^\bullet - {}^\bullet b + c^\bullet - {}^\bullet c + d^\bullet - d^\bullet = 0 & \textit{places are bounded} \\
m_0 \geq {}^\bullet a & \textit{Firing of } a \\
m_0 + c^\bullet - {}^\bullet c \geq {}^\bullet a & \\
m_0 + a^\bullet - {}^\bullet a + c^\bullet - {}^\bullet c + d^\bullet - {}^\bullet d \geq {}^\bullet a & \\
m_0 + a^\bullet - {}^\bullet a \geq {}^\bullet b & \textit{Firing of } b \\
m_0 + a^\bullet - {}^\bullet a + c^\bullet - {}^\bullet c \geq {}^\bullet b & \\
m_0 + a^\bullet - {}^\bullet a + c^\bullet - {}^\bullet c + d^\bullet - {}^\bullet d \geq {}^\bullet b & \\
m_0 + 2a^\bullet - 2^\bullet a + c^\bullet - {}^\bullet c + d^\bullet - {}^\bullet d \geq {}^\bullet b & \\
m_0 \geq {}^\bullet c & \textit{Firing of } c \\
m_0 + a^\bullet - {}^\bullet a \geq {}^\bullet c & \\
m_0 + a^\bullet - {}^\bullet a + b^\bullet - {}^\bullet b \geq {}^\bullet c & \\
m_0 + a^\bullet - {}^\bullet a + b^\bullet - {}^\bullet b + c^\bullet - {}^\bullet c \geq {}^\bullet c & \\
m_0 + a^\bullet - {}^\bullet a + c^\bullet - {}^\bullet c \geq {}^\bullet d & \textit{Firing of } d \\
m_0 + a^\bullet - {}^\bullet a + b^\bullet - {}^\bullet b + c^\bullet - {}^\bullet c \geq {}^\bullet d &
\end{array} \right.$$

Of course, all nine variables $(m_0, {}^\bullet a, a^\bullet, {}^\bullet b, b^\bullet, {}^\bullet c, c^\bullet, {}^\bullet d, d^\bullet)$ must be greater than or equal to zero. In addition to these linear constraints, one among two alternative sets of equations should be imposed in order to ensure that places are distributed according to the mapping of events : places located on A should satisfy ${}^\bullet b = {}^\bullet c = 0$, places located on B should statisfy ${}^\bullet a = {}^\bullet d = 0$.

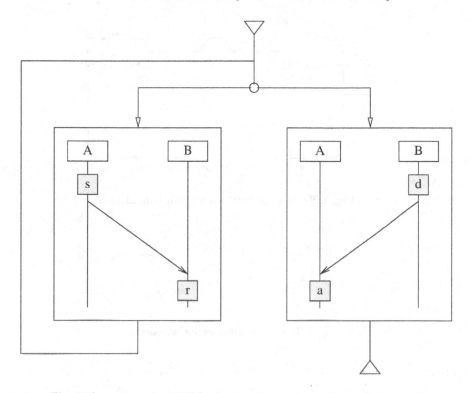

Fig. 5. An non-regular HMSC: the simple asynchronous transfer protocol

This defines two polyhedral cones. Their extremal rays are the places of the distributable (bounded) Petri net N in figure 2. It is easy to check that $\mathcal{L}(H)$ (which turns out to be regular) is equal to $\mathcal{L}(N)$. The Petri net N contains redundant places which can be safely discarded without changing its language. This results in the net in figure 3, which can be transformed into the pair of communicating automata in figure 4 (emissions resp. receptions of auxiliary messages are represented by occurences $!i$ resp. $?i$).

4.2   A Non-regular HMSC Language

The second case study is about the simple asynchronous transfer protocol defined by the HMSC H in figure 5. Action s stands for a message sending, r for a receiving, d for a disconnection request, and a for a disconnection acknowledgement. The commutative image of $\mathcal{L}(H)$ is given by the expression $(sr)^*(s^* + d + da)$. Each (possibly unbounded) place $(m_0, {}^\bullet a, a^\bullet, {}^\bullet b, b^\bullet, {}^\bullet c, c^\bullet, {}^\bullet d, d^\bullet)$ of the net $N = \mathcal{N}_H$ which realizes the (general) Petri net closure $\overline{\mathcal{L}}(H)$ of $\mathcal{L}(H)$ should satisfy the following set of linear equations and inequations:

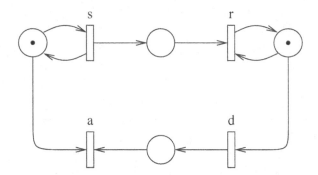

Fig. 6. Synthesized Petri net without redundant places

A::   **B::**

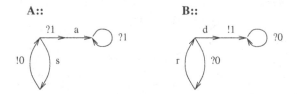

Fig. 7. Communicating automata

$$
\begin{cases}
m_0 \geq 0 & \text{\textit{variables are non-negative}} \\
{}^\bullet s \geq 0, s^\bullet \geq 0, {}^\bullet r \geq 0, r^\bullet \geq 0 \\
{}^\bullet d \geq 0, d^\bullet \geq 0, {}^\bullet a \geq 0, a^\bullet \geq 0 \\
s^\bullet - {}^\bullet s \geq 0 & \text{\textit{inequations on cycles}} \\
s^\bullet - {}^\bullet s + r^\bullet - {}^\bullet r \geq 0 \\
m_0 \geq {}^\bullet s & \text{\textit{Firing of} s} \\
m_0 + s^\bullet - {}^\bullet s \geq {}^\bullet r & \text{\textit{Firing of} r} \\
m_0 \geq {}^\bullet d & \text{\textit{Firing of} d} \\
m_0 + d^\bullet - {}^\bullet d \geq {}^\bullet a & \text{\textit{Firing of} a}
\end{cases}
$$

Distribution constraints impose either ${}^\bullet r = {}^\bullet d = 0$ or ${}^\bullet s = {}^\bullet a = 0$. This defines two polyhedral cones. Their extremal rays are: $d^\bullet + {}^\bullet a$, $m_0 + {}^\bullet a$, $m_0 + s^\bullet + {}^\bullet s + {}^\bullet a$, $m_0 + s^\bullet + {}^\bullet s$, m_0, $s^\bullet$, $r^\bullet$, $d^\bullet$, $a^\bullet$, $m_0 + r^\bullet + {}^\bullet r$, $m_0 + r^\bullet + {}^\bullet r + {}^\bullet d$, $s^\bullet + {}^\bullet r$, $m_0 + {}^\bullet d$. Some rays define redundant places and can be safely discarded. The synthesized Petri net is shown in figure 6. This net may be transformed into the pair of communicating automata in figure 7 ($!i$ resp. $?i$ represent emissions resp. receptions of auxiliary messages). These communicating automata have been derived under the assumption that the communication medium consists in a pair of unbounded reliable channels. The place between s and r in the Petri net is unbounded, and since the communication medium acts as a memory, the communication channel from agent A to agent B is also unbounded.

5   Conclusion

The results which have been presented in this paper call for several comments.

First of all, the undecidability results shown in section 2 indicate that one has an alternative between two antagonistic views upon HMSCs:
1) One may regard HMSCs as complete specifications. In that case, one is led to only consider HMSCs with regular behaviour, as otherwise verification and realization would become unfeasible. The loss of expressiveness is in our opinion a serious drawback at an early stage in the design of telecommunication systems.
2) One may regard HMSCs as incomplete specifications. One must in that case define the meanings of HMSCs as closures of their normal behaviours with respect to such or such class of realizations, e.g. distributable Petri nets or communicating automata. Verification on general HMSCs' behaviours is unfeasible, but verification on their closures is effective for well chosen classes of realizations – Petri nets for instance. We feel that this pragmatic view is far more suitable.

High level message sequence charts express positive facts on system behaviour. Results shown in section 3 about verification on Petri net realizations of HMSCs suggest that it would be desirable to extend HMSCs so that both positive and negative facts could be expressed in a single formalism. This should not be confused with Harel's distinction between compulsory and optional events in HMSCs.

Finally, this paper only considered closures of HMSCs' behaviours with respect to Petri nets. Considering other classes and comparing their advantages is an open field for research. Incidentally, the Petri net closure of a HMSC shows an interesting property: the flow of tokens in the synthesized net seems to induce a minimal covering of the order on events in the HMSC. This could provide a way of minimizing communications while preserving behaviour.

References

1. Alur, R., Yannakakis, M.: Model Checking of Message Sequence Charts. Proc. Concur, LNCS **1664** (1999) 114–129
2. Badouel, E., Caillaud, B., Darondeau, Ph.: Distributing Finite Automata through Petri Net Synthesis. (draft available from the authors)
3. Berstel, J.: Transductions and Context-Free Languages. Teubner Studienbücher, Stuttgart (1979)
4. Caillaud, B.: Bounded Petri Net Synthesis Techniques and their Applications to the Distribution of Reactive Automata. JESA **9–10** no.33 (1999) 925–942
5. Damm, W., Harel, D.: LCSs: Breathing Life into Message Sequence Charts. Report CS98/09, Weizmann Institute of Technology (1998)
6. Darondeau, Ph.: Deriving Unbounded Petri Nets from Formal Languages. Proc. Concur, LNCS **1466** (1998) 533–548
7. Darondeau, Ph.: Region Based Synthesis of P/T-Nets and its Potential Applications. Proc. ICATPN, LNCS **1825** (2000) 16–23

8. Diekert, V., Métivier, Y.: Partial Commutation and Traces. Research report 1996/02, Universität Stuttgart Fakultät Informatik (1996)
9. Diekert, V., Rozenberg, G. (editors): The Book of Traces. World Scientific, Singapore (1995)
10. Eilenberg, S., Schützenberger, M.: Rational Sets in Commutative Monoids. Journal of Algebra **13** (1969) 173–191
11. Esparza, J.: On the Decidability of Model-checking for several mu-calculi and Petri Nets. Proc. Caap, LNCS **787** (1994) 115–129
12. Fischer, P.C., Rosenberg, A.L.: Multitape One-Way Nonwriting Automata. JCSS **2** (1968) 88–101
13. Harel, D., Kugler, H.: Synthesizing State-Based Object Systems from LSC Specifications. Report MCS99/20, Weizmann Institute of Technology (1999)
14. Henriksen, J.G., Mukund, M., Narayan Kumar, K., Thiagarajan, P.S.: On Message Sequence Graphs and Finitely Generated Regular MSC Languages. Proc. Icalp, LNCS **1853** (2000) 675–686
15. Henriksen, J.G., Mukund, M., Narayan Kumar, K., Thiagarajan, P.S.: Regular Collections of Message Sequence Charts. Proc. MFCS, LNCS **1893** (2000) 405–414
16. TU-TS Recommendation Z.120: Message Sequence Chart 1996 (MSC96). Technical Report, ITU-TS, Geneva (1996)
17. Jancar, P., Moeller, F.: Checking Regular Properties of Petri Nets, Proc. Concur, LNCS **962** (1995) 348–362
18. Mauw, S., Reniers, M.A., High-Level Message Sequence Charts. Proc. Eighth SDL Forum, Elsevier Science Publishers B.V. (1997) 291–306
19. Mayr, E.: An Algorithm for the General Petri Net Reachability Problem. SIAM Journal on Computing **13** (1984) 441–460
20. Mukund, M., Narayan Kumar, K., Sohoni, M.: Synthesizing distributed finite-state systems from MSCs. Proc. Concur, LNCS **1877** (2000) 521–535
21. Muscholl, A., Peled, D., Su, Z.: Deciding Properties for Message Sequence Charts. Proc. Fossacs, LNCS **1378** (1998) 226–242
22. Pelz, E.: Closure Properties of Deterministic Petri Nets. Proc. Stacs, LNCS **247** (1987) 373–382
23. Peterson, J.L.: Computation Sequence Sets. JCSS **13** (1976) 1–24
24. van Glabbeek, R.J., Weijland, W.P.: Branching Time and Abstraction in Bisimulation Semantics. Proc. IFIP Congress, North Holland / IFIP (1989) 613–618

Industrial Applications of Model Checking

Alessandro Cimatti

ITC-IRST – Centro per la Ricerca Scientifica e Tecnologica
Via Sommarive 18, 38055 Povo, Trento, Italy
cimatti@irst.itc.it

Abstract. Formal methods have a great potential of application in the development of industrial critical systems. In certain application fields, formal methods are even becoming part of standards. Among formal methods, Model Checking is proving particularly effective, especially thanks to its ability to automatically analyze complex designs and to produce counterexamples. However, the application of formal methods in the industrial development practice is by no means trivial. Formal methods can be costly, slow down the development, and require training and changes to the development cycle. In this paper, the application of Model Checking techniques in the development of industrial critical systems is discussed, by focusing on two projects where Model Checking has been successfully applied under different conditions.

1 Introduction

The use of embedded software systems in (safety) critical industrial applications, such as railways or plant control systems, is continuously increasing. Compared to traditional (e.g. relay) systems, embedded software allows to provide flexible and complex functions at reasonable costs. The main problem, however, is to guarantee the correctness, the safety and the quality of such systems. Although existing software engineering techniques provide structured methodologies for design, implementation and testing of software, the degree of insurance they can provide is often not sufficient in the development of critical systems. For these reasons, formal methods have a great potential of application in the development of industrial critical systems [3]. They can provide for unambiguous specification languages, and mechanically assisted debugging methods, such as Model Checking [12,9], can be applied in the early stages of the development cycle. This is a significant advantage with respect to traditional software testing, which can miss important bugs because of the limited coverage achievable in practice. Furthermore, the feedback provided by testing comes too late in the development cycle, i.e. once the system has been built. For this potential, in certain application fields, formal methods are even becoming part of standards and regulations [2, 10].

The practical application of formal methods in the development of industrial products, however, is not an easy task. Indeed, formal methods can be costly, slow down the process of development, and require changes on the development

F. Cassez et al. (Eds.): MOVEP 2000, LNCS 2067, pp. 153–168, 2001.
© Springer-Verlag Berlin Heidelberg 2001

cycle, and training. Overall, the industrial take up of Formal Methods greatly depends on the cost/benefits ratio of the introduction of the new technology into the industrial development process. In general, it is of paramount importance to introduce formal methods selectively, concentrating on the most critical parts of design, and in the suitable phases of the development cycle. Furthermore, a tighter integration of the formal verification tools within the standard development process can widen the usability of verification methods by design engineers limiting the required amount of training. In this respect, it is very important to be able to adapt and customize the verification tools to the specific problem at hand. In summary, the well known state explosion problem arising in model checking [4], i.e. the amount of computational resources needed to complete a verification, is only one of the problems to be tackled for an effective application of formal methods in the development of industrial critical systems.

Technology transfer projects have been carried out at IRST aiming at the effective application of formal methods, Model Checking in particular, to the design of (safety) critical systems [6,5,1,7]. In the following, we focus on two rather different industrial projects, where formal methods have been applied in the development of industrial safety-critical systems. The first project, described in section 2, aimed at the design of a limited but very complex communication protocol, and was carried out by a small team, composed by experts in formal methods. The second project, described in section 3, aimed at the development of a large embedded system, and was carried out by a larger, heterogeneous team tackling the integration of formal specification and verification methods along the different phases of the development process (from functional requirements to architectural design, to testing). For each of the projects we provide an informal description of the system being designed, and we focus on the methodological aspects regarding the integration of formal (specification and verification) techniques within the development cycle, the problems faced and the adopted solutions. In section 4 we draw some conclusions.

2   Formal Design of a Communication Protocol

The goal of the project described in this section was the development of a complex communication protocol, called Safety Layer, used as basis for several computer-based, distributed safety-critical products. A previous implementation, obtained with traditional software development methods, had required an expensive activity of debugging on the field, and the resulting system was difficult to maintain and extend. Formal methods were thus applied by a small team, to produce develop a new, high-quality design specification, to be provided to the implementation team.

2.1   Informal Description of the Protocol

The Safety Layer is a communication protocol intended to provide reliable communication for distributed safety critical systems, e.g. Automatic Train Control

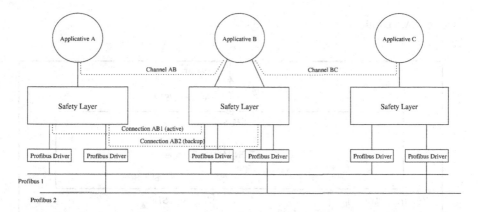

Fig. 1. The Safety Layer

systems, track-to-train communication systems, interlocking systems. Typically, such systems are based on several computing stations connected via field bus. The Safety Layer provides applicative programs (running on different units) with point to point communication channels. Figure 1 depicts applicative programs A, B and C, running on different units, connected by point-to-point bidirectional channels AB and BC. Such channels are protected against data corruption and out-of-order reception by means of CRC (Cyclic Redundancy Checksum) protection, authentication mechanisms, sequence numbering and final shutdown in presence of repeated errors. The interface to the application program is extremely simple, i.e. only send and receive primitives are available. The Safety Layer is configured off-line, i.e. the applicative-level channels are fixed at design time.

Besides guaranteeing the safety of communication channels to the applicative programs, the role of the Safety Layer is to enhance dependability, i.e. to make the channels available for the applicative programs as much as possible. Therefore, each unit running the Safety Layer is connected to two independent field buses. The PROFIBUS [15] drivers provide the Safety Layer with connection-oriented communication primitives. The role of the Safety Layer is to hide this redundancy from the application program, which only can see a reliable communication channel. The Safety Layer tries to maintain two connections, one per PROFIBUS, for each point-to-point channel to the application level. In Figure 1, the channel AB between applicatives A and B is realized through the two connections AB1 and AB2. In the case of nominal behavior of the protocol, one connection is active, through which data can be transmitted, while the other is in standby. (Notationally, the former is called the *active* connection, while the latter is called the *backup* connection.) Even when no data is transmitted, a minimum rate of transmission is guaranteed on both connections, by means of special control telegrams, called connection monitoring. This mechanism is used to reduce the time needed to detect problems, such as disturbance on the bus,

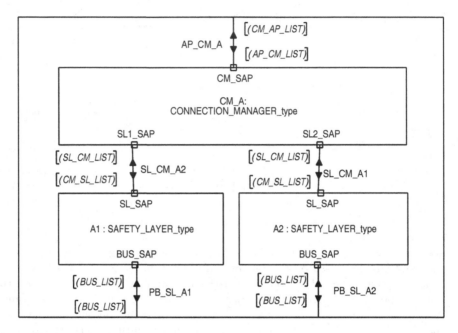

Fig. 2. The interconnection diagram of the Safety Layer.

or malfunctioning of hardware components. Such problems may be revealed by messages with corrupted CRC or out-of-order sequence numbers, or by time-outs. When a problem arises on the backup bus, the backup connection is reset, and the reconnection procedure is retried. The active connection is not affected. The protocol can thus work properly in a degraded mode, when only one connection is available, but this is completely hidden to the applicative program. If a problem arises on the active connection, and the backup connection is working properly, then the *switch-over* procedure is undertaken. The switch-over is a distinguishing mechanism of the protocol. When a switch-over occurs, the backup connection becomes active, and will be used to transmit applicative data, while the (previously) active connection is reset and restarted in standby.

2.2 Formal Specification

In this project, formal methods were supported by OBJECTGEODE [16], a commercial toolset for the development of real-time distributed systems. OBJECT-GEODE provides editors for StateChart [11] and for the SDL [13] graphical specification language. SDL designs can be (interactively) simulated and analyzed by an explicit-state model checker. Requirements can be formalized in expressed as assertions or as Message Sequence Charts (MSC) [14]. Execution

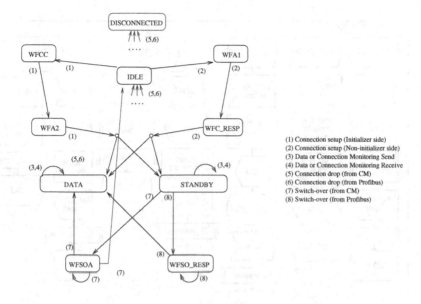

(1) Connection setup (Initializer side)
(2) Connection setup (Non-initializer side)
(3) Data or Connection Monitoring Send
(4) Data or Connection Monitoring Receive
(5) Connection drop (from CM)
(6) Connection drop (from Profibus)
(7) Switch-over (from CM)
(8) Switch-over (from Profibus)

Fig. 3. A simplified view of the SL machine.

traces generated via simulation or as counterexamples during model checking
can be shown as MSC.

In order to make the design specifications understandable by the development
team, notations with different degrees of formality were adopted and combined.
A structural view of the design was provided by SDL interconnection diagrams,
by decomposing the system into blocks connected by channels. Figure 2 depicts
the interface and the structure of each of the Safety Layer boxes in figure 1. At
the interface, there are an (upward) connection with the applicative program,
and two (downward) connections with the PROFIBUS. Channels are labeled
by message lists, describing the sets of messages which can be sent in the two
directions, and providing the formal (high-level) specification of the interfaces of
the system modules. The design is decomposed into three blocks. The two lower
level SL blocks are identical: each of them is able to handle a single connection,
and is not even aware of the existence of the other SL machine. The upper
Connection Manager (CM) block is responsible for the high level operation of
the channel: it is not aware of the details of the status of the SL machines, but
has a clear view of the redundancy of the channel, and enforces control on the
SL machines according to the events which are signaled by them.

The blocks in figure 2 were refined into asynchronously connected processes.
The corresponding state machines were informally described with high level
StateCharts. (Figure 3 represents (a simplified view of) each SL machine.) Although many details of the design (e.g. the conditions associated to the various
transitions) are abstracted away, these diagrams were extremely useful as graph-

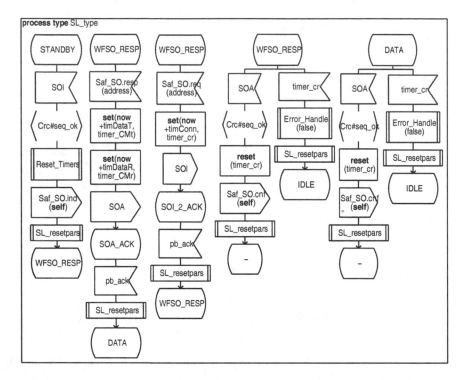

Fig. 4. The SDL specification of the (8) transitions of the SL machine in figure 3

ical road-map for the detailed specification of the machines. The StateChart descriptions of the machines are detailed in SDL in order to provide an executable design specification of the operations to be carried out in each situation. In Figure 4 we show the SDL description of the transitions corresponding to the "Switch-over from PROFIBUS" functionality, labeled with (8) in the StateChart in figure 3. The function is undertaken by the SL machine handling the backup connection (state STANDBY), when a Switch-over indication is received by the peer partner. (The details of the protocol can be found in [8].) For each of the transition in figure 3, there is (at least) a corresponding transitions in figure 4, leading from the same start to the same end states. The SDL provided a very detailed guideline: after a very short training, the SDL design was directly used by the implementation team.

2.3 Formal Verification

Formal verification was tightly integrated within the design process, following a cyclic design/specificy/validate process. At each cycle, the design was extended

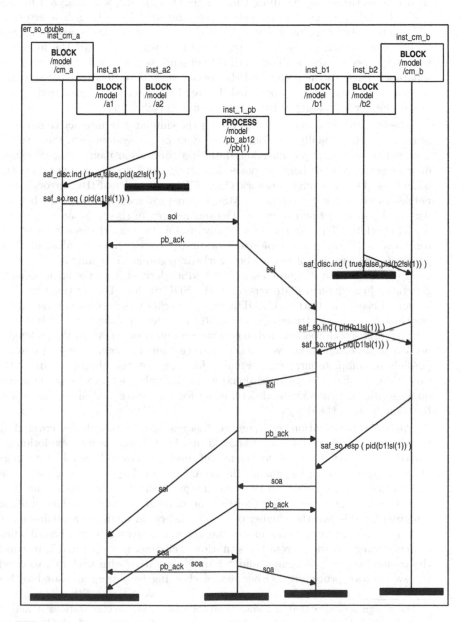

Fig. 5. The MSC of an error occurred during a double switch-over (revealed in an intermediate version of the model).

with new features (e.g. handling PROFIBUS errors), and was analyzed in OB-JECTGEODE with interactive simulations, and model checking. The errors or anomalous behaviors revealed were traced by means of MSC's and analyzed; then a new version of the model was produced which included the modifications suggested by the analysis, until convergence was reached. Notice that the separation between the design and the model used in verification (the so-called semantic gap) was greatly contained, being the formal model analyzed by the model checker a substantial part of the design specification.

The first step of every cycle was to run the simulator in interactive mode, in order to check manually the nominal behavior of the system (e.g. the setup of both active and backup connection, data and connection monitoring exchange, drop of active and/or backup connection, single and double switch-over), and some typical error handling scenarios (e.g. CRC errors, PROFIBUS errors, channel delays, etc.). The corresponding MSC's were produced, analyzed, and became part of the specification document. The second step of the cycle was to perform model checking. This step was extremely useful: the model checker found automatically a large number of errors or unexpected behaviors. Most of these problems were so complicate to be nearly impossible for a human analyst to conceive. For instance, figure 5 shows the MSC derived from the error scenario generated in an intermediate version of the SDL model[1]. During this phase, an advanced use of the OBJECTGEODE model checker was necessary. First, different choices of search strategy proved useful in different situations: for instance, breadth-first search was selected to generate counterexamples of minimal length. Second, state compression was used to reduce memory occupation and made it possible to complete large runs. Finally, filtering (i.e. the ability to hinder the execution of some selected transitions) was extremely useful to focus the search on a specific operation mode, thus allowing for a selective analysis of the various functionalities of the design.

After several iterations convergence was reached, i.e. the design covered all the situations and bugs no longer showed up. At this point a state explosion occurred, i.e. it was not possible for the model checker to cover the whole state space of the design. In order to enhance the confidence in the correctness, the model checker was run overnight on the final design with different initial conditions and different search strategies, limiting the number of states to three millions (empirically, this was the number of states that could fit in the available memory). In some of the runs, the model checker was activated with a breadth-first search strategy, starting from the situations "channel non operative", to check the channel set-up procedures, and "channel operative with backup", to check the switch-over procedures. Other model checking runs were activated with a

---

[1] The design was validated in a configuration where two partner stations A and B, each modeled by three processes, implement a point-to-point channel AB over the field bus, modeled as a nondeterministic process. When one of the SL process sends a telegram, the PROFIBUS process can either send the telegram to the partner SL process and return the suitable acknowledgement, or "flush" the message and return to the source SL a failure notification.

depth-first search strategy. These runs revealed no exception (dynamic error), deadlock, or stop condition (unexpected inputs, role incongruence of the SL's). Furthermore, they covered the 100% of the control states and about 75% of the transitions (the remaining 25% corresponded to entries in the event/state matrix that had been introduced for completeness, and but that were expected to be never activated). However, the strongest reason for being confident in the correctness of the design was that an error was detected in intermediate versions of the model, this was always done within up to a few thousands states analyzed. Once the design specification was completed, the software was implemented directly from the design, in a fraction of the planned time, and showed no error during testing. Overall, the ability to find bugs, i.e. falsification, appeared to be much more important, useful and cost-effective than verification.

3   Formal Design of an Embedded Control System

The aim of the second project was to develop a large, complex Embedded System with the support of the formal modeling and verification techniques provided by OBJECTGEODE. Compared to the activity described in previous section, this project was much larger and required the coordination of the activity of several (specification, design, implementation, testing) teams. In this section we focus on the problems related to the effective integration of formal methods in the development process.

3.1   Informal Description of the Embedded System

The Embedded System under design must operates within of a complex environment, interacting with it by means of a number of heterogeneous sensors and actuators. The sensors convey information concerning the physical status of the environment, e.g. indicating the faulty status of a controlled device. Actuators of different kind allow the Embedded System to control the operations according to a certain set of rules and the status of the external environment. Furthermore, human operators may send commands, select operation modes, and provide additional information to respond to data requests.

The main functionality of the Embedded System is to determine a safe behavior consistent with the constraints specified by the environment. In order to do so, the Embedded System is required to analyze the information acquired from different sources, integrate it, and respond suitably to the resulting conditions. These functions can be performed according to the different operation modes selected by a human operator, or autonomously entered depending on information conveyed by sensors. The system must be able to tolerate faults without producing unsafe behaviors, possibly entering degraded operation modes, maintaining some of its basic functionalities.

For dependability reasons, the Embedded System adopts an architecture based on redundancy, shown in figure 6. At the hardware level (below the dashed line), the Embedded System is built on several independent hardware platforms,

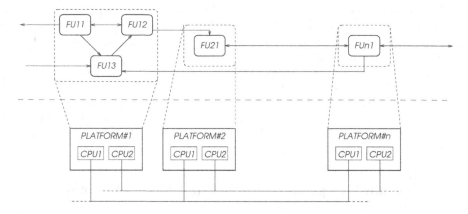

Fig. 6. The Embedded System architecture

each running a pair of CPUs, with a 2-out-of-2 exclusion logic, a run-time checking mechanism ensuring that the application program is executed consistently. At the software level (above the dashed line), the Embedded System is composed of several distributed programs, running on the different platforms. Each platform runs one or more *"functional units"*, connected in a point-to-point paradigm, provided by the communication protocol described in previous section. In the nominal mode, one of the platforms is in charge of performing the high level functions of the Embedded System and commanding the other platforms. The other platforms take care of interacting with the external environment, performing logging activities, commanding the actuators, and so on. The Embedded System also implements a form of functional redundancy, by doubling the platforms able to perform the functions of the master platform. Two such units are run in parallel, one actually performing the task while the other is in a "hot standby" status. A master/slave switch protocol is used to guarantee that a correctly functioning platform is in charge.

3.2 The Structured Formal Specification Methodology

In order to introduce formal methods into the development process of the Embedded System, the following problems were tackled. First, formal methods had to be additional on the previously adopted process, without requiring an extensive training of the people involved. Second, given the size of the team and the timing constraints, it had be possible to parallelize the activities. Furthermore, model checking had to be applicable in the early stages of the process, as an advanced debugger, and in a selective manner, restricting only to certain parts of the design. Figure 7 depicts the adopted approach. In standard practice, informal system requirements are the refined into (informal) system specifications and test specifications. These, in turn, are refined into system code and test

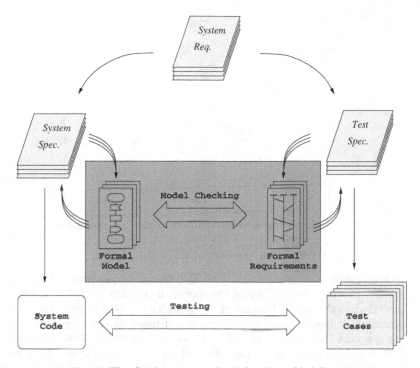

Fig. 7. The development cycle of the Embedded System

suites, that are used in the testing phase. The shaded box represents the additional, formal parts. As for the Safety Layer project, system specifications are a combination of informal and formal elements. Mechanical support was provided by OBJECTGEODE, and StateChart and SDL diagrams were integrated with the informal system description. The idea of deriving formal requirements (i.e. the properties to be model checked) from the test descriptions allowed to limit the effort required to set up the model checking problems. Given these ingredients, formal verification becomes possible early in the development process, before the system code is available for simulation. The feedback provided by model checking is extremely useful in pinpointing problems not only in the system but also in the test specifications.

This general schema was customized to the architecture of the Embedded System, by taking advantage of the structure for Functional Unit (FU), outlined in figure 8. A FU performs a reactive loop, first acquiring the inputs, then executing the state transitions, and finally delivering the outputs to the other units and to the environment. A FU is organized hierarchically, as a tree of finite state machines (or simply machines from now on), each with its own persistent state. A machine at a given level is invoked by the "father" machine at the upper level, and can activate its "sons" machines, according to a call-

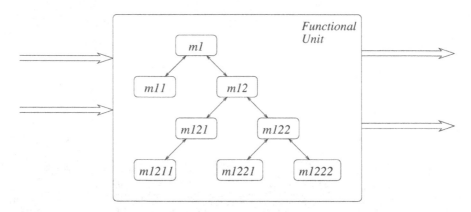

Fig. 8. The software architecture of a functional unit

return synchronous mechanism. Call and return signals may deliver a variable number of values, depending on the specific activation modality. Machines were identified as the basic elements of a compositional design procedure: a detailed specification mechanism for machines was defined, associating to each machine the specifications, and a centralized repository was set up. This allowed different (e.g. design, verification, coding, testing) teams to proceed in a pipeline chain, on different parts of the design which were scaled on different phases of the development process. As in previous section, the specification combines informal and formal aspects, associating to each of the machines a detailed description of the interface, the state variables bing read and modified, a high level State-Chart view of the transitions, a detailed specification based on SDL, and other information.

3.3   Customization of the Formal Verification Tools

In order to start the model checking activity, several problems had to be faced, mainly due to the limitations of OBJECTGEODE in handling such a large design. In particular, SDL do not support hierarchical modeling in a satisfactory way. Furthermore, OBJECTGEODE provides a very simple mechanism for handling environments, and does not support abstractions. This was clearly a problem, given the choice of decomposing the design in independently specified machines. We tackled these problems by designing and developing a mechanical support tool, called SDLSDL, for the automated generation of formal verification problems from the repository of design elements. Figure 9 describes the underlying idea. The tool receives in input a declaration of the FUs to be taken into account, and, for each FU, the description of the hierarchy of machines it contains. The tool cross-checks the information concerning the topology of the hierarchies in the functional units using the interface descriptions for each machine, making sure that the specified connections are possible. The output of the

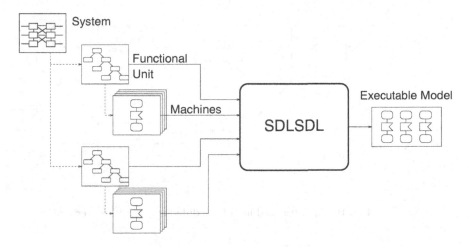

Fig. 9. The SDLSDL conversion

tool is a unique finite state machine (represented in standard SDL) that can be directly provided in input to the OBJECTGEODE model checker.

The SDLSDL tool relies on an extension to SDL that was designed in order to express in a compact and meaningful way synchronous control transfer between machines, as well as asynchronous communication between functional units. The extended language, called SDL$^+$, includes call and return constructs to model synchronous control transfer between machines. Furthermore, a simple language was designed to describe the topology of the system, and of each functional unit composing it. The language describes in a precise way the hierarchical structures. At this level, it is possible to specify that certain machines are "fake", i.e. empty place holders in the hierarchy. This allows to implement a simple form of abstraction, selecting relevant parts of a model, e.g. depending on the test that we intend to execute on it. This proved extremely useful to "hide" certain parts of the design which were not considered to be relevant for the model checking run being set up, or that simply were not ready at the time the verification problem was set up. The mechanical generation of model checking problems starting form the basic components greatly reduces the manual effort required to connect the components into a single model, and to set up the environment of the analyzed subsystem, a tedious and error-prone activity.

Two main possibilities were identified to model functional units starting from independent descriptions of machines. The first is to model each functional unit as an SDL process, and each machine of the unit as an SDL service, representing procedural invocations by input/output handshaking protocols. This solution allows for the observation of intermediate control states, but it requires the introduction of intermediate states to represent the points of control transfer. These additional states cause a combinatorial explosion, often making model checking infeasible, but allow to inspect more closely the behavior of the model.

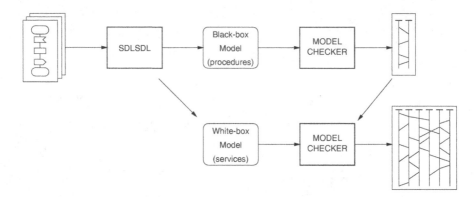

Fig. 10. An integrated use of the different SDLSDL conversions

The second possibility is to describe each functional unit as an SDL process, and each machine of the unit as an SDL procedure. This solution avoids the intermediate states problem caused by the services: procedural invocations can be directly represented via the SDL procedure call mechanism, without requiring the introduction of additional control states. On the other hand, removing the intermediate states decreases the model traceability: when a misbehavior of a functional unit is found, it becomes hard to detect which machine caused it, since no intermediate control state is recorded within the trace by OBJECTGEODE. The SDLSDL tool implements both possibilities, producing an executable SDL model of the system, where either procedures or services can be used to model machines. This ability to generate different models proved useful in practice, as depicted in figure 10. Once the more compact, procedure-based model produces an abstract bug trace, this can be used to drive the search over the more expensive, service-based model to produce a detailed version of the bugs trace.

Even with the SDLSDL support tool available, model checking the whole Embedded System could not be considered a reasonable goal for the OBJECT-GEODE model checker. However, by using the model checker for early debugging, significant results were obtained. The specification and validation methodology was applied to selected functionalities of the Embedded System, focusing on critical functionalities of the master functional unit, in particular the startup protocol for the Embedded System, and some functionalities related to the handling of vital commands coming from the environment. It was possible to complete the model checking runs under selected environmental hypothesis. As a results, some under-specifications and misalignments between the specifications of the various machines were identified. More importantly, when model checking the properties derived from of two of the test specifications, two problems were discovered which might had potentially led the Embedded System to unsafe behaviors. The structured specification methodology is currently in use for the ongoing project.

4   Conclusions

In this paper, two applications of formal methods to the design of safety critical systems are described. In the first, the design a complex communication protocol for distributed systems was tackled by a small team composed by experts in formal methods. In the second, the development of a complex, embedded control system was tackled by a large team. In order to achieve the project goals, formal methods were tightly integrated in (and adapted to) the development process, and heavily used in specification and verification to support the design phase. Model checking techniques were used to automatically analyze the specifications, and pinpoint several subtle errors and unexpected behaviors in early stages of the design.

Overall, formal methods have a great potential of applicability in the development of industrial critical systems, but there are several conditions that need to be achieved in order for them to be cost-effective. First, the application of formal methods must be motivated, e.g. by the critical functions carried out by the system, or by the regulatory standards. Furthermore, the formal activity must be selectively limited to the most critical parts/functions of the system, and integrated with the existing development processes. As a final remark, in our experience it was always necessary to pay the price of the formal methods team becoming expert in the application domain. This activity, however, appears to payoff constantly with the discovery of large amounts of under-specifications in the informal requirements and designs. Furthermore, domain expertise allows to produce the right abstractions in the models, and therefore to apply model checking more effectively.

Acknowledgements. The technology transfer activity carried out at IRST since 1995 in the application of formal methods to the development of industrial critical systems benefited from the essential contributions of Piergiorgio Bertoli, Fausto Giunchiglia, Paolo Pecchiari, Marco Pistore, Marco Roveri, Roberto Sebastiani, Paolo Traverso, Adolfo Villafiorita, Gabriele Zacco. This paper is based [1] and [8].

References

1. P.G. Bertoli and A. Cimatti P. Traverso. Integrating formal methods into the development cycle of a safety critical embedded software system. In *Proceedings of the 5th International Workshop on Formal Methods for Industrial Critical Systems (FMICS2000)*, number 91 in GMD report, pages 187–201, 2000.
2. J. Bowen. Formal Methods in Safety-Critical Standards. Oxford University Computing Laboratory Technical Report, 1995.
3. J. Bowen. The Industrial Take-Up of Formal Methods. Oxford University Computing Laboratory Technical Report, 1995.
4. J. R. Burch, E. M. Clarke, K. L. McMillan, D. L. Dill, and L. J. Hwang. Symbolic Model Checking: 10^{20} States and Beyond. *Information and Computation*, 98(2):142–170, June 1992.

5. A. Chiappini, A. Cimatti, C. Porzia, G. Rotondo, R. Sebastiani, P. Traverso, and A. Villafiorita. Formal specification and development of a safety-critical train management system. In *Proceedings of 18th international Conference on Computer Safety, Reliability and Security (SAFECOMP'99)*, number 1698 in Lecture Notes in Computer Science, 1999.

6. A. Cimatti, F. Giunchiglia, G. Mongardi, D. Romano, F. Torielli, and P. Traverso. Formal Verification of a Railway Interlocking System using Model Checking. *Journal on Formal Aspects in Computing*, (10):361–380, 1998.

7. A. Cimatti, F. Giunchiglia, P. Pecchiari, B. Pietra, J. Profeta, D. Romano, and P. Traverso. A Provably Correct Embedded Verifier for the Certification of Safety Critical Software. In *Proc. Computer-Aided Verification (CAV'97)*, Haifa, Israel, June 1997. Also IRST-Technical Report 9701-04, IRST, Trento, Italy.

8. A. Cimatti, P.L. Pieraccini, R. Sebastiani, P. Traverso, and A. Villafiorita. Formal specification and validation of a vital communication protocol. In *Proceedings of the World Congress on Formal Methods (FM99)*, number 1709 in Lecture Notes in Computer Science, pages 1584–1603, 1999.

9. E.M. Clarke and E.A. Emerson. Synthesis of synchronization skeletons for branching time temporal logic. In *Logic of Programs: Workshop*. Springer Verlag, May 1981. Lecture Notes in Computer Science No. 131.

10. European Commitee for Electrotechnical Standardization. European Standard - Railway Applications: Software for Railways Control and Protection Systems. EN 50128, 1995.

11. D. Harel and E. Gery. Executable Object Modeling with Statecharts. In *Proceedings of the 18th international conference on Software engineering*, pages 246–257. ACM, March 1996.

12. G.J. Holzmann. *Design and Validation of Computer Protocols*. Prentice Hall, 1991.

13. ITU-T. *CCITT specification and description language (SDL)*, March 1993. ITU-T Recommendation Z.100.

14. ITU-T. *Message Sequence Chart (MSC)*, October 1996. ITU-T Recommendation Z.120.

15. Profibus Nutzerorganization. *Profibus Standard*, July 1996. DIN 19 245.

16. VERILOG. *ObjectGEODE Documentation*. Available at *www.verilogusa.com*.

Formal Methods in Practice: The Missing Links. A Perspective from the Security Area

Dominique Bolignano, Daniel Le Métayer, and Claire Loiseaux

Trusted Logic
www.trusted-logic.fr

Abstract. Our goal in this paper is not to enrich the literature with yet another defence of formal methods, but rather to build on our experience of using and studying formal methods in security to provide an industrial point of view, with a strong emphasis on practicality. We also hope that, even if we take our inspiration mainly in the security area, most of our observations on formal methods are relevant to other application domains as well. The term "security" itself can be used in various contexts with different meanings. We use it here in the sense of security of information, as defined by the standard triptych: confidentiality, integrity and availability.

1 Introduction

The role and impact of formal methods in software engineering has always been a controversial issue and an ideal topic for lively debates and conference panels. Some of these debates turned into dogmatic pleas dividing the world into (roughly speaking) two camps, the believers and the scepticals, with little hope for reconciliation. A number of papers have also been published putting forward the significance of formal methods for software engineering. Until recently, however, the advocators of formal methods looked more or less like apostles preaching in the desert and suffering the scepticism of "real developers". But things are changing slowly and the situation is no longer so bleak for formal methods, at least in specific areas. One strong reason which may lead to a wider acceptance of formal methods is the need for software with specific non functional requirements such as quality, robustness, dependability, or security.

Our goal in this paper is not to enrich the literature with yet another defence of formal methods, but rather to build on our experience of using and studying formal methods in security to provide an industrial point of view, with a strong emphasis on practicality. We also hope that, even if we take our inspiration mainly in the security area, most of our observations on formal methods are relevant to other application domains as well. The term "security" itself can be used in various contexts with different meanings. We use it here in the sense of security of information, as defined by the standard triptych: confidentiality, integrity and availability.

In the next section, we identify a number of challenges and pitfalls for formal methods and we put forward our approach based on the notion of multiple

F. Cassez et al. (Eds.): MOVEP 2000, LNCS 2067, pp. 169–180, 2001.

views linked by consistency relations. The next sections illustrate this approach with two industrial products: TL-FIT and TL-CAT. Section 3 introduces TL-FIT, a programming environment which is well suited to the development of software for security certifications. TL-CAT is a test suite generator; it produces automatically test suites from a specification and a test strategy. The conclusion identifies avenues for further research.

2   Challenges and Pitfalls

In order to avoid any prejudice in a discussion about formal methods, it is better to start with a reminder of the original needs: in other words, what are we looking for, what are the criteria that will be used to assess a method, whether formal or not? We believe that the ultimate goal of the methods that we consider here is to increase confidence in software. This is especially the case when security matters because security is a notoriously difficult area, with potentially very important assets at stake. Generally speaking, the confidence in a system increases with the level of rigour used in its development. But rigour is a subjective matter and the use of a formalism can be a way to impose it. The second critical issue, which should not be looked over, is efficiency. A project leader may well be keen on adopting a method with the promise of getting higher quality software, but he could become reluctant when realising that the method incurs prohibitive costs. These costs in the case of formal methods can be measured in terms of training and potentially longer (initial) development cycles. So we are left with two conflicting goals: how can we, as cheaply as possible, increase, as much as possible, our confidence that a system satisfies specific security requirements? Keeping these goals in mind, we provide now a few observations about the current situation; we first consider the relationship between formal methods and informal (or semi-formal) methods. Then we generalise the discussion and justify the stress on "missing links" in the title.

2.1   Formal and Informal: Integration Rather than Opposition

The first question that can be asked by the sceptical concerns the very need of formalism to increase the level of confidence. There are plenty of techniques in software engineering with precisely this aim: development methods, code review, testing, quality assessment, etc. All these techniques have proved useful indeed and it should be out of question to dismiss them and pretend formal methods would make them obsolete. This would not only be unacceptable in practice, but also unfounded:

- It would be unfounded because formality is not a virtue per se; the ultimate goal is rigour, and formality can be one way to impose rigour, but not necessarily the single one. A well understood and properly applied development method can also be a way to achieve rigour; systematic testing following explicit strategies is another, complementary step towards rigour.

— It would be unacceptable in practice because software engineers have accumulated a lot of expertise in using these techniques and it would not be very wise to undervalue all this knowledge and impose a switch to a completely different working environment.

These arguments may look common sense, but it must be said that they have been largely overlooked by the formal methods community in the past and this is probably one of the main reasons for the relatively modest acceptance of tools such as Z [?] or B [?]. Most of the work in this community seemed to rely on the assumption that developers should experiment a dramatic culture shift and become some kinds of mathematicians. As a result, these endeavours have led to very sophisticated and impressive specification and verification tools, but these tools remain totally unconnected to the development environments used in industry. Even worse, they remain also largely unconnected to the semi-formal methods that have been used for decades and which have culminated with the emergence of UML [?] (it should be noticed however that efforts have been devoted recently on the definition of a formal semantics for specific aspects of UML, in particular under the initiative of the pUML group [?]).

Another reason why formal method proponents should definitely not hold informal methods in contempt is that the very ends of the development process are, by essence, informal because they relate to human beings:

— The start of the process is a collection of (functional or security) requirements expressed in a natural language.
— The end of the process (validation) is also informal in nature since its purpose is to convince the client (or the certification body) that the system really satisfies the original requirements.

There is no reason to believe that the final client will necessarily be impressed by the fact that the overall design and development have been conducted in a formal framework using a collection of well identified transformations, refinement rules and proof techniques. Many mistakes can still fall outside the scope of formal methods: the properties might be properly proven but irrelevant, they may not express what they were intended to, they may rely on unrealistic (or not well understood) assumptions. In addition, the client is not necessarily an expert on formal methods (and even less likely on the specific tool used for this development) and he might not take its soundness for granted. In any case, a theorem prover is a piece of software itself and it is not immune to programming errors. All these comments point to the same conclusion: using formal methods is not enough; it is necessary to establish the connection with the "external" (non formal) world. This connection can take different forms (traceability between different documents, informal proof sketches, translation between logical formalisms and graphical notations, etc.) but it is a requisite for the successful use of formal methods.

Security is an excellent area for illustrating these arguments because certifications rely on an international standard called the Common Criteria for information technology security evaluation [?] (Common Criteria in the sequel).

Seven evaluation levels are specified in the Common Criteria: from EAL1 to EAL7 (EAL stands for Evaluation Assurance Level). Depending on the evaluation level, different certification documents have to be provided in different formats: they can be informal, semi-formal or formal. All the documents considered at levels EAL1 to EAL4 are informal. EAL5 requires a semi-formal definition of the functional specification and the high-level design and a formal specification of the security policy model. Level EAL7 goes further and imposes a formal definition of the functional specification and the high-level design as well. As a result, all the levels above EAL4 (which are concerned by formal methods) involve different description styles (formal, semi-formal and informal). For example, the "assurance components" required at these levels include test components with their justification; also, providing formal specifications and proofs does not mean dispensing with informal explanations (traceability). As far as tools are concerned, the Common Criteria do not recommend the use of specific products, but the developer should provide enough evidence to convince the evaluators of their soundness. Of course, resorting to standard or widely used tools is a definite advantage in this process.

At first sight, this section may look overly critical about formal methods. The real point we want to make here however is not against formal methods themselves, but against a trend to study and develop them in isolation. Formal methods will always have to live with informal and semi-formal methods and they should be designed so that cooperation between them is as harmonious as possible. So we believe that the real challenge today is not to design new sophisticated specification languages or powerful proof techniques but rather to provide ways of integrating formal techniques in an otherwise informal or semi-formal environment. Such an objective should not be seen as a simple engineering problem: it is not clear whether anyone today can offer good enough solutions to problems such as proof explanations, traceability between informal and formal specifications, verifications on semi-formal documents, reusability of semi-formal descriptions to construct formal specifications, etc.

2.2   Establish Links

The outcome of a development can be seen as a set of documents expressed in different languages (natural language, graphical notation, restricted language, mathematical notation, etc.). Typical examples of documents are requirements, use cases, statecharts, class diagrams, high-level designs, low-level designs, formal specifications, source codes, test strategies, test suites, etc. Pursuing the ideas suggested in the previous section naturally leads us to consider the links between these documents. In other words, we would like to take each of these documents as a specific view of the system, with specific consistency relationships between them. Two significant features of views should be stressed at this point:

- They are partially redundant: the information they convey may overlap, even if expressed in different ways. For example the external (or publicly accessible) operations of the system should appear in the specification as

well as in the high-level design; information about authorised call sequences can be found in the use cases as well as in the specification and the test suites; information about input/output relationships appear in use cases, specifications, test cases, etc.
- They can (and usually are) provided by different parties (analyst, software architect, developer, tester, etc.). So each view reflects the way one particular party sees the system.

As a consequence, unless specific measures are taken, there is no reason why these views should necessarily be consistent. This can be taken as a fatality, but also as a great opportunity. As stated in the introduction, the ultimate goal of the methods considered here is to increase confidence in software. Now, the best way to improve confidence is to be able to rely on a collection of representations of this software (ideally originating from different sources) and to check for their consistency. The level of confidence in a software can then be defined as the result of three factors:

- The number of available representations.
- The number of different sources.
- The level of confidence in the consistency checking methods.

The notion of "view" has been used in the same spirit in a variety of contexts: in the software architecture community [?], in semi-formal development methods [?], in data bases etc. Very little has been done however on the problem of checking the consistency of different views (in particular, the verifications offered in most UML tools are really minimal) . Of course the problem is compounded when the views are expressed in different formalisms. Two main approaches have been proposed to deal with heterogeneous views:

- The first approach consists in translating each view into a single common representation in a general purpose formalism (Z for example in [?]. The overall consistency of the views then boils down to the internal consistency of the global view.
- The second approach is based on a collection of mutual consistency checks between the individual views. Each check is tailored to the specific formalisms involved.

Each approach has its own advantages and drawbacks. The first one may not be generally applicable because it assumes that a common encompassing formalism can be found, which is likely to introduce severe restrictions in the styles that can be used to define the views. In addition, it can lead to cumbersome specifications and proofs. The second approach is more in the spirit of views (separation of issues) but it yields a number of verifications which grows quadratically with the number of views.

We still believe that the second approach is more promising for pragmatic reasons:

- First, it is not necessary in practice to check all the pairs of views for consistency. Some views may not be related to each other (think of functional test cases and high-level design for example); the consistency between two views may be implied by other consistency properties involving these views (for example, refinement relations are transitive), etc.

− The second reason has to do with the efficiency criterion identified in the introduction. The important point is that the consistency checking process can be incremental since each verification between two views increases the level of confidence on the whole system. In addition, the verification algorithms can be made automatic and efficient because they are specific to the given views. This contrasts with the translation into a single formalism which leads to verifications using a general purpose theorem prover, with little hope for mechanisation.

We can rely again on the Common Criteria to illustrate the principles put forward in this section. One significant class of documents that we haven't mentioned so far is called the "Representation Correspondence Rationale". As the name suggests, the role of this class of components is to provide evidence about the consistency of different documents. These documents may be expressed in different formalisms and the general rule is that the rationale should be as formal as the less formal of the documents involved. For example, the rationale between a formal security policy model and an informal functional specification has to be expressed informally. On the other hand, the rationale between a formal functional specification and a formal high-level design (refinement) must be a formal proof. Other examples of rationales include refinement relations between high-level design and low-level design and test cases (between functional specifications or low-level design and implementations).

3   TL-FIT: Linking Formal and Informal Descriptions

A serious impediment to the certification at the highest levels of the Common Criteria is the extra cost incurred by the application of formal methods. It is the case indeed that the use formal methods currently imposes a dramatic change in terms of methodology. As a consequence, it is very difficult to build on the documents produced for, say an EAL4 certification, to prepare an EAL7 certification. Our opinion however is that this state of affairs is not without remedy. Following the discussion of section 2, we believe that it is the consequence of the current absence of link between formal and informal methods rather than inherent to formal methods themselves. As stated in section 2, the key issue is rigour; formalism is one way to achieve rigour, but it does not have to be the single one; there is no reason why informal or semi-formal descriptions should necessarily be sloppy. This idea is at the core of the TL-FIT environment, whose goal is precisely to favour rigour in the informal mode as well as in the semi-formal and the formal modes. Proceeding this way makes it easier to factorise efforts and to build on one level to go further up in the hierarchy.

More precisely, the TL-FIT environment is based on the notion of view suggested in the previous section. Views are organised in a two-dimensional space inspired by the Common Criteria:

- The first dimension expresses the refinement levels: it includes the functional specification, the high-level design, the low-level design and the implementation.
- The second dimension corresponds to the description mode: informal, semi-formal or formal.

For a given description mode, the Common Criteria impose that all the refinement levels are present. Of course, not all description modes need to be provided for a given development. For example, the semi-formal and formal modes are not relevant for EAL1 certifications. Their presence in the same space however is a crucial factor as far as evolutivity is concerned. Each document in this two-dimensional space follows the same pattern. The pattern defines a module (or system) as a set of fields including its interface (operations accessible from outside), set of global variables, invariant, protocol (sequences of authorised calls to interface operations), call graph and set of classes. Classes themselves include a set of local variables, a local invariant and links to other classes. Operations are defined by several attributes: pre-condition, post-condition, control graph, set of read variables, set of modified variables, set of called operations, etc. In addition, both variables and operations have visibility attributes (public or private).

Despite the fact that they follow the same pattern, the documents may look quite differently depending on their position in the two-dimensional space. The unique pattern can be seen as a structure of fields which can be parameterised in two ways:

- First, the fields of a document may be optional or mandatory depending on its position in the space. For example, the control graph of an operation has to be provided only for the low-level design representations; the protocol, the pre-conditions and the call graph are not required for informal descriptions.
- The second parameterisation mean is the formalism used to define the fields. The informal descriptions are expressed in a natural language. The semi-formal descriptions are based on restricted languages with a well-defined syntax. These languages are typically graphical notations or "Claims languages" (severely restricted versions of natural languages with a limited vocabulary and grammar). The formal descriptions rely on a language with not only a well-defined syntax, but also a well-defined semantics. This separation in three categories is consistent with the Common Criteria.

As suggested in section 2, the different views include a number of redundancies. These redundancies form the basis for a variety of consistency checkings. Consistency properties can be divided in three classes:

- Internal consistency constraints (within a single description).
- Refinement relations (between two descriptions in the same mode).
- Traceability relations (between two descriptions at the same refinement level, but in different modes).

More fundamentally, the consistency properties can either be syntactical or semantical. Of course semantical properties can only be checked in the formal mode. Among the syntactical properties that are checked in TL-FIT, we can mention:

1. The set of operations in the interface of the module is equal to the set of public operations in its classes.
2. All the variables occurring in the pre-condition or the post-condition of an operation must also appear in either in the set of read variables or the set of modified variables (and vice versa).
3. The protocol associated with a module should not involve any operation which does not belong to its interface.
4. The call graph of a module should agree with the call sets of its operations.
5. The links associated with a class should agree with the definitions of its operations.
6. The set of operations in a given class in the low-level design should include the set of operations of the same class (if present) in the high-level design.
7. The call graph of the low-level design should not introduce new dependencies between operations occurring in the call graph of the high-level design.
8. The sets of operations of a module should be identical in the informal and the formal modes.
9. The sets of read and modified variables associated with an operation in a semi-formal description should be identical in the corresponding formal description.

The first five properties are internal consistency constraints; the following two are refinement relations and the last two are traceability relations.

The following are examples of semantical properties generated by TL-FIT:

1. The protocol associated with a module should not specify successions of operations that are forbidden by the specifications (pre-condition and post-condition) of these operations.
2. The specification of an operation should not invalidate the invariant associated with its class.
3. The invariant of a module in the high-level design should imply the invariant of the same module in the functional specification.
4. The pre-condition of an operation in the high-level design should imply the pre-condition of the same operation in the low-level design.
5. The post-condition of an operation in the low-level design should imply the post-condition of the same operation in the high-level design.

The first two properties are internal consistency constraints; the last three are refinement relations. There is no semantical traceability relation since semantical properties can only involve descriptions in the formal mode.

Two important points should be made concerning the tools for consistency checking:

1. All syntactic consistency verifications are completely automatic. They are based on set operations and graph manipulation algorithms.

2. The semantic verifications cannot be mechanised in whole generality. Semantical properties can be translated into a theorem prover and have then to be checked with the help of the user. This interaction cannot be avoided without further restrictions on the logical language used to specify properties. We believe that it should be possible though to take advantage of the specific form of the properties to be proven in this context for the design of special purpose proof strategies.

As far as the product itself is concerned, we should mention that TL-FIT has been developed on the top of Objecteering, the UML environment proposed by Softeam. We believe that UML is ideally suited to this kind of development because its notation is rich enough and widely accepted in industry. Its notation might even be too rich for our purpose, but we exploit only specific aspects of UML (namely class diagrams, statecharts and activity diagrams) that are tailored to meet our needs.

To conclude this section, we would like to point out a further advantage of integrating formal methods in a wider context including informal and semi-formal descriptions. The benefits of using formal methods become clearer with the two-dimensional space. The above discussion shows that moving towards the formal end of the spectrum entails further constraints but also significant rewards. The constraint is that is necessary to provide more information to the system (because syntax is no longer enough, semantics has also to be considered). The reward however is that new tools can exploit this extra information (checking the semantics aspects of your documents). Looking that way, formalisation is just a step further, adding new links and increasing confidence in the software.

4   TL-CAT: Linking Specifications and Test Suites

Testing is another major issue which has not been considered with enough attention by the formal methods community in the past. Claims have even been made at some stage that formal methods would make testing irrelevant. After all, what is the point of testing a software that has been proven correct? Even when it didn't take so extreme forms, the general feeling was that testing was an essentially practical business, with little room for formalisation. Fortunately this hostile mood has evolved significantly during the last decade, mainly under the initiative of the communication protocols community [?,?]. Several research projects are now devoted to the generation of test suites from specifications. The specifications considered in this context are generally expressed as some kind of transition system and the generation is mainly control-oriented. This is well suited to protocol testing, but testing other classes of applications generally requires taking also data values into account [?]. In this section, we present TL-CAT (Computer Assisted Testing), a commercial tool for the automatic generation of test suites which takes data as well as control into account.

The two main inputs of TL-CAT are a specification of the application and a description of the test strategy. Specifications are provided using a simple "condition-action" language. Basically, an application is defined as a collection of state variables and operations expressed as sets of pairs (C,A) where:

1. C is a condition (on the state variables and the parameters of the operation) that has to be satisfied for the action to apply.
2. A is the action: it specifies a transformation of the state variables.

Two kinds of strategies can be defined by the tester (or picked up from a library of pre-defined strategies):

1. Data-oriented strategies, which impose the selection of data in specific domains associated with the specification. The minimal strategy consists in choosing one combination of data to exercise each pair (C,A). Richer strategies involve further decompositions of the domains. Examples of such strategies include: interval bounds, decomposition of specific expressions such as "or" connectors, exhaustive coverage of small domains, etc.
2. Control-oriented strategies, which impose specific orderings between test cases. For example, the tester may want to test operation Op1 under condition C1 after several applications of Op2 and Op3. Such strategies are expressed in an extended regular language.

Strategies are not exclusive, but additional. The goal of TL-CAT is to generate a collection of test suites that is sufficient to cover the requirements expressed by all the strategies.

TL-CAT is implemented using a dedicated constraint solver. As usual, the solver may fail to solve a particular constraint for two reasons: either the constraint does not have any solution, or it does have solutions but the strategy of the solver is not powerful to discover it. As in most constraint solvers, it is then up to the user to decide that a test case is not feasible, or to help the solver by providing a solution or a hint (instantiation of a specific variable for example). This kind of interaction is offered by the system because the language of properties is not decidable, but the system can also be used in a batch mode in which it just tries to produce all the possible test cases and keeps track of the remaining ones.

We believe that test suite generation as exemplified in this section illustrates the principles of section 2 in several ways:

1. First, and most importantly, it represents a way of integrating formal methods in a more traditional development environment. Far from dismissing the testers' skills, the tool makes it possible for them to express their expertise through the design of test strategies and focus on the really significant part of their job, rather than the repetitive and boring task of inventing sets of data values.
2. It should also be stressed that the links that are established between specifications and test data are valuable not only for testing the first version of the software; this link is of great value to support software evolution; in particular, it makes non-regression testing easier.

3. The benefit of using a systematic test generator should not be measured only in terms of reduced testing times, but also in terms of quality. The test strategies can be provided as a justification for the test suites and help convince outsiders (for example certification bodies) that the key features of the software have been properly tested.

5 Conclusion

The approach put forward in this paper is very much in line with the idea that a proof is nothing more than a "social process" [?]. The notion of an absolute proof is illusory, especially in the area of software engineering. It is only when many authoritative people have approved it that we can get some confidence in a mathematical proof. Putting it in our context, it is only when many links have been established (and checked by relialable tools) between development documents produced by various people that we can get some confidence in the software. These considerations take us far away from the purist view of formal methods solving grand problems in isolation from the rest of the world.

We have illustrated our philosophy with two examples showing ways of establishing links between a variety of documents, with a special emphasis on the links between informal and formal descriptions. Of course there are still a lot of challenges to be met, or missing links to be discovered. Let us just mention some of them which have become conspicuous in the context of security certifications but are more generally relevant.

The first observation that can be made by an outsider getting interested in formal methods is the plethora of tools (academic if not industrial) available. Many of them seem to rely on similar grounds (set theory, type theory, transition systems) but they still offer subtle variations and different syntaxes. More importantly, being able to conduct a proof using one of the existing theorem provers seems to remain the privilege of few experts; even worse, the required expertise is not so much in formal methods generally speaking than in one particular system. Coming back to our original goal of improving confidence, it should be clear that neither a client nor a certification body can really be expected to possess expertise in a large set of theories and theorem provers. In fact, it is even not clear whether the idiosyncrasies of specific provers should really matter when the goal is to prove relatively simple refinement relations or invariant preservations. It does not seem to be out of reach to produce proof sketches in a relatively neutral style, that could then be translated into the internal languages of specific tools. A standard mathematical notation, possibly augmented with a restricted natural language, would be ideal for this purpose. Some work has already be done in this direction, but we feel that there is a strong need for further research and tools.

Another issue which is becoming increasingly important for the application of formal methods to security is compositionality. We have some ideas about specifying security properties of individual components; but what happens when these components are linked together to form a system? Is it possible to build on the work done at the level of components to derive useful information about the system? An interesting, and timely, question to this respect is the independent certification of a system and its components. Again, preliminary work has been done on this topic, in particular in the software architecture community, but much more has to be done to meet the needs.

To conclude this paper, we can mention yet another challenge which is motivated by current security certifications. The Common Criteria require a formal definition of the security policy model from level EAL5 upwards. A number of specific models have been proposed in the literature, but they have very different flavours and there is nothing like a widely recognised framework for defining a security policy model. Following our pragmatic approach, we believe that such a model should be designed with verifications in mind, which means that general purpose, Turing complete, models should be avoided if possible. Further work should be done to study the applicability of the "Domain Specific Languages" approach in this context in order to design a language that could lead to automatic verifications (at least of simple security policies).

References

1. Abrial, J. R.: "Assigning programs to meaning". *Cambridge University Press* 1996.
2. Bochmann, G., Petrenko, A.: "Protocol testing: review of methods and relevance for software testing". *Proc. of the ACM int. Symposium on software testing and analysis* 1994.
3. Booch,G., Rumbaugh, J., Jacobson, I.: "The Unified Modeling Language user guide". *Addison-Wesley* 1998.
4. Bowman, H., Boiten, E., Derrick, J., Steen, M.: "Viewpoint consistency in ODP, a general interpretation". *Proc. of the 1st IFIP int. Workshop on formal methods for open object-based distributed systems, Chapman & Hall* 1996, pp. 189–204.
5. "The Common Criteria for Information Technology Security Evaluation". *http://www.commoncriteria.org/docs/aboutus.html.*
6. De Millo, R. A., Lipton, R. J., Perlis, A. J.: "Social processes and proofs of theorems and programs". *Communications of the ACM*, 22(5) 1979, pp. 271–280.
7. Fernandez, J-C., Jard, C., Jéron, T., Viho, C.: "An experiment in automatic generation of test suites for protocols with verification technology". *Science of Computer Programming*, Vol. 28, 1997, pp. 123–146.
8. Fradet, P., Le Métayer, D., Périn, M.: "Consistency checking for multiple view software architecture". *Proc. 7th ACM SIGSOFT Symposium on the Foundations of Software Engineering*, Springer Verlag, LNCS 1687, 1999, pp. -410-428.
9. Kruchten, P-B.: "The 4+1 view model of architecture". *IEEE Software*, 12(6), 1995, pp. 42–50.
10. "The Precise UML (PUML) group". *http://www.cs.york.ac.uk/puml/.*
11. Spivey, J.: "The Z reference manual". *Prentice Hall*, 1992.
12. Van Aertryck, L., Benveniste, M., Le Métayer, D.: "Casting: a formally based software test generation method". *IEEE int. Conference on formal engineering methods*, 1997, pp. 101–111.

Annotated Bibliographies

Verification of Systems with an Infinite State Space

Javier Esparza

Institut für Informatik, Technische Universität München, Germany
esparza@in.tum.de

During the last two decades, an important effort has been devoted to the development of verification techniques and their application. Significant achievements have been obtained, and efficient tools have been developed for *automatic* verification of *finite-state systems* (i.e., systems with finitely many configurations), based essentially on reachability analysis algorithms. All major constructors of hardware and software controllers have already created verification groups that use these techniques. This is particularly true after the recent occurrence of costly errors like the Pentium bug and the Ariane crash.

However, while the finite-state framework is well suited for reasoning about e.g., logical circuits, it cannot deal with essential aspects in the behaviors of software systems like communication protocols. For this we must be able to reason about models which may have *infinitely* many configurations.

There are different "sources of infinity". A simple analysis permits to identify at least the following five:

(1) **Data manipulation:** Software systems manipulate data structures and variables ranging over infinite data domains, e.g., integer counters.
(2) **Control structures:** Procedures lead to potentially unbounded call stacks, while process creation leads to unboundedly many concurrent processes.
(3) **Asynchronous communication:** Asynchronous communication leads to unbounded queues for the messages interchanged by different processes. A natural model for asynchronous communicating systems are automata with unbounded FIFO queues (FIFO-channel systems). This model is the basis of widely used specification languages like SDL, the ITU-T (CCITT) international standard language for the specification of telecommunication protocols.
(4) **Parametrization:** Many distributed systems are designed for an arbitrary number k of processes. The problem is to validate the system for all possible values of k, or to determine the values of k for which the system is correct. Strictly speaking, we deal here with an infinite family of systems. However, the family can usually be seen as one single infinite-state system.
(5) **Real-time constraints:** The behaviors of systems like communication protocols involve various mechanisms based on timing constraints, e.g time-outs. Models of these systems use real-valued clocks to measure delays between events. Since the time domain is infinite, these models have infinitely many configurations.

In the lecture I introduce some of the main techniques developed in the last years for dealing with these points, like symbolic forward and backward search,

F. Cassez et al. (Eds.): MOVEP 2000, LNCS 2067, pp. 183–186, 2001.
© Springer-Verlag Berlin Heidelberg 2001

accelerations, and widenings. The concepts are illustrated by applying them to a simple but interesting class of parametrized systems called *broadcast protocols*. Therefore the lecture is biased towards point (4) above. The results on broadcast protocols are taken from the following papers:

J. Esparza, A. Finkel and R. Mayr: On the Verification of Broadcast Protocols. Proceedings of LICS'99, IEEE Computer Society, 352–359 (1999).

G. Delzanno, J. Esparza and A. Podelski: Constraint-based Analysis of Broadcast Protocols. Proceedings of CSL '99 Lecture Notes in Computer Science 1683, 50–66 (1999).

G. Delzanno and J.-F. Raskin: Symbolic Representation of Upwards Closed Sets. Proceedings of TACAS '00. Lecture Notes in Computer Science 1683, 426–440 (2000).

G. Delzanno: Automatic Verification of Parameterized Cache Coherence Protocols. Proceedings of CAV '00. Lecture Notes in Computer Science 1683, 53–68 (2000).

Forward and backward search, accelerations, and widenings can also be applied to other sources of infinity, not only to parametrized systems. However, a detailed presentation would take too much time. Therefore, in the lecture I just mention a number of papers in which the same techniques are applied to models for (1), (2), (3) and (5) above. The references are listed below. Notice that the list is not a systematic bibliography, and that many important papers are missing.

Data manipulation. An interesting approach is to apply constraint programming techniques. Here is a nice paper on it:

G. Delzanno and A. Podelski: Model Checking in CLP. Proceedings of TACAS '99, Lecture Notes in Computer Science 1579, 223–239 (1999).

Control structures. Verification problems for systems with one unbounded stack has been intensely studied in the last years. These systems can model the control structure of procedural programs. Here are three of my own papers on this topic.

A. Bouajjani, J. Esparza and O. Maler: Reachability Analysis of Pushdown Automata: Application to Model-Checking. Proceedings of CONCUR '97, Lecture Notes in Computer Science 1243, 135–150 (1997).

J. Esparza, D. Hansel, P. Rossmanith and S. Schwoon: Efficient Algorithms for Model Checking Pushdown Systems. Lecture Notes in Computer Science 1683, 232–247 (2000).

J. Esparza and J. Knoop: An Automata-theoretic Approach to Interprocedural Dataflow Analysis. Proceedings of FOSSACS '99, Lecture Notes in Computer Science 1578, 14–30 (1999).

The group of Bernhard Steffen at the University of Dortmund has also done much work on this problem. They have applied the theory to dataflow analysis problems with very good results. Their (many) papers can be accessed online.

Asynchronous communication. The two papers below study the problem of computing an approximation of the set of reachable states of a system with FIFO-channels.

B. Boigelot and P. Godefroid: Symbolic Verification of Communication Protocols with Infinite State Spaces using QDDs. Proceedings of CAV '96, Lecture Notes in Computer Science 1102, 1–12 (1996).

A. Bouajjani and P. Habermehl: Symbolic Reachability Analysis of FIFO-Channel Systems with Nonregular Sets of Configurations. Proceedings of ICALP '97, Lecture Notes in Computer Science 1256, 560–570 (1998).

The next two papers consider the particular case in which the channels are lossy, i.e., may lose messages. Interestingly, some problems which are undecidable for systems with perfect FIFO-channels become decidable for systems with lossy channels.

P.A. Abdulla and B. Jonsson: Verifying programs with unreliable channels. Information and Computation 127(2):91–101 (1996).

P.A. Abdulla, A. Bouajjani and B. Jonsson: On-the-Fly Analysis of Systems with Unbounded, Lossy FIFO Channels. Proceedings of CAV '98, Lecture Notes in Computer Science 1427, 305–318 (1998).

Parametrization. Two of the first papers to study the problem of systems with an unbounded number of processes are

S.M. German and A.P. Sistla: Reasoning about systems with many processes. Journal of the ACM, 39(3):675-735 (1992).

E.A. Emerson and J. Srinivasan. A decidable temporal logic to reason about many processes. In Proceedings of the Ninth Annual ACM Symposium on Principles of Distributed Computing, 233-246 (1990).

Automata have been used to verify arrays and rings of processes of unbounded length. A recent paper on this approach is

P.A. Abdulla, A. Bouajjani, B. Jonsson and M. Nilsson: Handling Global Conditions in Parametrized System Verification. Proceedings of CAV '99, Lecture Notes in Computer Science 1633, 134–145 (1999).

Real-time. This topic has generated lots of literature in the last years, and it is the subject of the MOVEP'2k talks by Larsen and Petterson, and by Sifakis. I just mention here one of the seminal papers.

R. Alur and D.L. Dill. A theory of timed automata. Theoretical Computer Science, 126(2):183-235 (1994). Fundamental Study.

Testing Transition Systems: An Annotated Bibliography

Ed Brinksma and Jan Tretmans

University of Twente *
Faculty of Computer Science, Formal Methods and Tools Group
P.O. Box 217, 7500 AE Enschede, The Netherlands
{brinksma,tretmans}@cs.utwente.nl
http://fmt.cs.utwente.nl

Abstract. Labelled transition system based test theory has made remarkable progress over the past 15 years. From a theoretically interesting approach to the semantics of reactive systems It has developed into a field where testing theory is (slowly) narrowing the gap with testing practice. In particular, new test generation algorithms are being designed that can be used in realistic situations whilst maintaining a sound theoretical basis. In this paper we present an annotated bibliography of labelled transition system based test theory and its applications covering the main developments.

1 Formal Testing Theory

Formal testing theory was introduced by Rocco De Nicola and Matthew Hennessy in their seminal paper [DNH84], further elaborated in [DN87,Hen88]. Their original motivation was to characterise interesting formalisations of the notion of *observable behaviour* for transition systems using an idealised but intuitive formalisation of testing. It contributed to the semantic theory of reactive systems, and was not intended as a theory about actual testing. One of the main behavioural preorders or *implementation relations* of [DNH84], so called *must*-testing, was in fact an alternative characterisation of the standard semantic model for CSP [Hoa85], the *failures* model (at least, in the absence of infinite internal computations). Their approach actually required the formal observability of *deadlock* behaviour. This assumption was further exploited by Phillips in [Phi87], and independently by Langerak [Lan90], to define testing scenarios that allow for the testing of alternative behaviour after the observation of deadlocks, the so called *refusals* model. Abramsky showed in [Abr87] that by the introduction of still stronger assumptions (e.g., the unbounded copying

---

* Supported by the Dutch Technology Foundation STW under project STW TIF.4111: *Côte de Resyste – COnformance TEsting of REactive SYSTEms*, and by the Netherlands Organization for Scientific Research NWO under the Van Gogh project for French-Dutch cooperation VGP 62-480: *Automatic Generation of Conformance Tests*.

F. Cassez et al. (Eds.): MOVEP 2000, LNCS 2067, pp. 187–195, 2001.

of behaviours under test), even classical behavioural equivalences like *bisimulation* can be characterised by testing scenarios. An overview of the theory of behavioural equivalences and preorders for transition systems, including the testing-based notions and their further extensions, can be found in the classical surveys by Van Glabbeek [Gla90,Gla93].

2   Test Frameworks

To arrive at a useful formal model for actual testing a well-defined framework of basic terminology, concepts and methods is needed. The ISO International Standard on conformance testing [ISO91] has been a very influential, informal source in this respect. A short overview can be found in [Ray87], a more critical a posteriori assessment in [Ray97]. A first attempt to come to a more formal interpretation can be found in [BAL+90], with subsequent elaborations in [TKB92,Tre94, Tre99]. This has led itself to standardisation activity culminating in [ISO96], with related expositions in [CFP94,HST96].

3   Formal Test Generation

The first attempts to use De Nicola-Hennessy testing theory for finding algorithms to derive tests automatically from formal specifications were made by Brinksma in [Bri87,Bri88]. This work, which used the specification language LOTOS [ISO89,BB87] as a defining notation for the transition systems, led to the so called *canonical tester* theory. This approach has led to a whole series of modifications and extensions, the main ones being [PF90,Tre90,Doo91,Dri92,Led92]. Publications on specific test generation algorithms and (in some cases) their implementations can be found in [Eer87,Ald90,Wez90,DAV93,TPB96]. All these approaches assume that the testing process can communicate *synchronously* with the system under test (SUT), i.e., that each communication can be viewed as a joint action of system and tester, as in most process algebras [Mil89,Hoa85, BK85,ISO89].

4   Asynchronous Test Contexts

In practice the assumption of synchronous communication is seldom fulfilled. Initially, the problem was handled by applying existing theory on a transformation of the original formal specification. In this transformation the original transition system is 'plugged' into a context of input an output queues that enabled the asynchronous communication of inputs (test stimuli) and outputs (test responses) between tester and SUT [TV92,VTKB93]. In this way the existing theory could simply be 'lifted' to all sorts of asynchronous scenarios. The disadvantage of this approach, however, was that one had to have different transformations for each (static) communication interface. Moreover, as the communication queues were in most cases unbounded, they caused infinite state spaces even in the case of finite state specifications, which complicated the test generation problem considerably.

A major step forward was made by interpreting transition systems as descriptions of input/output-automata (I/O-automata) [LT89,Seg93]. In this model the property that test inputs cannot be blocked by the SUT is covered by the assumption of *input enabledness* (the I/O-condition), which says that in each state transitions for all input actions are defined. The impossibility to refuse test outputs is obtained by having the analogous requirement for the tester process. This semantic requirement on SUT and tester allows for a uniform and simplified treatment of whole classes of asynchronous testing scenarios and has related refusal and failure models that are in a certain sense simpler than their synchronous counterparts. These ideas were first explored by Phalippou and Tretmans [Pha94a,Pha94b,Tre96a,Tre96b]. Heerink has subsequently refined these ideas by refining the I/O-condition in the sense that either all or none of the input actions are enabled, allowing for the treatment of *bounded* communication media [HT97,Hee98]. This work also allows for the treatment of multiple *Points of Control and Observation* (PCO) that exist in practical situations. The multiple I/O-paradigm for testing turns out to be a natural saturation point of the whole theory, in the sense that all relevant other implementation relations can be obtained as special cases. An overview of the main ideas can be found in [BHT97].

5   Test Generation Tools

The ideas behind many of the reported test generation algorithms have been tried out in small, academic prototypes, but there are only a few examples of larger test tool developments linked to academic research in general, and transition system based testing in particular. An important point in this respect was the development of the test tool TVEDA [CGPT96]. Although not developed on the basis of a formal theory of testing, most of its underlying principles can be justified in terms of the I/O-theories of [Pha94b,Tre96b]. A more recent test tool that uses algorithms from the domain of model checking is TGV [FJJV96, FJJV97,JM99]. The ideas underlying TVEDA and TGV have been combined into TestComposer which is part of the commercial SDL tool set Object-Geode [KJG99].

In the Dutch *Côte de Resyste* project [STW96] the tool TorX is developed which is the first larger test tool that is completely based on a formal model of conformance testing [BFV+99,Tre99]. TorX accepts specifications in LOTOS and Promela; Promela is the input language for the model checker SPIN [Hol91,Spi]. The implementation of TorX uses the state-space exploration algorithms of SPIN for its Promela part [VT98], while for its LOTOS part it relies on the Cæsar-Aldebaran tool set [Gar98].

Among the other tools for formal transition system based test generation are VVT-RT which uses CSP as the input specification language [PS97], and SaMsTaG and Autolink which derive tests from SDL specifications but which have a slightly different and less formal approach [GSDD97,SEK+98]. The I/O testing paradigm is also used in hardware validation [HT99].

6   Current Developments

Current theory and tools can generate tests from transition systems based specifications, however, it is difficult to steer the test generation process and to know how much of the specification has been tested. Some of the tools use user-specified *test purposes* to steer the test generation (TGV, AUTOLINK), while others use a random approach (TORX). The problem of finding criteria for how to select the tests with the largest chance of detecting errors is one of the major research issues [Bri93,Pha94b,HT96,CV97,CG97]. Among the other research items of current interest are the representation and treatment of data aspects in test generation, the combination between conformance testing and performance testing, formal verification of test suites [JJM00], and distributed testing [JJKV98]. On the practical side we see increasing activities in applying the techniques and tools to realistic industrial case studies [KVZ98], while also comparison of different algorithms and tools is investigated in an experimental setting [BFV$^+$99, DBRV$^+$00,HFT00].

7   Other Formal Approaches to Testing

There are two other important 'schools' of formal methods based testing. The one with the longest tradition is based on Mealy-machines (also known as the FSM-approach); for overviews see [LY96,Pet00]. The link between this theory and transition systems based testing is studied in [Tan97].

Both the FSM and the transition system based approaches mainly deal with the dynamic aspects of system behaviour. An existing formal approach to testing the static aspects of systems, such as data structures and their operations, uses abstract data type (ADT) theory as its basis, see e.g., [Ber91,Gau95,LGA96] and [Mar95] for a corresponding tool. It is generally assumed that this approach can be combined with either of the control-oriented approaches [GJ98].

References

[Abr87]   S. Abramsky. Observational equivalence as a testing equivalence. *Theoretical Computer Science*, 53(3):225–241, 1987.

[Ald90]   R. Alderden. COOPER, the compositional construction of a canonical tester. In S.T. Vuong, editor, *FORTE'89*, pages 13–17. North-Holland, 1990.

[BAL$^+$90]   E. Brinksma, R. Alderden, R. Langerak, J. van de Lagemaat, and J. Tretmans. A formal approach to conformance testing. In J. de Meer, L. Mackert, and W. Effelsberg, editors, *Second Int. Workshop on Protocol Test Systems*, pages 349–363. North-Holland, 1990. Also: Memorandum INF-89-45, University of Twente, The Netherlands.

[BB87]   T. Bolognesi and E. Brinksma. Introduction to the ISO specification language LOTOS. *Computer Networks and ISDN Systems*, 14:25–59, 1987.

[Ber91]   G. Bernot. Testing against formal specifications: A theoretical view. In S. Abramsky and T. S. E. Maibaum, editors, *TAPSOFT'91, Volume 2*, pages 99–119. Lecture Notes in Computer Science 494, Springer-Verlag, 1991.

[BFV⁺99]   A. Belinfante, J. Feenstra, R.G. de Vries, J. Tretmans, N. Goga, L. Feijs,
           S. Mauw, and L. Heerink. Formal test automation: A simple experiment. In
           G. Csopaki, S. Dibuz, and K. Tarnay, editors, *Int. Workshop on Testing of
           Communicating Systems 12*, pages 179–196. Kluwer Academic Publishers,
           1999.
[BHT97]   E. Brinksma, L. Heerink, and J. Tretmans. Developments in testing transi-
           tion systems. In M. Kim, S. Kang, and K. Hong, editors, *Int. Workshop on
           Testing of Communicating Systems 10*, pages 143–166. Chapman & Hall,
           1997.
[BK85]   J.A. Bergstra and J.W. Klop. Algebra of communicating processes with
           abstraction. *Theoretical Computer Science*, 37(1):77–121, 1985.
[Bri87]   E. Brinksma. On the existence of canonical testers. Memorandum INF-
           87-5, University of Twente, Enschede, The Netherlands, 1987.
[Bri88]   E. Brinksma. A theory for the derivation of tests. In S. Aggarwal and
           K. Sabnani, editors, *Protocol Specification, Testing, and Verification VIII*,
           pages 63–74. North-Holland, 1988. Also: Memorandum INF-88-19, Uni-
           versity of Twente, The Netherlands.
[Bri93]   E. Brinksma. On the coverage of partial validations. In M. Nivat, C.M.I.
           Rattray, T. Rus, and G. Scollo, editors, *AMAST'93*, pages 247–254. BCS-
           FACS Workshops in Computing Series, Springer-Verlag, 1993.
[CFP94]   A.R. Cavalli, J.P. Favreau, and M. Phalippou. Formal methods in confor-
           mance testing: Results and perspectives. In O. Rafiq, editor, *Int. Workshop
           on Protocol Test Systems VI*, number C-19 in IFIP Transactions, pages 3–
           17. North-Holland, 1994.
[CG97]   O. Charles and R. Groz. Basing Test Coverage on a Formalization of Test
           Hypotheses. In M. Kim, S. Kang, and K. Hong, editors, *Int. Workshop on
           Testing of Communicating Systems 10*, pages 109–124. Chapman & Hall,
           1997.
[CGPT96]   M. Clatin, R. Groz, M. Phalippou, and R. Thummel. Two approaches link-
           ing test generation with verification techniques. In A. Cavalli and S. Bud-
           kowski, editors, *Eight Int. Workshop on Protocol Test Systems*. Chapman
           & Hall, 1996.
[CV97]   J.A. Curgus and S.T. Vuong. Sensitivity analysis of the metric based test
           selection. In M. Kim, S. Kang, and K. Hong, editors, *Int. Workshop on
           Testing of Communicating Systems 10*, pages 200–219. Chapman & Hall,
           1997.
[DAV93]   K. Drira, P. Azéma, and F. Vernadat. Refusal graphs for conformance
           tester generation and simplification: A computational framework.   In
           A. Danthine, G. Leduc, and P. Wolper, editors, *Protocol Specification,
           Testing, and Verification XIII*, number C-16 in IFIP Transactions. North-
           Holland, 1993.
[DBRV⁺00] L. Du Bousquet, S. Ramangalshy, C. Viho, A. Belinfante, and R.G. de
           Vries.   Formal Test Automation: The Conference Protocol with
           TGV/TORX. In G. von Bochmann, R. Probert, and H. Ural, editors, *Test-
           Com 2000*. Kluwer Academic Publishers, 2000. To appear.
[DN87]   R. De Nicola. Extensional equivalences for transition systems. *Acta Infor-
           matica*, 24:211–237, 1987.
[DNH84]   R. De Nicola and M.C.B. Hennessy. Testing equivalences for processes.
           Theoretical Computer Science, 34:83–133, 1984.
[Doo91]   P. Doornbosch. Test Derivation for Full LOTOS. Memorandum INF-91-51,
           University of Twente, Enschede, The Netherlands, 1991. Master's Thesis.

[Dri92]   K. Drira. *Transformation et Composition de Graphes de Refus: Analyse de la Testabilité*. PhD thesis, Laboratoire d'Automatique et d'Analyse des Systemes du CNRS, Toulouse, France, 1992.

[Eer87]   H. Eertink. The implementation of a test derivation algorithm. Memorandum INF-87-36, University of Twente, Enschede, The Netherlands, 1987.

[FJJV96]   J.-C. Fernandez, C. Jard, T. Jéron, and C. Viho. Using on-the-fly verification techniques for the generation of test suites. In R. Alur and T.A. Henzinger, editors, *Computer Aided Verification CAV'96*. Lecture Notes in Computer Science 1102, Springer-Verlag, 1996.

[FJJV97]   J.-C. Fernandez, C. Jard, T. Jéron, and C. Viho. An experiment in automatic generation of test suites for protocols with verification technology. *Science of Computer Programming – Special Issue on COST247, Verification and Validation Methods for Formal Descriptions*, 29(1–2):123–146, 1997.

[Gar98]   H. Garavel. OPEN/CÆSAR: An open software architecture for verification, simulation, and testing. In B. Steffen, editor, *Fourth Int. Workshop on Tools and Algorithms for the Construction and Analysis of Systems (TACAS'98)*, pages 68–84. Lecture Notes in Computer Science 1384, Springer-Verlag, 1998.

[Gau95]   M.-C. Gaudel. Testing can be formal, too. In P.D. Mosses, M. Nielsen, and M.I. Schwartzbach, editors, *TAPSOFT'95: Theory and Practice of Software Development*, pages 82–96. Lecture Notes in Computer Science 915, Springer-Verlag, 1995.

[GJ98]   M.-C. Gaudel and P.R. James. Testing algebraic data types and processes: A unifying theory. In J.F. Groote, B. Luttik, and J. van Wamel, editors, *Third Int. Workshop on Formal Methods for Industrial Critical Systems (FMICS'98)*, pages 215–230, Amsterdam, The Netherlands, 1998. CWI.

[Gla90]   R.J. van Glabbeek. The linear time – branching time spectrum. In J.C.M. Baeten and J.W. Klop, editors, *CONCUR'90*, Lecture Notes in Computer Science 458, pages 278–297. Springer-Verlag, 1990.

[Gla93]   R.J. van Glabbeek. The linear time – branching time spectrum II (The semantics of sequential systems with silent moves). In E. Best, editor, *CONCUR'93*, Lecture Notes in Computer Science 715, pages 66–81. Springer-Verlag, 1993.

[GSDD97]   J. Grabowski, R. Scheurer, Z.R. Dai, and Hogrefe. D. Applying SaMsTaG to the B-ISDN protocol SSCOP. In M. Kim, S. Kang, and K. Hong, editors, *Int. Workshop on Testing of Communicating Systems 10*, pages 397–415. Chapman & Hall, 1997.

[Hee98]   L. Heerink. *Ins and Outs in Refusal Testing*. PhD thesis, University of Twente, Enschede, The Netherlands, 1998.

[Hen88]   M. Hennessy. *Algebraic Theory of Processes*. Foundations of Computing Series. The MIT Press, 1988.

[HFT00]   L. Heerink, J. Feenstra, and J. Tretmans. Formal Test Automation: The Conference Protocol with PHACT. In G. von Bochmann, R. Probert, and H. Ural, editors, *TestCom 2000*. Kluwer Academic Publishers, 2000. To appear.

[Hoa85]   C.A.R. Hoare. *Communicating Sequential Processes*. Prentice-Hall, 1985.

[Hol91]   G.J. Holzmann. *Design and Validation of Computer Protocols*. Prentice-Hall Inc., 1991.

[HST96]   D. Hogrefe, Heymer. S., and J. Tretmans. Report on the standardization
            project "Formal Methods in Conformance Testing". In B. Baumgarten,
            H.-J. Burkhardt, and A. Giessler, editors, *Int. Workshop on Testing of
            Communicating Systems 9*, pages 289–298. Chapman & Hall, 1996.

[HT96]   L. Heerink and J. Tretmans. Formal methods in conformance testing:
            A probabilistic refinement. In B. Baumgarten, H.-J. Burkhardt, and
            A. Giessler, editors, *Int. Workshop on Testing of Communicating Systems
            9*, pages 261–276. Chapman & Hall, 1996.

[HT97]   L. Heerink and J. Tretmans. Refusal testing for classes of transition sys-
            tems with inputs and outputs. In T. Mizuno, N. Shiratori, T. Higashino,
            and A. Togashi, editors, *Formal Desciption Techniques and Protocol Speci-
            fication, Testing and Verification FORTE X /PSTV XVII '97*, pages 23–38.
            Chapman & Hall, 1997.

[HT99]   J. He and K.J. Turner. Protocol-Inspired Hardware Testing. In G. Csopaki,
            S. Dibuz, and K. Tarnay, editors, *Int. Workshop on Testing of Communi-
            cating Systems 12*, pages 131–147. Kluwer Academic Publishers, 1999.

[ISO89]   ISO. *Information Processing Systems, Open Systems Interconnection, LO-
            TOS - A Formal Description Technique Based on the Temporal Ordering
            of Observational Behaviour*. International Standard IS-8807. ISO, Geneve,
            1989.

[ISO91]   ISO. *Information Technology, Open Systems Interconnection, Confor-
            mance Testing Methodology and Framework*. International Standard IS-
            9646. ISO, Geneve, 1991. Also: CCITT X.290–X.294.

[ISO96]   ISO/IEC JTC1/SC21 WG7, ITU-T SG 10/Q.8. *Information Retrieval,
            Transfer and Management for OSI; Framework: Formal Methods in Con-
            formance Testing*. Committee Draft CD 13245-1, ITU-T proposed recom-
            mendation Z.500. ISO – ITU-T, Geneve, 1996.

[JJKV98]   C. Jard, T. Jéron, H. Kahlouche, and C. Viho. Towards Automatic Distri-
            bution of Testers for Distributed Conformance Testing. In S. Budkowski,
            A. Cavalli, and Najm E., editors, *Formal Desciption Techniques and Pro-
            tocol Specification, Testing and Verification FORTE X /PSTV XVII '98*,
            pages 353–368. Kluwer Academic Publishers, 1998.

[JJM00]   C. Jard, T. Jéron, and P. Morel. Verification of Test Suites. In G. von
            Bochmann, R. Probert, and H. Ural, editors, *TestCom 2000*. Kluwer Aca-
            demic Publishers, 2000. To appear.

[JM99]   T. Jéron and P. Morel. Test generation derived from model-checking. In
            D. Halbwachs, N. nad Peled, editor, *Computer Aided Verification CAV'99*,
            pages 108–121. Lecture Notes in Computer Science 1633, Springer-Verlag,
            1999.

[KJG99]   A. Kerbrat, T. Jéron, and R. Groz. Automated Test Generation from SDL
            Specifications. In R. Dssouli, G. von Bochmann, and Y. Lahav, editors,
            SDL'99, The Next Millennium - Proceedings of the 9th SDL Forum, pages
            135–152. Elsevier Science, 1999.

[KVZ98]   H. Kahlouche, C. Viho, and M. Zendri. An industrial experiment in auto-
            matic generation of executable test suites for a cache coherency protocol.
            In A. Petrenko and N. Yevtushenko, editors, *Int. Workshop on Testing of
            Communicating Systems 11*, pages 211–226. Kluwer Academic Publishers,
            1998.

[Lan90]   R. Langerak. A testing theory for LOTOS using deadlock detection. In
            E. Brinksma, G. Scollo, and C. A. Vissers, editors, *Protocol Specification,
            Testing, and Verification IX*, pages 87–98. North-Holland, 1990.

[Led92]   G. Leduc. A framework based on implementation relations for imple-
            menting LOTOS specifications. *Computer Networks and ISDN Systems*,
            25(1):23–41, 1992.
[LGA96]   P. Le Gall and A. Arnould. Formal specifications and test: Correctness
            and oracle. In O.-J. Dahl, O. Owe, and M. Haveraaen, editors, 11th *ADT
            Workshop*. Lecture Notes in Computer Science, Springer-Verlag, 1996.
[LT89]   N.A. Lynch and M.R. Tuttle. An introduction to Input/Output Au-
            tomata. *CWI Quarterly*, 2(3):219–246, 1989. Also: Technical Report
            MIT/LCS/TM-373 (TM-351 revised), Massachusetts Institute of Technol-
            ogy, Cambridge, U.S.A., 1988.
[LY96]   D. Lee and M. Yannakakis. Principles and methods for testing finite state
            machines – a survey. *The Proceedings of the IEEE*, 84, August 1996.
[Mar95]   B. Marre. LOFT: A tool for assisting selection of test data sets from alge-
            braic specifications. In P.D. Mosses, M. Nielsen, and M.I. Schwartzbach,
            editors, *TAPSOFT'95: Theory and Practice of Software Development*,
            pages 799–800. Lecture Notes in Computer Science 915, Springer-Verlag,
            1995.
[Mil89]   R. Milner. *Communication and Concurrency*. Prentice-Hall, 1989.
[Pet00]   A. Petrenko. In *These Proceedings*, 2000.
[PF90]   D. H. Pitt and D. Freestone. The derivation of conformance tests
            from LOTOS specifications. *IEEE Transactions on Software Engineering*,
            16(12):1337–1343, 1990.
[Pha94a]   M. Phalippou. Executable testers. In O. Rafiq, editor, *Int. Workshop on
            Protocol Test Systems VI*, number C-19 in IFIP Transactions, pages 35–50.
            North-Holland, 1994.
[Pha94b]   M. Phalippou. *Relations d'Implantation et Hypothèses de Test sur des
            Automates à Entrées et Sorties*. PhD thesis, L'Université de Bordeaux I,
            France, 1994.
[Phi87]   I. Phillips. Refusal testing. *Theoretical Computer Science*, 50(2):241–284,
            1987.
[PS97]   J. Peleska and M. Siegel. Test automation of safety-critical reactive sys-
            tems. *South African Computer Journal*, 19:53–77, 1997.
[Ray87]   D. Rayner. OSI conformance testing. *Computer Networks and ISDN Sys-
            tems*, 14:79–98, 1987.
[Ray97]   D. Rayner. Future directions for protocol testing, learning the lessons from
            the past. In M. Kim, S. Kang, and K. Hong, editors, *Int. Workshop on
            Testing of Communicating Systems 10*, pages 3–17. Chapman & Hall, 1997.
[Seg93]   R. Segala. Quiescence, fairness, testing, and the notion of implementa-
            tion. In E. Best, editor, *CONCUR'93*, pages 324–338. Lecture Notes in
            Computer Science 715, Springer-Verlag, 1993.
[SEK+98]   M. Schmitt, A. Ek, B. Koch, J. Grabowski, and D. Hogrefe. – AUTOLINK
            – Putting SDL-based Test Generation into Practice. In A. Petrenko and
            N. Yevtushenko, editors, *Int. Workshop on Testing of Communicating Sys-
            tems 11*, pages 227–243. Kluwer Academic Publishers, 1998.
[Spi]   Spin. On-the-Fly, LTL Model Checking with SPIN.
            URL: http://netlib.bell-labs.com/netlib/spin/whatispin.html.
[STW96]   Dutch Technology Foundation STW. *Côte de Resyste* – COnformance
            TEsting of REactive SYSTEms. Project proposal STW TIF.4111, Uni-
            versity of Twente, Eindhoven University of Technology, Philips Research
            Laboratories, KPN Research, Utrecht, The Netherlands, 1996. URL:
            http://fmt.cs.utwente.nl/CdR.

[Tan97]   Q. Tan. *On Conformance Testing of Systems Communicating by Ren-*
            dezvous. PhD thesis, Université de Montréal, Montréal, Canada, 1997.
[TKB92]   J. Tretmans, P. Kars, and E. Brinksma. Protocol conformance testing:
            A formal perspective on ISO IS-9646. In J. Kroon, R. J. Heijink, and
            E. Brinksma, editors, *Fourth Int. Workshop on Protocol Test Systems*,
            number C-3 in IFIP Transactions, pages 131–142. North-Holland, 1992.
            Extended abstract of Memorandum INF-91-32, University of Twente, The
            Netherlands, 1991.
[TPB96]   Q.M. Tan, A. Petrenko, and G. von Bochmann. Modeling Basic LOTOS by
            FSMs for conformance testing. In P. Dembiński and M. Średniawa, editors,
            Protocol Specification, Testing, and Verification XV, pages 137–152. IFIP
            WG6.1, Chapman & Hall, 1996. Also: publication # 958, Université de
            Montréal, Département d'Informatique et de Recherche Opérationnelle.
[Tre90]   J. Tretmans. Test case derivation from LOTOS specifications. In S.T.
            Vuong, editor, *FORTE'89*, pages 345–359. North-Holland, 1990. Also:
            Memorandum INF-90-21, University of Twente, The Netherlands.
[Tre94]   J. Tretmans. A formal approach to conformance testing. In O. Rafiq,
            editor, *Int. Workshop on Protocol Test Systems VI*, number C-19 in IFIP
            Transactions, pages 257–276. North-Holland, 1994.
[Tre96a]   J. Tretmans. Conformance testing with labelled transition systems: Im-
            plementation relations and test generation. *Computer Networks and ISDN
            Systems*, 29:49–79, 1996.
[Tre96b]   J. Tretmans. Test generation with inputs, outputs and repetitive quies-
            cence. *Software—Concepts and Tools*, 17(3):103–120, 1996. Also: Technical
            Report No. 96-26, Centre for Telematics and Information Technology, Uni-
            versity of Twente, The Netherlands.
[Tre99]   J. Tretmans. Testing concurrent systems: A formal approach. In J.C.M
            Baeten and S. Mauw, editors, *CONCUR'99 – 10th Int. Conference on
            Concurrency Theory*, volume 1664 of *Lecture Notes in Computer Science*,
            pages 46–65. Springer-Verlag, 1999.
[TV92]   J. Tretmans and L. Verhaard. A queue model relating synchronous and
            asynchronous communication. In R.J. Linn and M.Ü. Uyar, editors, *Proto-
            col Specification, Testing, and Verification XII*, number C-8 in IFIP Trans-
            actions, pages 131–145. North-Holland, 1992. Extended abstract of Mem-
            orandum INF-92-04, University of Twente, Enschede, The Netherlands,
            1992, and Internal Report, TFL RR 1992-1, TFL, Hørsholm, Denmark.
[VT98]   R.G. de Vries and J. Tretmans. On-the-Fly Conformance Testing using
            SPIN. In G. Holzmann, E. Najm, and A. Serhrouchni, editors, *Fourth Work-
            shop on Automata Theoretic Verification with the* SPIN *Model Checker*,
            ENST 98 S 002, pages 115–128, Paris, France, November 2, 1998. Ecole
            Nationale Supérieure des Télécommunications. Also to appear in *Software
            Tools for Technology Transfer*.
[VTKB93]   L. Verhaard, J. Tretmans, P. Kars, and E. Brinksma. On asynchronous
            testing. In G. von Bochmann, R. Dssouli, and A. Das, editors, *Fifth Int.
            Workshop on Protocol Test Systems*, IFIP Transactions. North-Holland,
            1993. Also: Memorandum INF-93-03, University of Twente, The Nether-
            lands.
[Wez90]   C. D. Wezeman. The CO-OP method for compositional derivation of con-
            formance testers. In E. Brinksma, G. Scollo, and C. A. Vissers, editors,
            Protocol Specification, Testing, and Verification IX, pages 145–158. North-
            Holland, 1990.

Fault Model-Driven Test Derivation from Finite State Models: Annotated Bibliography

Alexandre Petrenko

Centre de Recherche Informatique de Montreal (CRIM),
550 Sherbrooke West, Suite 100, Montreal, H3A 1B9, Canada
Petrenko@crim.ca

Abstract. The annotated bibliography highlights work in the area of algorithmic test generation from formal specifications with guaranteed fault coverage, i.e., fault model-driven test derivation. A fault model is understood as a triple, comprising a finite state specification, conformance relation and fault domain that is the set of possible implementations. The fault model can be specialized to Input/Output FSM, Labeled Transition System, or Input/Output Automaton and to a number of conformance relations such as FSM equivalence, reduction or quasi-equivalence, trace inclusion or trace equivalence and others. The fault domain usually reflects test assumptions, as an example, it can be the universe of all possible I/O FSMs with a given number of states, a classical fault domain in FSM-based testing. A test suite is complete with respect to a given fault model when each implementation from the fault domain passes it if and only if the postulated conformance relation holds between the implementation and its specification. A complete test suite is said to provide fault coverage guarantee for a given fault model.

Alur, R., Courcoubetis, C., and Yannakakis, M.: Distinguishing Tests for Nondeterministic and Probabilistic Machines. In: Proceedings of the 27th ACM Symposium on Theory of Computing (1995) 363-372

The complexity of state distinguishability problems for nondeterministic and probabilistic finite state machines is studied.

Bhattacharyya, A.: Checking Experiments in Sequential Machines. John Wiley & Sons (1989)

The book provides an overview of an early work on checking experiments and fault detection in sequential circuits.

Bochmann, G. v., Das, A., Dssouli, R., Dubuc, M., Ghedamsi, A., and Luo, G.: Fault Models in Testing. In: Proceedings of IFIP TC6 Fourth International Workshop on Protocol Test Systems. North-Holland (1991) 17-30

The paper provides an inventory of various fault models used for specification-based hardware and software testing. Various types of specifications are covered in the survey.

F. Cassez et al. (Eds.): MOVEP 2000, LNCS 2067, pp. 196–205, 2001.

Bochmann, G. v. and Petrenko, A.: Protocol Testing: Review of Methods and Relevance for Software Testing. In: Proceedings of ACM International Symposium on Software Testing and Analysis. Seattle USA (1994) 109-123

The paper reviews existing protocol testing methods, including methods for FSM and LTS-based test derivation for various fault models.

Boroday, S. Yu.: Distinguishing tests for nondeterministic finite state machines. In: Proceedings of the 11th International Workshop on Testing of Communicating Systems (IWTCS'98). Russia (1998) 101-107

The following fault model is considered. The specification is a completely defined nondeterministic FSM. The conformance relation is the reduction relation. The fault domain is the set of all completely defined deterministic FSMs each of which is a reduction either of the specification machine or of another auxiliary completely defined nondeterministic FSM. No upper bound on the number of states in deterministic FSMs is assumed, a finite test suite complete for this fault model does not always exist. A necessary and sufficient condition for its existence and a method for deriving a minimal adaptive test suite are presented.

Boroday, S. Yu.: Simple Fault Checking For Automata Generated By A Fault Function. Cybernetics and System Analysis. Plenum Publishing New York. Vol. 31, No. 6. (1995) 835-841

It presents a method for deriving a test suite complete with respect to the fault model that includes a completely defined deterministic I/O FSM, equivalence relation between such machines and fault domains comprising deterministic submachines of a given nondeterministic FSM (a fault function as in the FF-method) such that faults affect either a single state or single transition without increasing the number of states in implementations.

Chow, T. S.: Testing Software Design Modeled by Finite-State Machines. IEEE Transactions on Software Engineering. Vol. SE-4, No. 3. (1978) 178-187

The method of Vasilevskii is detailed and slightly modified allowing for arbitrary (and not necessarily suffix-closed) characterization sets. It became known as the W-method.

Friedman, A. D., and Menon, P. R.: Fault Detection in Digital Circuits. Prentice-Hall (1971)

Chapter 3 explains checking experiments on minimal completely defined deterministic I/O FSMs.

Fujiwara, S., Bochmann, G. v., Khendek, F., Amalou, M., and Ghedamsi, A.: Test Selection Based on Finite State Models. IEEE Transactions on Software Engineering. Vol. SE-17, No. 6. (1991) 591-603

The method of Vasilevskii (the W-method) is improved to the Wp-method. In this method, the transition checking phase relies on subsets (state identifiers) of the characterization set W used in the state checking phase (as in the W-method).

Gill, A.: Introduction to the theory of finite-state machines. Mc Graw-Hill. New York (1962)

One of the first books where FSM-based testing is explained in detail.

Gonenc, G.: A Method for the Design of Fault Detection Experiments. IEEE Transactions on Computers. Vol. C-19. June (1970) 551-558

The Hennie's approach is further elaborated in a more formal way for the class of FSMs possessing distinguishing sequences. The method became known as the D-method.

Grunsky, I. S., and Petrenko, A.: Design of Checking Experiments with Automata Describing Protocols. Automatic Control and Computer Sciences. Allerton Press Inc. USA. No. 4 (1988)

The problem of deriving tests with complete coverage of restricted faults in implementations of a completely defined deterministic I/O FSM is first formulated assuming that each implementation FSM is equivalent to a deterministic submachine of a nondeterministic FSM (called a fault function). It is demonstrated that the fault function generalizes other existing FSM fault models. A method for deriving a test suite with complete fault coverage is proposed.

Grunsky, I. S.: Testing of Automata: from Experiments to Representations by Means of Fragments. In: Proceedings of the 11th International Workshop on Testing of Communicating Systems (IWTCS'98). Russia (1998) 3-14.

An overview of several important results in FSM testing published in the Russian literature, some of the referred papers are not available in English.

Hennie, F. C.: Fault Detecting Experiments for Sequential Circuits. In: Proceedings of the IEEE 5th Annual Symposium on Switching Circuits Theory and Logical Design. Princeton (1964) 95-110

Fundamental principles of the transition checking approach are first enunciated. The specification is assumed to be a minimal, deterministic, completely defined and strongly connected I/O FSM. The basic procedure yields a single test (checking experiment) for machines that have a distinguishing sequence provided that faults do not increase the number of states in implementations. Extended (though presented informally) procedures allow faults to double the number of states and apply to machines with two or more characterizing sequences (instead of a distinguishing sequence).

Holzmann, G. J.: Design and Validation of Computer Protocols. Prentice Hall (1991)

Chapter 9 is about conformance testing.

Hsieh, E. P.: Checking Experiments for Sequential Machines. IEEE Transactions on Computers. Vol. C-20, No. 10. (1971) 1152-1166.

The transition checking approach (pioneered by Hennie) is further elaborated for a special class of FSMs with Simple I/O sequences. The latter were later rediscovered under the name of UIO sequences.

Kohavi, Z.: Switching and Finite Automata Theory. McGraw-Hill Computer Science Series. New York (1970)

Chapter 13 is about state-identification and fault-detection experiments. Minimal completely defined deterministic I/O FSMs are considered.

Koufareva, I., Petrenko, A., and Yevtushenko, N.: Test Generation Driven by User-defined Fault models. In: Proceedings of the 12th International Workshop on Testing of Communicating Systems (IWTCS'99). Hungary (1999) 215-233

A method is proposed for deriving a test suite complete with respect to the following fault model: a completely defined deterministic I/O FSM, equivalence relation between such machines and fault domains comprising all deterministic submachines of a given nondeterministic FSM (a fault function). The latter represents faults defined by the user. Faults can increase the number of states in implementations.

Lee, D., and Yannakakis, M.: Testing Finite-State Machines: State Identification and Verification. IEEE Transactions of Computers. Vol. 43, No. 3 (1994) 306-320

The complexity of deriving distinguishing and Simple (UIO) sequences from a completely defined FSM is studied. Efficient algorithms are presented.

Lee, D., and Yannakakis, M.: Principles and Methods of Testing Finite-State Machines-A survey. Proceedings of the IEEE. Vol. 84, No. 8. (1996) 1090-1123

The paper contains an analysis of testing problems and existing solutions based on minimal completely defined nondeterministic I/O FSMs. Some extensions to the basic framework are also discussed. It includes an extended list of references.

Lukyanov, B. D.: Distinguishing and Control Experiments with Nondeterministic Automata. Cybernetics and System Analysis. Plenum Publishing. New York. Vol. 31, No 5. (1995) 691-696

Adaptive and preset experiments with nondeterministic I/O FSM are analyzed.

Luo, G., Bochmann, G. v., and Petrenko, A.: Test Selection based on Communicating Nondeterministic Finite State Machines using a Generalized Wp-Method. IEEE Transactions on Software Engineering. Vol. SE-20, No. 2. (1994) 149-162

The fault model considered in this paper includes a minimal completely defined nondeterministic I/O FSM, the equivalence relation between FSMs and the universe of all nondeterministic FSMs with a given number of states. It is demonstrated that the Wp-method can be extended to derive a test suite complete for this fault model.

Luo, G., Petrenko, A., and Bochmann, G. v.: Selecting Test Sequences for Partially Specified Nondeterministic Finite State Machines. In: Proceedings of the IFIP Seventh International Workshop on Protocol Test Systems. Japan (1994) 95-110

The fault model considered in this paper includes a partially defined nondeterministic I/O FSM, the quasi-equivalence (weak conformance) relation between FSMs and the universe of all completely defined nondeterministic FSMs with a given number of states. The so-called HSI-method that is based on harmonized state identifiers, subsets of a characterization set, first proposed for partially defined deterministic FSMs, yields a test suite complete for this fault model.

Moore, E. F.: Gedanken - Experiments on Sequential Machines. In: Automata Studies. Princeton University Press. Princeton New Jersey (1956) 129-153

It is one of most referred papers in black box testing. A conceptual framework for FSM-based testing is proposed. The notions of simple and multiple checking (black box) experiments are introduced. The proposed approach for deriving a checking experiment requires the explicit enumeration of all FSMs with a given number of states. The resulting experiments allow one not only to detect a fault but also to locate it. Machine identification is thus achieved.

Naito, S., and Tsunoyama, M.: Fault Detection for Sequential Machines by Transition-Tours. In: Proceedings of the IEEE International Symposium on Fault Tolerant Computer Systems (1981) 238-243

A transition tour gives a test sequence that covers every transition of a deterministic FSM and is complete with respect to all output (but not transfer) faults. The method became known as the T-method.

Petrenko, A.: Checking Experiments with Protocol Machines. In: Proceedings of IFIP Fourth International Workshop on Protocol Test Systems. North-Holland (1991) 83-94

The paper provides a summary of results in the FSM-based testing previously obtained with the author's participation in the ex-USSR.

Petrenko, A., and Yevtushenko, N.: Test Suite Generation for a FSM with a Given Type of Implementation Errors. In: Proceedings of IFIP 12th International Symposium on Protocol Specification, Testing, and Verification. USA (1992) 229-243

It presents a method for deriving a test suite complete with respect to the fault model that includes a completely defined deterministic I/O FSM, equivalence relation between such machines and fault domains comprising all deterministic submachines of a given nondeterministic FSM (called a fault function-based method, the FF-method). The latter represents faults defined by the user. It is assumed that no fault increases the number of states in implementations.

Petrenko, A., Bochmann, G. v., and Dssouli, R.: Conformance Relation and Test Derivation. In: Proceedings of IFIP Fifth International Workshop on Protocol Test Systems, 1993. North-Holland (1994) 157-178

The paper contains a survey of FSM-based test derivation methods with complete fault coverage. The idea of encoding an LTS by an I/O FSM in failure semantics is first presented. The notion of multiple checking experiments becomes thus applicable to the LTS model and bridge between the FSM and LTS-based testing is established.

Petrenko, A., Yevtushenko, N., Lebedev, A., and Das, A.: Nondeterministic State Machines in Protocol Conformance Testing. In: Proceedings of IFIP Fifth International Workshop on Protocol Test Systems, 1993. North-Holland (1994) 363-378

The paper present a method for deriving tests complete with respect to the following fault model. A completely defined nondeterministic I/O FSM from a special class, the reduction relation between FSMs and the universe of all completely defined deterministic FSMs with a given number of states. The paper also contains preliminary results for testing FSM in context.

Petrenko, A., Yevtushenko, N., Bochmann, G. v., and Dssouli, R.: Testing in Context: Framework and Test Derivation. Computer Communications (special issue on protocol engineering). 19 (1996) 1236-1249

A framework for testing FSM in context is presented. It is demonstrated that the problem can be reduced to testing in isolation w.r.t. the fault model that includes a partially defined nondeterministic I/O FSM, the reduction relation between FSMs and the universe of all completely defined deterministic FSMs with a given number of states.

Petrenko, A., Yevtushenko, N., and Bochmann, G. v.: Fault Models for Testing in Context. In: Proceedings of IFIP Joint International Conference on Formal Description Techniques for Distributed Systems and Communication Protocols, and Protocol Specification, Testing, and Verification. Germany (1996) 163-178

The paper proposes various fault models appropriate for test generation with complete fault coverage when the implementation is embedded in a context and studies the relationships between them.

Petrenko, A., Yevtushenko, N., and Bochmann, G. v.: Testing Deterministic Implementations from Nondeterministic FSM Specifications. In: Proceedings of the 9th International Workshop on Testing of Communicating Systems. Germany (1996) 125-140

The following fault model is considered: a completely or partially defined non-deterministic I/O FSM, the reduction relation between FSMs and the universe of all completely defined deterministic FSMs with a given number of states. The proposed method yields a test suite complete for this fault model.

Petrenko, A., Bochmann, G. v., and Yao, M.: On Fault Coverage of Tests for Finite State Specifications. Computer Networks and ISDN Systems (special issue on protocol testing). 29, December (1996) 81-106

The paper analyzes the existing techniques for fault coverage of a given test suite for finite state models.

Petrenko, A., and Yevtushenko, N.: Fault Detection in Embedded Components. In: Proceedings of 10th International Workshop on Testing of Communicating Systems. Korea (1997) 272-287

An efficient method is proposed for reducing the problem of testing in context to testing in isolation w.r.t. the following fault model: a partially defined nondeterministic I/O FSM, the reduction relation between FSMs and the universe of all completely defined deterministic FSMs with a given number of states.

Poage, J. F., and McCluskey, Jr., E. J.: Derivation of Optimal Test Sequences for Sequential Machines. In: Proceedings of the IEEE 5th Symposium on Switching Circuits Theory and Logical Design (1964) 121-132

The specification is a completely defined deterministic I/O FSM (Mealy machine). Faults are represented by a set of deterministic I/O FSMs. The latter are explicitly constructed from a given (small) set of structural faults in a sequential circuit. A method for deriving tests with complete fault coverage is proposed based on a notion of a product of deterministic FSMs.

Rezaki, A., and Ural. H.: Construction of Checking Sequences Based on Characterization Sets. Computer Communications. Vol. 18, No. 12 (1995) 911-920

The Hennie's approach is further elaborated in a more formal way. The relationship between a single and multiple checking experiments is established.

Sidhu, D. P., and Leung, T. K.: Formal Methods for Protocol Testing: A Detailed Study. IEEE Transactions on Software Engineering. Vol. SE-15, No. 4. (1989) 413-426

The paper reviews several basic FSM-based test derivation methods and presents a case study of experimental estimation of tests for their fault coverage. Note that Theorem 3 holds only under certain assumptions.

Starke, P. H.: Abstract Automata. North-Holland/American Elsevier. (1972)

It contains among other interesting things the theory of nondeterministic I/O FSMs used for testing.

Tan, Q. M., Petrenko, A., and Bochmann, G. v.: Modeling Basic LOTOS by FSMs for Conformance Testing. In: Proceedings of the 15th International IFIP Symposium on Protocol Specification, Testing and Verification. Poland (1995) 123-138

The idea of modeling an LTS by an I/O FSM is further elaborated for trace semantics and failure semantics. It is demonstrated that the proposed transformations preserve the relations used for testing. Thus, test suites for the LTS model with complete fault coverage can be derived via detour to the FSM model.

Tan, Q. M., Petrenko, A., and Bochmann, G. v.: A Framework for Conformance Testing of Systems Communicating through Rendezvous. In: Proceedings of the 26th IEEE International Symposium on Fault-Tolerant Computing. Japan (1996) 230-238

Several fault models for the LTS model are considered. For a given LTS specification a fault domain includes the universe of all LTSs with the given action set and the number of states not exceeding a given bound, the conformance relation can be one of the following. Trace inclusion, trace equivalence, failure reduction, failure equivalence, or nondeterminism reduction. The upper bounds for the complexity of tests complete w.r.t. each of these fault models are established.

Tan, Q. M., Petrenko, A., and Bochmann, G. v.: Checking Experiments with Labeled Transition Systems for Trace Equivalence. In: Proceedings of the 10th International Workshop on Testing of Communicating Systems. Korea (1997) 167-182

The fault model includes an LTS, trace equivalence and the universe of all LTSs with the given action set and the number of states not exceeding a given bound. The analogues of the W-, Wp-, HIS- (Harmonized State Identification) methods originally developed for the I/O FSM model are proposed to generate test suites complete w.r.t. this fault model directly from the LTS.

Tan, Q. M., Petrenko, A.: Test Generation for Specifications Modeled by Input/Output Automata. In: Proceedings of the 11th International Workshop on Testing of Communicating Systems. Russia (1998) 83-99

The fault model includes a reduced input-enabled and transition-deterministic I/O Automaton (I/O Transition System), trace equivalence and the set of all such automata with a given number of states. A method is proposed to generate a test suite complete with respect to this fault model. The method is an analogue of the FSM-based HSI-method.

Trakhtenbrot, B. A., Barzdin, Y. M.: Finite Automata, Behaviour and Synthesis. North-Holland (1973)

The statistical properties of FSMs, including ones related to testing, are studied, among other topics.

Ural, H.: Formal Methods for Test Sequence Generation. Computer Communications. Vol. 15, No. 5. (1992) 311-325

The paper discusses several basic I/O FSM-based test derivation methods and some variations of them.

Vasilevskii, M. P.: Failure Diagnosis of Automata. Cybernetics. Plenum Publishing Corporation. New York No. 4 (1973) 653-665

A method for deriving a complete test suite from a minimal completely defined deterministic I/O FSM is proposed. The number of states in the implementations is assumed not to exceed a given bound. The method was later detailed by Chow and became known as the W-method. Polynomial upper and lower bounds on the length of tests are proved.

Yannakakis, M., and Lee, D.: Testing Finite-State Machines: Fault Detection. Journal of Computer and System Sciences. 50 (1995) 209-227

Randomized algorithms for deriving a checking sequence (single experiment) from a reduced FSM are proposed.

Yao, M., Petrenko, A., and Bochmann, G. v.: Conformance Testing of Protocol Machines without Reset. In: Proceedings of the 13th IFIP Symposium on Protocol Specification, Testing and Verification. Belgium (1993) 241- 253

The transition checking approach (pioneered by Hennie) is further improved for FSMs with Simple I/O (UIO) sequences.

Yevtushenko, N., and Petrenko, A.: Synthesis of Test Experiments in Some Classes of Automata. Automatic Control and Computer Sciences. Allerton Press Inc. USA No. 4 (1990)

Harmonized State Identifiers (HSI) are first proposed as an alternative to a characterization set W. State identifiers are said to be harmonized if any two identifiers contains a common prefix that tells apart the corresponding states. Replacing the W set in the W-method by HSI gives the HSI-method for a reduced deterministic I/O FSM. This method unifies test derivation for both completely and partially defined machines. An extension of this method for a subclass of nondeterministic I/O FSM is also suggested.

Yevtushenko, N., and Petrenko, A.: Method of Constructing a Test Experiment for an Arbitrary Deterministic Automaton. Automatic Control and Computer Sciences. Allerton Press Inc. USA. No. 5 (1990)

The paper considers the fault model that includes a deterministic I/O FSM possibly partially defined and unreduced, the quasi-equivalence (weak conformance) relation and the universe of all completely defined I/O FSMs with a given number of states. It presents the first known method for deriving a test suite complete with respect to this fault model.

Mobile Processes: A Commented Bibliography

Silvano Dal Zilio

Microsoft Research

Abstract. We propose a short bibliographic survey of calculi for mobile processes. Contrasting with other similar exercises, we consider two related, but distinct, notions of mobile processes, namely *labile processes*, which can exhibit dynamic changes in their interaction structure, as modelled in the π-calculus of Milner, Parrow and Walker for example, and *motile processes*, which can exhibit motion, as modelled in the ambient calculus of Cardelli and Gordon. A common characteristic of the algebraic frameworks presented in this paper is the use of names as first class values and the support for the dynamic generation of new, fresh names.

1   Introduction

Process algebras have proved to be valuable mathematical tools to reason about the behaviour of concurrent and communicating systems. For more than ten years now, research has been conducted on semantics of higher-order processes that allow communication channels or even processes to be carried across by communications. Process calculi featuring the ability to dynamically create and exchange channel names are often referred to as *mobile*, a term popularised by the seminal introduction to the π-calculus [1], a prominent example of calculus with mobile processes.

1. Robin Milner, Joachim Parrow, David Walker: A Calculus of Mobile Processes, (parts I and II). Information and Computation **100**(1) (1992) 1–77
2. Robin Milner: Communicating and Mobile Systems: the Pi-Calculus. Cambridge University Press (2000)

Unfortunately, the term mobility is overloaded with meaning and the notion of mobility supported by the π-calculus encompasses only part of all the abstractions meaningful to mobility in a distributed system. For instance, the π-calculus does not directly model phenomena such as the distribution of processes within different localities, their migrations, or their failures.

As a matter of fact, the term mobility is related to two distinct notions. First, mobility is a property of systems undergoing frequent changes. In this situation, we say that the system is *labile*, by analogy with the labile compounds of a chemical reaction. Another notion associated with mobility is related to systems capable of changing their physical location. We say that these systems are *motile*, borrowing a term commonly used in biology to describe living form demonstrating movement by independent means.

F. Cassez et al. (Eds.): MOVEP 2000, LNCS 2067, pp. 206–222, 2001.

Labile systems are well modelled by the π-calculus, which can represents systems that dynamically reorganize their communication structure throughout time. But as we said earlier, the π-calculus does not directly models motile systems. Based on this distinction, and to grasp the core meaning of location and process migration, process calculi with explicit locations, such as the *ambient calculus* of Cardelli and Gordon [3], have been recently proposed.

3. Luca Cardelli, Andrew D. Gordon: Mobile Ambients. In Proc. of FoSSaCS, Springer LNCS 1378 (1998) 140–155

This paper offers a short bibliographic survey of calculi for mobile processes. Contrasting with other similar exercises, we consider both labile and motile process calculi and we concentrate especially on the π-calculus, the ambient calculus, and some extension of π with distribution primitives.

This commented bibliography is not meant as an introduction to the π-calculus or the ambient calculus. In particular, we do not define these calculi, nor give hints at their syntax or semantics, as we cite several introductory materials that answer this purpose. Instead, this paper is an attempt to explain the differences and similarities between the two different notions of mobility that motivated the design of the π and ambient calculi, and to attract notice to interesting research problems arisen from the study of mobility.

We organize the rest of the paper as follows. Section 2 is concerned with labile process calculi, that is, calculi featuring mobility of names, and more particularly with the π-calculus. We suppose that the reader is familiar with process calculus and their equational theory, such as found in [2] for example. Familiarity with distributed programming languages and type systems would also be an advantage. In Section 3, we present calculi with distributed and migrating processes, namely motile calculi. We start by considering extension of the π-calculus with explicit locations and primitives for location failures and process migration. Then we look at the ambient calculus, an archetypal calculus for the mobility of computations.

Since bibliographical references make an important part of this paper, we provide them directly within the text. The complete list of references is provided at the end of this paper.

2 Mobility of Names

As explained in introduction of this paper, the notion of mobility in process calculi often refers to the capability for a process to exchange names as values. The idea of using channel names as data, together with the ability to generate fresh and unique names, is the basis on which the π-calculus is founded.

In his 1991 Turing award Lecture, Milner [4] gives an illuminating account on the concepts of interaction and naming. The study of the relation between computation and naming is further developed in Gordon's survey on *nominal calculi* [5], that we discuss in the following section.

4. Robin Milner: Elements of Interaction. Communications of the ACM **36**(1) (1993) 78–89
5. Andrew D. Gordon: Notes on Nominal Calculi for Security and Mobility. In Proc. of FOSAD, Springer LNCS (2001), to appear

2.1   The Significance of Names

In his Turing award lecture, Milner argues that when one talks about mobility in a system of interacting agents, what really matters is not the mobility of the agents per se (an agent can even not exist), but rather the movement of the access paths to the agents. These access paths — channel names in the π-calculus or references in object-oriented terminology — are the key element we actually need to reason about.

As noted by Gordon [5], this emphasis on the role of naming in the comprehension of computational systems is not isolated. Indeed, contemporarily to the π-calculus definition, Needham [6] was advocating the importance of the notion of *pure names* in the formalization of distributed objects. In his own words, a pure name is *"nothing but a bit pattern that is an identifier, and is only useful for comparing for identity with other bit patterns — which includes looking up in tables in order to find other information."* Compare this definition with the usage of (channel) names in the π-calculus, where a process can read from a named channel, emit in a named channel, or test the equality of two names.

Another example of research on the significance of pure names can be found in the nu-calculus of Pitts and Stark [7], a typed lambda-calculus extended with state in the form of dynamically generated names, in which pure names are introduced in order to models the effect of adding references to a functional language like ML.

6. Roger M. Needham: Names. In S. Mullender (ed.): Distributed Systems, Addison-Wesley (1989) 89–101
7. Andrew M. Pitts, Ian D. B. Stark: Observable Properties of Higher Order Functions that Dynamically Create Local Names, or: What's New? In Proc. of MFCS, Springer LNCS 711 (1993) 122–141

2.2   The π-Calculus

As the λ-calculus, from which many similarities can be drawn, the π-calculus is a parsimonious algebraic framework built from a reduced number of operators, yet expressive enough to model a wide range of computational systems and data structures.

A good introduction to the π-calculus can be found in Milner's tutorial book [2], a preliminary version of which exists as a LFCS research report [8]. Sangiorgi and Walker provide a reference book on the π-calculus theory [9], with emphasis on proof techniques. Related papers, more targeted towards the application to concurrent and distributed programming languages, are Benjamin

Pierce's introduction to the π-calculus for the engineer [10], and Peter Sewell's report on applied pi [11].

Beside these papers, the reader interested by a thorough presentation of the π-calculus will benefit from the notable bibliography on mobile processes compiled by Kohei Honda. Other interesting collections of resources are the bibliography and web pages on mobile process calculi maintained by Uwe Nestmann and Björn Victor and available at the following address: http://move.to/mobility.

8. Robin Milner: The Polyadic π-Calculus: a Tutorial. Technical Report ECS-LFCS-91-180, University of Edinburgh (1991)
9. Davide Sangiorgi, David Walker: The π-Calculus: a Theory of Mobile Processes. Cambridge University Press (2001)
10. Benjamin C. Pierce: Foundational Calculi for Programming Languages. In A. B. Tucker (ed.): Handbook of Computer Science and Engineering, CRC Press (1996)
11. Peter Sewell: Applied Pi – A Brief Tutorial. Technical Report 498, University of Cambridge (2000)
12. Kohei Honda: Selected Bibliography on Mobile Processes. Unpublished notes, available electronically (1998)
13. Uwe Nestmann, Björn Victor: Calculi for Mobile Processes: Bibliography and Web Pages. Bulletin of the EATCS **64** (1998) 139–144

The definition of the π-calculus is not steady and many different evolution of π can be found in the literature. The π-calculus is actually more a family of calculi than just a unique calculus. Such evolutions, briefly summarized in [11], include asynchronous, internal or receptive version of the π-calculus; extensions with primitive for testing the (in)equality of names; etc. In addition, several process calculi based on name-passing has been proposed: the fusion calculus of Parrow and Walker, a simplification of π with a more symmetric form of communication; the spi-calculus of Abadi and Gordon, an extension of π designed for the description and analysis of cryptographic protocols; the join-calculus of Fournet, Gonthier et al; the blue-calculus of Boudol; etc.

14. Joachim Parrow, Björn Victor: The Fusion Calculus: Expressiveness and Symmetry in Mobile Processes. In Proc. of LICS, IEEE Computer Society Press (1998) 176–185
15. Martìn Abadi, Andrew D. Gordon: A Calculus for cryptographic protocols: the spi calculus. Information and Computation **148** (1999) 1–70
16. Cédric Fournet, Georges Gonthier: The Reflexive Chemical Abstract Machine and the Join-Calculus. In Proc. of POPL, ACM Press (1996) 372–385
17. Gérard Boudol: The π-Calculus in Direct Style. Higher-Order and Symbolic Computation **11** (1998) 177–208

There are also definitions of higher-order process calculi, like CHOCS for instance [18], where whole processes and not simply names can be exchanged during communication. Interestingly enough, Sangiorgi proved that it is possible to encode a primitive for higher-order communication in π [19].

18. Bent Thomsen: Plain CHOCS. A Second Generation Calculus for Higher
    Order Processes. Acta Informatica **30**(1) (1993) 1–59
19. Davide Sangiorgi: From pi-Calculus to Higher-Order pi-Calculus – and Back.
    In Proc. of TAPSOFT, Springer LNCS 668 (1993) 151–166

In the remainder of this section, we follow the style of [12] and present a selection of articles following a somewhat arbitrary decomposition into topics.

2.3   Equational Theory and Properties of Processes

The operational semantics of concurrent systems are commonly defined using labelled transition systems. For example, the π-calculus semantics given in [1] is based on such a presentation. Nonetheless, the now conventional dynamic semantics of π is based on a reduction relation defined on top of a *structural congruence* relation that identifies processes up to elementary rearrangements. This presentation, first introduced in [20] and inspired by the chemical abstract machine of Berry and Boudol, allows for a simple and compact definition of the reduction rules in which the sub-processes having to interact appear in contiguous position. It also accounts for much of the elegance and simplicity of the π-calculus semantics.

20. Robin Milner: Functions as Processes. Mathematical Structures in Computer
    Science **2** (1992) 119–141
21. Gérard Berry, Gérard Boudol: The Chemical Abstract Machine. Theoretical
    Computer Science **96** (1992) 217–248

There exist several definitions of behavioural equivalences for π-calculus processes based on labelled-semantics, like for example the early and late bisimulations defined in [1]. See [11,12] for a general account on these equivalences and [22] for a good introduction to the semantics of concurrent process calculi.

In the reduction-based semantics, an interesting notion of equivalence is obtained using barbed equivalence. See also Honda and Yoshida reduction-based equivalence for an asynchronous process calculus [24].

The use of reduction-based equivalences is interesting because these kinds of equivalences are amenable to comparison between different calculi and semantics. Moreover, experience show that it is easier to define a reduction semantics for a calculi with explicit locations than to define (the equivalent) labelled transition semantics.

22. Robin Milner: Semantics of Concurrent Processes. In J. van Leeuwen (ed.):
    Handbook of theoretical computer science, Elsevier (1990) 1203–1241
23. Robin Milner, Davide Sangiorgi: Barbed Bisimulation. In Proc. of ICALP,
    Springer LNCS 623 (1992) 685–695
24. Kohei Honda, Nobuko Yoshida: On Reduction-Based Process Semantics.
    Theoretical Computer Science **152**(2) (1995) 437–486

Another general method to express and verify properties of processes is to use a logical system. In the case of CCS, for example, a modal logic known as Hennessy-Milner logic has been defined that can be used as an alternative characterization of bisimulation equivalences: two processes are equivalent if and only if they satisfies the same formulas. Milner, Parrow and Walker have extended this logic to mobile processes in [26]. Another interesting reference is the work of Mads Dam [27] on an extension of the modal μ-calculus used to define a proof system for π.

25. Matthew Hennessy, Robin Milner: Algebraic laws for Non-Determinism and Concurrency. Journal of the ACM **32** (1985) 137–161
26. Robin Milner, Joachim Parrow, David Walker: Modal Logics for Mobile Processes. Theoretical Computer Science **114**(1) (1993) 149–171
27. Mads Dam: Model Checking Mobile Processes. Information and Computation **129**(1) (1996) 35–51

2.4   The π-Calculus as a Programming Model

One of the major successes of the π-calculus is its use in the validation of concepts for concurrent programming languages; in almost the same manner that functional programming has been established from the computational model provided by the λ-calculus. In particular, programming languages directly based on the π-calculus have been proposed. Examples are Pict, developed by Pierce and Turner at the University of Edinburgh, and the join-calculus, a programming language based on the homonymous process calculus [16], developed at INRIA.

The theoretical foundations of these programming languages take support from the study of abstract machines for intermediate languages derived from π. For instance, Pict is based on an asynchronous version of π without choice operator [28]. See [29] for a study on how to encode choice. Likewise, the join-calculus is obtained as a restriction of π that makes it easier to implement in a distributed scenario [30].

28. David N. Turner: The Polymorphic Pi-Calculus: Theory and Implementation. PhD thesis, University of Edinburgh (1995)
29. Uwe Nestmann, Benjamin C. Pierce: Decoding Choice Encodings. In Proc. of CONCUR, Springer LNCS 119 (1996) 179–194
30. Cédric Fournet: Le join-calcul: un calcul pour la programmation répartie et mobile. PhD thesis, École Polytechnique (1998)

Other theoretical foundations for the design of concurrent programming languages are provided by studies on how to model various computational model in π. Fundamental studies include the encoding of the functional and object-oriented paradigm in the π-calculus — including actors and concurrent objects. For instance, a complete tutorial on the different encoding of the λ-calculus in the π-calculus, extending the initial article of Milner on the encoding of functions as processes [20], can be found in [31]. See also Part VI of [9].

31. Davide Sangiorgi: Interpreting Functions as pi-Calculus Processes: a Tutorial. INRIA Research Report 3470 (1999)

The study of objects using process calculus (and process calculus techniques) is also particularly fruitful. For instance, the π calculus has been used in semantics of concurrent object-oriented programming languages [32] and to prove the validity of program transformations [33].

32. Cliff B. Jones: A π-Calculus Semantics for an Object-Based Design Notation. In Proc. of CONCUR, Springer LNCS 715 (1993) 158–172
33. Davide Sangiorgi: Typed pi-Calculus at Work: A Correctness Proof of Jones's Parallelisation Transformation on Concurrent Objects. Theory and Practice of Object Systems, **5**(1) (1999) 25–33

The π-calculus as also been used in interpretations of typed calculi of objects [34,35,36] and as a model for Obliq [37], an object-based programming language with distributed and mobile objects developed by Cardelli [38]. Other interesting works are concerned with the study of dedicated nominal calculi proposed as formalism to reason about concurrent objects [39,40,41].

34. Davide Sangiorgi: An Interpretation of Typed Objects Into Typed π-Calculus. Information and Computation **143**(1) (1998) 34–73
35. Josva Kleist, Davide Sangiorgi: Imperative Objects and Mobile Processes. In Proc. of PROCOMET, Chapman & Hall (1998)
36. Silvano Dal Zilio: An Interpretation of Typed Concurrent Objects in the Blue Calculus. In Proc. of IFIP TCS, Springer LNCS 1872 (2000) 409–424
37. Josva Kleist, Massimo Merro, Uwe Nestmann: Local pi-Calculus at Work: Mobile Objects as Mobile Processes. In Proc. of IFIP TCS, Springer LNCS 1872 (2000) 390–408
38. Luca Cardelli: A language with distributed scope. Computing Systems **8**(1) (1995) 27–59
39. Kohei Honda, Mario Tokoro: An Object Calculus for Asynchronous Communication. In Proc. of ECOOP, Springer LNCS 512 (1991) 133–147
40. Vasco T. Vasconcelos: Typed Concurrent Objects. In Proc. of ECOOP, Springer LNCS 821 (1994) 100–117
41. Andrew D. Gordon, Paul D. Hankin: A Concurrent Object Calculus: Reduction and Typing. In Proc. of HLCL, Elsevier ENTCS **16**(3) (1998)

2.5   Verification and Type Systems

In the case of the π-calculus, verification is related to the action of checking bisimilarity relations or checking whether a process satisfies some given logical specification, for instance expressed in a temporal or modal logic. An interesting example of verification problem is given by the work of Abadi and Gordon on the spi-calculus, in which processes represent protocols and security properties are stated in terms of behavioural equivalences.

A substantial number of works related to verification for mobile processes concentrate on *finite control processes* [42], a class of processes that correspond to CCS finite state processes. See for instance the mobility Workbench, an automated tool for analysing π-calculus processes developed by Faron Moller and Björn Victor [43], and work in the HAL environment [45].

42. Mads Dam: On the Decidability of Process Equivalences for the π-Calculus. SICS Research Report 94-20 (1994)
43. Björn Victor, Faron Moller; The Mobility Workbench – a Tool for the π-Calculus. In Proc. of CAV, Springer LNCS 818 (1994) 428–440
44. Marco Pistore, Davide Sangiorgi: A Partition Refinement Algorithm for the π-Calculus. In Proc. of CAV, Springer LNCS 1102 (1996) 38–49
45. Gianluigi Ferrari, Stefania Gnesi, Ugo Montanari, Marco Pistore, Gioia Ristori: Verifying Mobile Processes in the HAL Environment. In Proc. of CAV, Springer LNCS 1427 (1998)

Due to the presence of recursion and dynamic generation of names, and in contrast with the situation in CCS, processes can exhibit an infinite-state behaviour. Therefore, model checking for mobile processes is related to the problem of verification of infinite-state and parameterised systems, a problem potentially undecidable. See the work of Esparza, among others, at the Technische Universität of Munich. An interesting proposition to automate the verification of "infinite" mobile processes (especially proofs of bisimilarity properties) relies on the use of theorem prover, such as Coq [46] or Isabelle [47].

46. Daniel Hirschkoff: A Full Formalisation of π-Calculus Theory in the Calculus of Constructions. In Proc. of TPHOL, Springer LNCS 1275 (1997)
47. Christine Röckl, Javier Esparza: Proof-Checking Protocols using Bisimulations. In Proc. of CONCUR, Springer LNCS 1664 (1999) 525–540

Another technique used to verify properties of processes relies on type systems. This approach of verification is particularly useful because it is generally simpler to type a process than to verify a property given in a modal logic.

Type systems in mobile calculus, like in functional calculus, are useful to prevent so-called run-time errors, but also to enforce security policies, to specify synchronization behaviours, or to validate program transformations and equivalences. For example, type systems have been used to attack problems related to information flow analysis, to prove the correctness of cryptographic protocols, or to prove the absence of deadlock in a program.

The first notion of type for π-calculus processes, called *sort*, is defined in Milner's tutorial [8]. Works on extension of the sorting system are well summarized in [12], and include, among others, the addition of (second-order) polymorphism, subtyping [48] and linearity [49]. More precise type analysis, based on the extension of the sorting system with modal operators, have also been proposed [50, 51,52].

48. Benjamin C. Pierce, Davide Sangiorgi: Typing and Subtyping for Mobile Processes. Mathematical Structures in Computer Science **6**(5) (1996) 409–453
49. Naoki Kobayashi, Benjamin C. Pierce, David N. Turner: Linearity and the pi-Calculus. In Proc. of POPL, ACM Press (1996) 358–371
50. Nobuko Yoshida: Graph Types for Monadic Mobile Processes. In Proc. of FST & TCS, Springer LNCS 1180 (1996) 371–386
51. Gérard Boudol: Typing the Use of Resources in a Concurrent Calculus. In Proc. of ASIAN, Springer LNCS 1345 (1997) 239–253
52. Naoki Kobayashi: A Partially Deadlock-Free Typed Process Calculus. In Proc. of LICS, IEEE Computer Society Press (1997) 128–139

An original application of type systems to concurrent processes is in the definition of new behavioural equivalences. See [53] for an example. In this context, types are viewed as a way to establish a contract between a process and the possible contexts in which it can be executed, i.e., tested. Therefore, an equivalence defined using typed processes is coarser than its untyped counterpart and can be used to prove properties based on given assumption about the (execution) environment.

53. Benjamin C. Pierce, Davide Sangiorgi: Behavioral Equivalence in the Polymorphic pi-Calculus. In Proc. of POPL, ACM Press (1997) 242–255

2.6   Locality-Based Semantics

Before moving on to the next section of this presentation, concerned with motile process calculi, we briefly consider some early work on localities in CCS.

As pointed out in the introduction, mobility is strongly related to the concept of *locality*, which is the key notion used to represent where things are changing, or moving. In process calculi such as CCS, for example, it is possible to make the distributed structure of processes explicit by assigning different locations to each component of a parallel composition. Using this model of locations, it is possible to refine the usual behavioural equivalences defined between processes. An example of such equivalence is given in [55].

54. Ilaria Castellani, Matthew Hennessy: Distributed Bisimulations. Journal of the ACM, **36**(4) (1989) 887–911
55. Gérard Boudol, Ilaria Castellani, Matthew Hennessy, Astrid Kiehn: A Theory of Processes with Localities. Formal Aspects of Computing **6**(2) (1994) 165–200

Based on the same idea, Sangiorgi [56], and later Degano and Priami [57], have conducted related works in the context of mobile processes.

56. Davide Sangiorgi: Locality and Interleaving Semantics in Calculi for Mobile Processes. Theoretical Computer Science, **155**(1) (1996) 39–83

57. Pierpaolo Degano, Corrado Priami: Non Interleaving Semantics for Mobile Processes. Theoretical Computer Science **216**(1-2) (1999) 237–270

We mention this thread of research because it proposes an early treatment of the notion of locality in process calculi. Nevertheless, the notion of locality obtained with this approach is too syntactical and, consequently, is not adequate to deal with phenomenon such as the migration of processes. To get round this limitation, process calculi with an explicit notion of locality and explicit primitives for migrating processes have been proposed.

3 Mobility of Processes

The π-calculus is best used to model concurrent systems where interacting programs and processes can freely address each other and share resources. This is, for instance, the model commonly chosen to program systems of distributed objects over local area network, where a dedicated infrastructure can ensure the consistency of an abstract layer of services, like transparent routing of messages or failures recovery.

In programming over wide area network, such as the Internet, distribution introduces new issues of its own and breaks many postulates commonly assumed in concurrent system. See [58] for a good overview of the new problems faced in computations over large-scale network. In this paper, Cardelli points out that many events kept hidden in concurrent systems suddenly become apparent. Examples of such events, or *observable*, are the existence of explicit physical locations (because of the existence of latency in communication), the existence of virtual locations (because security policies can restrict the access to some protected resources), or the existence of failures.

Faced with these intrinsic differences, a new computing paradigm based on the migration of code or agents, instead of the migration of references, has been advocated.

58. Luca Cardelli: Abstractions for Mobile Computation. In J. Vitek and C. Jensen (eds.): Secure Internet Programming: Security Issues for Mobile and Distributed Objects, Springer LNCS 1603 (1999) 51–94

The existence of objective barriers to the free mobility of names makes the π-calculus an unsatisfactory choice for the modelling of computations over large-scale networks. But other limitations exist that require the definition of a new model, like the ability to represent containment or repudiation behaviours. For example, once a name has been communicated in π, it is impossible to withdraw the knowledge or the capabilities associated with this name to the receiving process. Likewise, even if the π-calculus has proved useful in modelling concurrent objects, it is difficult to use π to model groups of objects, a very important notion in component-based systems. Indeed, groups are important for defining set of objects sharing a common behaviour — the involvement in a transaction, a strategy regarding the concurrent access to resources, etc. — or a common attribute — for example a given security policy. At the opposite, models based on explicit locations, such as the ambient calculus, provide an easy way to define "containment" or sharing properties.

The phenomena discussed in this introduction have little to do with (pure) concurrency or name mobility, and are therefore not directly captured by labile process calculi. Considering their significance in the understanding and the modelling of computations over large-scale networks, they nevertheless require an extensive theoretical treatment. For this reason, several motile process calculi have been defined, which directly include locations and primitives for moving processes.

3.1   Distributed Process Calculi

An early attempt to add an explicit notion of location to a process calculus is the work of Amadio and Prasad on π_1 [59]. In this paper, authors remark that while site failure is an essential aspect of distributed systems, it was not adequately modelled in the π-calculus. To model failures, they propose a process calculus in which processes are run at distributed locations. Their calculus provides operators to kill locations, to test the status of locations (ping), and to spawn processes at remote locations.

59. Roberto Amadio, Sanjiva Prasad: Localities and Failures. In Proc. of FST & TCS, Springer LNCS 880 (1994) 205–216
60. Roberto Amadio: An Asynchronous Model of Locality, Failure, and Process Mobility. In Proc. of COORDINATION, Springer LNCS 1282 (1997)

Riely and Hennessy have considered subsequent distributed versions of π. In [61,62] they describe a foundational language for specifying dynamically evolving networks of distributed processes, Dpi, which extends π with notions of remote execution and migration. Novel features of Dpi are that (channel) names are endowed with permissions and that the holder of a name may only use it in the manner allowed by these permissions. See also the model of distribution and failure proposed, independently, for the join-calculus [65].

In the works of Hennessy and Riely, the administration of permissions can be controlled using a type system: well-typed processes use their names in accordance with the permissions allowed by the types. For instance, types are used to guarantee that distributed agents cannot access the resources of a system without first being granted the capability to do so (the language studied allows agents to move between distributed locations and to augment their set of capabilities via communication with other agents). Another example of type system for distributed version of π is given in [66].

61. Matthew Hennessy, James Riely: Resource Access Control in Systems of Mobile Agents. In Proc. of HLCL, Electronic Notes in Theoretical Computer Science 16(3) (1998)
62. Matthew Hennessy, James Riely: A Typed Language for Distributed Mobile Processes. In Proc. of POPL, ACM Press (1998) 378–390

63. Peter Sewell: Global/Local Subtyping and Capability Inference for a Distributed π-Calculus. In Proc. of ICALP, Springer LNCS 1443 (1998) 695–706
64. Nobuko Yoshida, Matthew Hennessy: Subtyping and Locality in Distributed Higher Order Processes. In Proc. of CONCUR, Springer LNCS 1664 (1999) 557–572
65. Cédric Fournet, Georges Gonthier, Jean-Jacques Lévy, Luc Maranget, Didier Rémy; A Calculus of Mobile Agents. In Proc. of CONCUR, Springer LNCS 1119 (1996) 406–421
66. Roberto Amadio, Gérard Boudol, Cédric Lhoussaine: The Receptive Distributed pi-Calculus. In Proc. of FST & TCS, Springer LNCS 1738 (1999) 304–315

3.2   The Ambient Calculus

Very recently, Cardelli and Gordon have proposed a new process algebra, the ambient calculus [3], for describing systems with mobile computations. In this calculus, processes may reside within a hierarchy of locations, called *ambients*. Each location is a cluster of processes and sub-ambients that can move as a group.

Ambients provide an interesting abstraction that combines, within the same theoretical framework, notions such as *mobile computations*, i.e., computations that can dynamically change the place where they are executed and are continuously active before and after movement (like agents), the *sites* where these computations happen: processor, router, etc. and the *mobility* of these sites, such as found with mobile, or even simply temporarily disconnected, computers, or in the crossing of administrative boundary, like applets crossing a firewall.

In the ambient calculus, each ambient has a name — the counterpart of a channel name in the π-calculus — used to define a set of possible capabilities, namely the capability of entering, of exiting or of opening an ambient. The result is a concise process calculus permitting to describe both the mobility and the security behaviours of a system using the same primitives. Instead of extending an existing process calculus with a hierarchical system of locations, Cardelli and Gordon have designed a calculus of locations and migration primitives sufficiently expressive to encode π.

An equational theory for the ambient calculus, as well as the proof of some algebraic laws, is given in [67]. Other works are related to the definition of type systems, like for instance type systems to guarantee that certain ambients remain immobile, or that the execution environment cannot dissolved certain ambients [68,69].

67. Luca Cardelli, Andrew D. Gordon: Equational Properties of Mobile Ambients. In Proc. of FoSSaCS, Springer LNCS 1578 (1999)
68. Luca Cardelli, Andrew D. Gordon: Types for Mobile Ambients. In Proc. of POPL, ACM Press (1999) 79–92

69. Luca Cardelli, Giorgio Ghelli, Andrew D. Gordon: Mobility Types for Mobile Ambients. In Proc. of ICALP, Springer LNCS 1644 (1999) 230–239

To define stronger and finer properties of processes, Cardelli and Gordon have also defined a new logic for the ambient calculus [70,71], which includes both temporal modalities, to specify the behaviour of processes after some reductions, and space modalities, to specify the behaviour of sub-processes at a given location. The modal logic for ambients has also been used as the basis for a query language on semistructured data [72].

70. Luca Cardelli, Andrew D. Gordon: Anytime, Anywhere: Modal Logics for Mobile Ambients. In Proc. of POPL, ACM Press (2000) 365–377
71. Davide Sangiorgi: Extensionality and Intensionality of the Ambients Logics. In Proc. of POPL, ACM Press (2001) 4–13
72. Luca Cardelli, Giorgio Ghelli: A Query Language Based on the Ambient Logic. In Proc. of ESOP, Springer LNCS (2001), to appear

Another definition of process calculus based on mobile location is the Seal calculus of Vitek and Castagna. An interesting property of this calculus is that it allows expressing directly the possibility to seize a capability given at a certain point, something that can only be modelled in an ambient calculus equipped with a type system enforcing a linear use of capabilities.

73. Jan Vitek, Guiseppe Castagna: Seal: A Framework for Secure Mobile Computations. In Internet Programming Languages, Springer LNCS 1686 (1999)

4   Summary

This paper loosely surveys ten years of research on mobile process calculus. Our choice was to concentrate on algebraic formalism based on the notion of naming, also called nominal calculi by Gordon [5], and we have therefore omitted other possible formalism like coordination languages (such as LINDA) or Hewitt's models of actors.

Although many work has already been achieved, there are still promising research developments to expect in the study of the concept of naming and interaction, notions at the core of Milner's action calculi, a unifying framework introduced to study various notions of concurrent interactive behaviour.

74. Robin Milner: Calculi for Interaction. Acta Informatica **33**(8) (1996) 707–737

Another promising research development is to extend the notion of naming, only used for processes at present, to the level of types or even logical formulas. Example of type systems based on pure names can be found in [50,51] and in the system of groups defined by Cardelli, Ghelli and Gordon for the ambient calculus [75], which has also been applied to the π-calculus [76,77]. A similar example, at the level of logic, can be found in the recent extension of the modal logic of ambients with a new quantifier to express the freshness of names [79], modelled after Gabbay and Pitts work [78].

75. Luca Cardelli, Giorgio Ghelli, Andrew D. Gordon: Ambient Groups and Mobility Types. In Proc. of IFIP TCS, Springer LNCS 1872 (2000) 332–347
76. Luca Cardelli, Giorgio Ghelli, Andrew D. Gordon: Secrecy and Group Creation. In Proc. of CONCUR, Springer LNCS 1877 (2000) 365–379
77. Silvano Dal Zilio, Andrew D. Gordon: Region Analysis and a π-calculus with Groups. In Proc. of MFCS, Springer LNCS 1893 (2000) 1–20
78. Murdoch J. Gabbay, Andrew M. Pitts: A New Approach to Abstract Syntax Involving Binders. In Proc. of LICS, IEEE Computer Society Press (1999) 214–224
79. Luca Cardelli, Andrew D. Gordon: Logical Properties of Name Restriction. In Proc. of FoSSaCS, Springer LNCS (2001), to appear

Acknowledgments. I would like to thank Uwe Nestmann and Peter Sewell for helpful comments. Luca Cardelli and Andy Gordon commented on a previous version of this text.

References

1. Robin Milner, Joachim Parrow, David Walker: A Calculus of Mobile Processes, parts I and II. Information and Computation **100** (1992) 1–77
2. Robin Milner: Communicating and Mobile Systems: the Pi-Calculus. Cambridge University Press (2000)
3. Luca Cardelli, Andrew D. Gordon: Mobile Ambients. In Proc. of FoSSaCS, Springer LNCS 1378 (1998) 140–155
4. Robin Milner: Elements of Interaction. Communications of the ACM **36**(1) (1993) 78–89
5. Andrew D. Gordon: Notes on Nominal Calculi for Security and Mobility. In Proc. of FOSAD, Springer LNCS (2001), to appear
6. Roger M. Needham: Names. In S. Mullender (ed.): Distributed Systems, Addison-Wesley (1989) 89–101
7. Andrew M. Pitts, Ian D. B. Stark: Observable Properties of Higher Order Functions that Dynamically Create Local Names, or: What's New? In Proc. of MFCS, Springer LNCS 711 (1993) 122–141
8. Robin Milner: The Polyadic π-Calculus: a Tutorial. Technical Report ECS-LFCS-91-180, University of Edinburgh (1991)
9. Davide Sangiorgi, David Walker: The π-Calculus: a Theory of Mobile Processes. Cambridge University Press (2001)
10. Benjamin C. Pierce: Foundational Calculi for Programming Languages. In A. B. Tucker (ed.): Handbook of Computer Science and Engineering, CRC Press (1996)
11. Peter Sewell: Applied Pi – A Brief Tutorial. Technical Report 498, University of Cambridge (2000)
12. Kohei Honda: Selected Bibliography on Mobile Processes. Unpublished notes, available electronically (1998)
13. Uwe Nestmann, Björn Victor: Calculi for Mobile Processes: Bibliography and Web Pages. Bulletin of the EATCS **64** (1998) 139–144
14. Joachim Parrow, Björn Victor: The Fusion Calculus: Expressiveness and Symmetry in Mobile Processes. In Proc. of LICS, IEEE Computer Society Press (1998) 176–185

15. Martìn Abadi, Andrew D. Gordon: A Calculus for cryptographic protocols: the spi calculus. Information and Computation **148** (1999) 1–70
16. Cédric Fournet, Georges Gonthier: The Reflexive Chemical Abstract Machine and the Join-Calculus. In Proc. of POPL, ACM Press (1996) 372–385
17. Gérard Boudol: The π-Calculus in Direct Style. Higher-Order and Symbolic Computation **11** (1998) 177–208
18. Bent Thomsen: Plain CHOCS. A Second Generation Calculus for Higher Order Processes. Acta Informatica **30**(1) (1993) 1–59
19. Davide Sangiorgi: From pi-Calculus to Higher-Order pi-Calculus – and Back. In Proc. of TAPSOFT, Springer LNCS 668 (1993) 151–166
20. Robin Milner: Functions as Processes. Mathematical Structures in Computer Science **2** (1992) 119–141
21. Gérard Berry, Gérard Boudol: The Chemical Abstract Machine. Theoretical Computer Science **96** (1992) 217–248
22. Robin Milner: Semantics of Concurrent Processes. In J. van Leeuwen (ed.): Handbook of theoretical computer science, Elsevier (1990) 1203–1241
23. Robin Milner, Davide Sangiorgi: Barbed Bisimulation. In Proc. of ICALP, Springer LNCS 623 (1992) 685–695
24. Kohei Honda, Nobuko Yoshida: On Reduction-Based Process Semantics. Theoretical Computer Science **152**(2) (1995) 437–486
25. Matthew Hennessy, Robin Milner: Algebraic laws for Non-Determinism and Concurrency. Journal of the ACM **32** (1985) 137–161
26. Robin Milner, Joachim Parrow, David Walker: Modal Logics for Mobile Processes. Theoretical Computer Science **114**(1) (1993) 149–171
27. Mads Dam: Model Checking Mobile Processes. Information and Computation **129**(1) (1996) 35–51
28. David N. Turner: The Polymorphic Pi-Calculus: Theory and Implementation. PhD thesis, University of Edinburgh (1995)
29. Uwe Nestmann, Benjamin C. Pierce: Decoding Choice Encodings. In Proc. of CONCUR, Springer LNCS 119 (1996) 179–194
30. Cédric Fournet: Le join-calcul: un calcul pour la programmation répartie et mobile. PhD thesis, École Polytechnique (1998)
31. Davide Sangiorgi: Interpreting Functions as pi-Calculus Processes: a Tutorial. INRIA Research Report 3470 (1999)
32. Cliff B. Jones: A π-Calculus Semantics for an Object-Based Design Notation. In Proc. of CONCUR, Springer LNCS 715 (1993) 158–172
33. Davide Sangiorgi: Typed pi-Calculus at Work: A Correctness Proof of Jones's Parallelisation Transformation on Concurrent Objects. Theory and Practice of Object Systems, **5**(1) (1999) 25–33
34. Davide Sangiorgi: An Interpretation of Typed Objects Into Typed π-Calculus. Information and Computation **143**(1) (1998) 34–73
35. Josva Kleist, Davide Sangiorgi: Imperative Objects and Mobile Processes. In Proc. of PROCOMET, Chapman & Hall (1998)
36. Silvano Dal Zilio: An Interpretation of Typed Concurrent Objects in the Blue Calculus. In Proc. of IFIP TCS, Springer LNCS 1872 (2000) 409–424
37. Josva Kleist, Massimo Merro, Uwe Nestmann: Local pi-Calculus at Work: Mobile Objects as Mobile Processes. In Proc. of IFIP TCS, Springer LNCS 1872 (2000) 390–408
38. Luca Cardelli: A language with distributed scope. Computing Systems **8**(1) (1995) 27–59

39. Kohei Honda, Mario Tokoro: An Object Calculus for Asynchronous Communication. In Proc. of ECOOP, Springer LNCS 512 (1991) 133–147
40. Vasco T. Vasconcelos: Typed Concurrent Objects. In Proc. of ECOOP, Springer LNCS 821 (1994) 100–117
41. Andrew D. Gordon, Paul D. Hankin: A Concurrent Object Calculus: Reduction and Typing. In Proc. of HLCL, Elsevier ENTCS 16(3) (1998)
42. Mads Dam: On the Decidability of Process Equivalences for the π-Calculus. SICS Research Report 94-20 (1994)
43. Björn Victor, Faron Moller; The Mobility Workbench – a Tool for the π-Calculus. In Proc. of CAV, Springer LNCS 818 (1994) 428–440
44. Marco Pistore, Davide Sangiorgi: A Partition Refinement Algorithm for the π-Calculus. In Proc. of CAV, Springer LNCS 1102 (1996) 38–49
45. Gianluigi Ferrari, Stefania Gnesi, Ugo Montanari, Marco Pistore, Gioia Ristori: Verifying Mobile Processes in the HAL Environment. In Proc. of CAV, Springer LNCS 1427 (1998)
46. Daniel Hirschkoff: A Full Formalisation of π-Calculus Theory in the Calculus of Constructions. In Proc. of TPHOL, Springer LNCS 1275 (1997)
47. Christine Röckl, Javier Esparza: Proof-Checking Protocols using Bisimulations. In Proc. of CONCUR, Springer LNCS 1664 (1999) 525–540
48. Benjamin C. Pierce, Davide Sangiorgi: Typing and Subtyping for Mobile Processes. Mathematical Structures in Computer Science 6(5) (1996) 409–453
49. Naoki Kobayashi, Benjamin C. Pierce, David N. Turner: Linearity and the pi-Calculus. In Proc. of POPL, ACM Press (1996) 358–371
50. Nobuko Yoshida: Graph Types for Monadic Mobile Processes. In Proc. of FST & TCS, Springer LNCS 1180 (1996) 371–386
51. Gérard Boudol: Typing the Use of Resources in a Concurrent Calculus. In Proc. of ASIAN, Springer LNCS 1345 (1997) 239–253
52. Naoki Kobayashi: A Partially Deadlock-Free Typed Process Calculus. In Proc. of LICS, IEEE Computer Society Press (1997) 128–139
53. Benjamin C. Pierce, Davide Sangiorgi: Behavioral Equivalence in the Polymorphic pi-Calculus. In Proc. of POPL, ACM Press (1997) 242–255
54. Ilaria Castellani, Matthew Hennessy: Distributed Bisimulations. Journal of the ACM, 36(4) (1989) 887–911
55. Gérard Boudol, Ilaria Castellani, Matthew Hennessy, Astrid Kiehn: A Theory of Processes with Localities. Formal Aspects of Computing 6(2) (1994) 165–200
56. Davide Sangiorgi: Locality and Interleaving Semantics in Calculi for Mobile Processes. Theoretical Computer Science, 155(1) (1996) 39–83
57. Pierpaolo Degano, Corrado Priami: Non Interleaving Semantics for Mobile Processes. Theoretical Computer Science 216(1-2) (1999) 237–270
58. Luca Cardelli: Abstractions for Mobile Computation. In J. Vitek and C. Jensen (eds.): Secure Internet Programming: Security Issues for Mobile and Distributed Objects, Springer LNCS 1603 (1999) 51–94
59. Roberto Amadio, Sanjiva Prasad: Localities and Failures. In Proc. of FST & TCS, Springer LNCS 880 (1994) 205–216
60. Roberto Amadio: An Asynchronous Model of Locality, Failure, and Process Mobility. In Proc. of COORDINATION, Springer LNCS 1282 (1997)
61. Matthew Hennessy, James Riely: Resource Access Control in Systems of Mobile Agents. In Proc. of HLCL, Electronic Notes in Theoretical Computer Science 16(3) (1998)
62. Matthew Hennessy, James Riely: A Typed Language for Distributed Mobile Processes. In Proc. of POPL, ACM Press (1998) 378–390

63. Peter Sewell: Global/Local Subtyping and Capability Inference for a Distributed π-Calculus. In Proc. of ICALP, Springer LNCS 1443 (1998) 695–706
64. Nobuko Yoshida, Matthew Hennessy: Subtyping and Locality in Distributed Higher Order Processes. In Proc. of CONCUR, Springer LNCS 1664 (1999) 557–572
65. Cédric Fournet, Georges Gonthier, Jean-Jacques Lévy, Luc Maranget, Didier Rémy; A Calculus of Mobile Agents. In Proc. of CONCUR, Springer LNCS 1119 (1996) 406–421
66. Roberto Amadio, Gérard Boudol, Cédric Lhoussaine: The Receptive Distributed pi-Calculus. In Proc. of FST & TCS, Springer LNCS 1738 (1999) 304–315
67. Luca Cardelli, Andrew D. Gordon: Equational Properties of Mobile Ambients. In Proc. of FoSSaCS, Springer LNCS 1578 (1999)
68. Luca Cardelli, Andrew D. Gordon: Types for Mobile Ambients. In Proc. of POPL, ACM Press (1999) 79–92
69. Luca Cardelli, Giorgio Ghelli, Andrew D. Gordon: Mobility Types for Mobile Ambients. In Proc. of ICALP, Springer LNCS 1644 (1999) 230–239
70. Luca Cardelli, Andrew D. Gordon: Anytime, Anywhere: Modal Logics for Mobile Ambients. In Proc. of POPL, ACM Press (2000) 365–377
71. Davide Sangiorgi: Extensionality and Intensionality of the Ambients Logics. In Proc. of POPL, ACM Press (2001) 4–13
72. Luca Cardelli, Giorgio Ghelli: A Query Language Based on the Ambient Logic. In Proc. of ESOP, Springer LNCS (2001), to appear
73. Jan Vitek, Guiseppe Castagna: Seal: A Framework for Secure Mobile Computations. In Internet Programming Languages, Springer LNCS 1686 (1999)
74. Robin Milner: Calculi for Interaction. Acta Informatica **33**(8) (1996) 707–737
75. Luca Cardelli, Giorgio Ghelli, Andrew D. Gordon: Ambient Groups and Mobility Types. In Proc. of IFIP TCS, Springer LNCS 1872 (2000) 332–347
76. Luca Cardelli, Giorgio Ghelli, Andrew D. Gordon: Secrecy and Group Creation. In Proc. of CONCUR, Springer LNCS 1877 (2000) 365–379
77. Silvano Dal Zilio, Andrew D. Gordon: Region Analysis and a π-calculus with Groups. In Proc. of MFCS, Springer LNCS 1893 (2000) 1–20
78. Murdoch J. Gabbay, Andrew M. Pitts: A New Approach to Abstract Syntax Involving Binders. In Proc. of LICS, IEEE Computer Society Press (1999) 214–224
79. Luca Cardelli, Andrew D. Gordon: Logical Properties of Name Restriction. In Proc. of FoSSaCS, Springer LNCS (2001), to appear

Author Index

Lecture Notes in Computer Science

For information about Vols. 1–2130
please contact your bookseller or Springer-Verlag